Praise for *The Power of Self-Healing*

"After 30 years of being a relationship therapist and best-selling author of the Mars/ Venus book series, one thing I've discovered is that having a great relationship with yourself and your body is the foundation to having healthy relationships with others. Dr. Fab shows us all how to do that right here in this book. Read it and be well. . . ."

— **Dr. John Gray**, author of *Men Are from Mars, Women Are from Venus*

"Wow! What an incredible book. Fabrizio Mancini is one of the world's greatest experts on health, healing, and energy; and here for the first time, he has put all of his ideas together in one place."

— **Brian Tracy**, author of *10 Great Ways to Live a Wonderful Life*

*"I've always said that you are not your circumstances, you are your possibilities. That's what I love so much about Dr. Fab and his new book, **The Power of Self-Healing**. Dr. Fab shows what's possible for each of us in the realm of natural health and healing. The principles in this book will impact many lives."*

— **Stedman Graham**, CEO of S. Graham & Associates; *New York Times* best-selling author of *You Can Make It Happen: A Nine-Step Plan for Success* and *Teens Can Make It Happen: Nine Steps to Success*

*"**The Power of Self-Healing** is your guide to transforming your brain and body in just three weeks. I have seen these principles literally change people's lives. I highly recommend it for you and your loved ones."*

— **Daniel G. Amen, M.D.**, Medical Director, Amen Clinics; author of *Use Your Brain to Change Your Age*

*"Being at the forefront of a new way of being isn't easy but is crucial if you want to stay informed about the most effective ways to live better. Dr. Fabrizio Mancini's new book, **The Power of Self-Healing**, shows us that we're at yet another new forefront. Read this book and learn how each of us has even more power than we ever thought possible to healing ourselves and living our best life, naturally. His 21-day program will get you on the road to a healthy you."*

— **Kathy Smith**, fitness icon; president of Kathy Smith Lifestyles; and author of the bestsellers *Feed Muscle, Shrink Fat Diet* and *Moving Through Menopause*

"Whether it's watching a cut as it heals from the deepest part upwards, to realizing that to heal our hearts and minds we must face and deal with our deepest inner emotional hurts, Dr. Mancini is well worth learning from."

— **Naomi Judd**, country music icon, motivational speaker, and former nurse

"It's much easier to experience great joy and love in your life when you have good health. That's why knowing how to unlock your body's self-healing power is a key to deep happiness. Thanks to **The Power of Self-Healing,** you can learn a simple yet transformative 21-day program that will put you on the road to extraordinary health, happiness, and love."

— **Marci Shimoff,** #1 *New York Times* best-selling author of
Love for No Reason and *Happy for No Reason*

"Dr. Fab is one of those special, rare, and gifted individuals I admire and love to watch work. His message is essential. His enthusiasm is infectious. **The Power of Self-Healing** contains the most powerful message you will find on the most essential skill we all must know. Thanks for helping me unlock my natural healing potential with the 21-day program. Let him help you unlock yours, and you'll be thankful forever, just like I am."

— **Mark Victor Hansen,** America's Ambassador of Possibility and co-founder of the #1 *New York Times* best-selling *Chicken Soup for the Soul* series

"As the founder of the world's most-visited natural-health website, I've researched many thousands of healing tools. My purpose for creating Mercola.com is to provide you with inexpensive and practical resources to take control of your health. Dr. Mancini's book is one of the better tools that will help you achieve that goal. Well worth the investment of your time to review."

— **Dr. Joe Mercola,** *New York Times* best-selling author
and founder of **Mercola.com**

"Dr. Mancini's inspiring new book, **The Power of Self-Healing,** offers you a refreshing and integrative way of awakening your natural-born powers to heal. Imagine, all in one book: the many known natural ways you can simply help heal yourself."

— **Dr. John F. Demartini,** author of *Count Your Blessings:
The Healing Power of Gratitude and Love*

"The masses are mystified about our cultural health challenges and how to solve them. In his book **The Power of Self-Healing,** Dr. Mancini masterfully communicates a life-changing truth—that we humans 'self-heal.' And further, from this powerful context he gives us an easy-to-follow plan that guides us into leveraging this amazing self-healing mechanism. This incredible health leader, through this book, has given you and me a tremendous gift."

— **Dr. Patrick Gentempo, Jr.,** founder of the Creating Wellness Alliance
and co-founder of the Chiropractic Leadership Alliance

"Fab is and has always been passionate about expanding one's realization of what's possible when it comes to our well-being. He is committed to and has created an approach that truly makes a difference. This book is a 21st-century holistic view of how you can improve your life physically, emotionally, and spiritually in a realistic and practical way—it is a must-read. Fab is a master of the total approach! You can say he is FABulous. Thanks, Dr. Fab!"

— **Rick Leffke**, CEO of R.C. Leffke & Associates, Inc.

*"Every once in a while the world is blessed with someone who envisions a better existence for humanity. Fabrizio is one of the special people who puts others and their well-being before his own. His book **The Power of Self-Healing** is a testament to his philosophy that we are in control, we have the power, and we just don't know it yet!"*

— **Petra Robinson**, fitness industry expert for Zumba Fitness

*"There could not be a more timely or relevant book than **The Power of Self-Healing**. Dr. Fabrizio Mancini's newest book is essential reading for anyone who is ready to take control of his or her destiny and live a longer, healthier life."*

— **Robin Crow**, author, speaker, and entrepreneur

"It has been my life's journey to help people find their own perfect health. Dr. Fab makes it easy by sharing the time-tested principles doctors and self-healing experts worldwide follow. I loved reading this book, and you will, too."

— **Beth Shaw**, founder of YogaFit and a leading expert in the mind-body fitness industry

"Being well is a delicate balance and focus on what's possible. Dr. Fab is one of our inspirations for what's possible in the realm of natural health and healing. We love Dr. Fab's simple 21-day plan. It's a foundation for your success."

— **Melissa Gregory** and **Denis Petukhov**, U.S. Olympians, six-time U.S. national medalists

"If you don't have your health, you don't have anything. Dr. Fabrizio Mancini's new book shares some powerful self-healing strategies that you need to know about."

— **Larry Benet**, CEO of the Speakers and Authors Networking Group (SANG)

"Finally, advice that will exponentially shift your health and your mind. Dr. Fabrizio Mancini—a recognized world leader in health—provides simple, authentic, and transformational information to forever alter your well-being. After reading this book, your body and soul will thank you."

— **Shawne Duperon**, six-time Emmy winner, **ShawneTV.com**

"Dr. Fab's message is powerful. There's no greater power than the power of self-healing. Learn how to unlock yours by reading this book as soon as you can. His 21-day self-healing program will begin your journey to the health you deserve."

— **Larry North**, author and leading expert in health, fitness, nutrition, and weight loss

"We all have the power of self-healing within us. Dr. Mancini teaches us how to harness this power for a healthier life now, and for a lifetime."

— **Dr. Eric Plasker**, best-selling author of *The 100 Year Lifestyle* and *The 100 Year Lifestyle Workout*

"Dr. Fabrizio Mancini is a true leader. That is, he is truly a leader worth following. He is a man of commitment: he is committed to his family, his friends, and to his profession. You will benefit from his message."

— **Bryan Flanagan**, vice president of sales and training, Zig Ziglar Corporation; founder of the Flanagan Training Group

"Dr. Fab walks the talk—he is on a personal mission to educate and inspire others by sharing with the world his profound belief in the power of self-healing. His words will move you, and compel you, to assess your own health and choices, and rouse you to make changes!"

— **Becky Halstead**, motivational speaker and founder of STEADFAST Leadership

"Simply put, when it comes to mind, body, and soul, Dr. Mancini is the authority."

— **Art Sellinger**, two-time National Long Drive Champion

*"I've invested my life in uplifting humanity's consciousness around the world through our entrepreneurial programs. I have worked with some of the greatest hearts and minds on the planet. Dr. Fab is one of those incredible people who has the perfect balance of heart and mind to help you tap into your greatest hidden resource that's just waiting to be unlocked and released. Thank you, Dr. Fab, for **The Power of Self-Healing** and your tremendous contributions to the world. If there is one thing I know, it is that our health is the greatest wealth that we possess."*

— **Dame DC Cordova**, CEO of Excellerated Business Schools®/Money & You® global organization

"My heartfelt applause goes to Dr. Fabrizio Mancini for his skilled diligence of empowering our minds with the knowledge that the power that made the body, heals the body. This book transforms our perceptions of our health and adds years to our lives."

— **Starr Shephard**, author, speaker, and global Demartini Method facilitator

"Dr. Fabrizio Mancini is the expert when it comes to the power of self-healing. He has years of expertise and understanding of how 'the only thing that heals the body is the body' and shares the best practices on how to make it happen. It's time for this information to be shared!"

— **Scott Schilling**, professional speaker and business-growth expert

*"**The Power of Self-Healing** is a masterpiece that blends Dr. Mancini's decades of incredible work with cutting-edge information and applicable practices to implement while reading the book. The 21-day self-healing plan is perfect for those who truly desire to live a vital, happy, and healthy life."*

— **Tami Walsh, M.A.**, president of TeenWisdom, Inc.

*"**The Power of Self-Healing** has the most important attributes of any book about health; the information presented is easily understandable, and there are clear action steps to follow. In other words, there are no excuses not to read and follow the sound advice Dr. Mancini provides! The rest, as always, is up to you."*

— **Dr. James L. Chestnut, B.Ed., M.Sc., D.C., C.C.W.P.**, president and head of research, The Wellness Practice Global Self-Health Corp.

"In simplicity there is elegance, and in this simple, yet amazingly powerful, well-written, and life-changing book, Dr. Fabrizio Mancini will capture your attention by providing you with a GPS system for unlocking your already ' built-in' healing potential—all in just 21 days!"

— **Dr. Larry Markson**, creator of The Cabin Experience and author of *Talking to Yourself Is Not Crazy*

*"**The Power of Self-Healing** might just be the most important subject we can learn about right now. Every aspect of our life is connected to our health. Read Dr. Fabrizio Mancini's new book and discover how to activate the innate healing power we all have inside ready to help us heal all aspects of our life today."*

— **Dr. Jason A. Deitch**, best-selling co-author of *Discover Wellness: How Staying Healthy Can Make You Rich*

*"Dr. Mancini's new book, **The Power of Self-Healing**, is an enlightening, common-sense approach to health. It is an exceptional guide for anyone interested in health, wellness, and self-healing. Each chapter inspires the reader as he or she opens another door to a healthier life. This book is more than transformational—it is a must-read and should be part of the country's preventative health plan of action."*

— **Dr. Eric Kaplan**, #1 best-selling author of *Dr. Kaplan's Lifestyle of the Fit & Famous, Dying to Be Young,* and *The 5 Minute Motivator*

"If you are interested in understanding your miraculous ability to be healthy naturally, read this book and follow Dr. Mancini's advice. He is a master on the subject."

— **Dr. Gilles A. LaMarche**, author of *The Art of Responsibility*

"The Power of Self-Healing has the potential to shift your life from despair to inspiration and health; it contains lifesaving principles that, if applied, will bring healing and gratitude. It is a gift to give to yourself and your loved ones."

— **Dr. Lise Janelle, D.C.**, founder of the Centre for Heart Living

"It is a special moment for the globe to have a powerful healer reveal so much of his lifetime of secrets. Dr. Mancini's work is a direct connect with important information that will alter the course of your destiny. Don't miss it!"

— **Dr. Ramah Wagner**, author of *The Health of Business*

"Dr. Fab reminds us that wellness, vitality, and healing always come from within. Most important, it matters not where in life we currently find ourselves as long as we make life-promoting changes that make profound differences in the long haul. Read, digest, and act!"

— **Dr. Liz Anderson-Peacock**, author, speaker, and developer of
The Best Version of You™

"The Power of Self-Healing reveals the secrets of the most powerful healing potential on the planet: the human body. Dr. Fabrizio Mancini's book eloquently and succinctly explains the benefits of looking within for health and optimal performance. The insightful advice, practical tips, and action steps that Dr. Mancini shares are only further testimony of the leadership he provides every day."

— **Christopher J. Colloca, D.C.**, CEO and founder of Neuromechanical
Innovations; co-author of the bestseller *GameChangers: The World's Leading
Entrepreneurs: How They're Changing the Game, and You Can Too!*

"This is a remarkable book. Even doctors and the most sophisticated tests can't always find the source of a health issue, but there is one authority that always knows—your own body. Dr. Mancini has organized his years of experience into a practical compendium that will empower you to unlock your innate natural healing abilities to create a vital, fulfilling, and healthy life. Dr. Mancini's guidance will provide you with the tools you need to take a more active role in your own well-being."

— **Mark Sanna, D.C.**, president and CEO, Breakthrough Coaching

THE
POWER
OF SELF-HEALING

ALSO BY DR. FABRIZIO MANCINI

CHICKEN SOUP FOR THE CHIROPRACTIC SOUL:
Stories of Inspiration, Healing, Laughter and a Lifetime of Wellness
(with Jack Canfield and Mark Victor Hansen)

FEELING FAB: Four Steps to Living a Fabulous Life

THE WELL-ADJUSTED SOUL:
Feel-Good Stories from the Heart of Chiropractic
(with Dr. Gilles A. LaMarche and Donald M. Dible, M.S.)

THE
POWER
OF SELF-HEALING

Unlock Your Natural
Healing Potential in 21 Days!

DR. FABRIZIO MANCINI

HAY HOUSE, INC.

Carlsbad, California • New York City
London • Sydney • Johannesburg
Vancouver • Hong Kong • New Delhi

613
man

1/13
BT

Published and distributed in the United States by: Hay House, Inc.: www.hayhouse .com® • *Published and distributed in Australia by:* Hay House Australia Pty. Ltd.: www .hayhouse.com.au • *Published and distributed in the United Kingdom by:* Hay House UK, Ltd.: www.hayhouse.co.uk • *Published and distributed in the Republic of South Africa by:* Hay House SA (Pty), Ltd.: www.hayhouse.co.za • *Distributed in Canada by:* Raincoast: www.raincoast.com • *Published in India by:* Hay House Publishers India: www.hayhouse.co.in

Cover & interior design: Tricia Breidenthal

The stories that appear throughout this book have been reprinted with permission from the individuals involved. In some cases, names and identifying details have been changed to preserve confidentiality.

The author of this book does not dispense medical advice or prescribe the use of any technique as a form of treatment for physical, emotional, or medical problems without the advice of a physician, either directly or indirectly. The intent of the author is only to offer information of a general nature to help you in your quest for emotional and spiritual well-being. In the event you use any of the information in this book for yourself, which is your constitutional right, the author and the publisher assume no responsibility for your actions.

Library of Congress Cataloging-in-Publication Data

Mancini, Fabrizio.
 The power of self-healing : unlock your natural healing potential in 21 days! / Fabrizio Mancini.
   p. cm.
  Includes bibliographical references.
  ISBN 978-1-4019-3621-1 (hardback)
 1. Self-care, Health. 2. Healing. 3. Mind and body therapies. I. Title.
 RA776.95.M26 2012
 613--dc23
                              2011033913

Tradepaper ISBN: 978-1-4019-3622-8
Digital ISBN: 978-1-4019-3623-5

16 15 14 13   7 6 5 4
1st edition, January 2012
4th edition, January 2013

Printed in the United States of America

In memory of my loving father, Giovanni Mancini

CONTENTS

FOREWORD

I encourage you to read this book very deliberately. It speaks to a fundamental truth that has become lost—or at the very least, obscured—in modern times. We seem to have forgotten that each and every one of us has built into our very existence the power to live our lives at a level of super health. Rather than looking within, we have become a people who are foolishly searching for the answers for living healthfully everywhere . . . everywhere, that is, but where the answers truly reside.

We are continuously being bombarded by messages telling us that healing will come to us from an external source: Take a pill—rather, a whole handful of pills—in order to make yourself well. Eat foods that have been genetically modified and contaminated with additives, refined carbohydrates, and overly processed to the point of tricking your body's "I've had enough" regulation. This has resulted in excessively high rates of obesity, heart disease, and a multiplicity of disorders that are all preventable.

Dr. Fabrizio, or "Fab," as he is known, has provided you with a guide for tapping into your own inborn potential for healing. He reminds you that you are the hero, your body is the hero, and your mind is the hero. Most emphatically, he assures you that your spirit is right there for you, a superhero that can and will remind you that when you finally come to completely trust in yourself—yes, yourself—you are trusting in the very wisdom that created you, and that wisdom is infinite and omnipresent and yours to access at will.

After reading and digesting this "fab"ulous book, you will have your eyes opened to the healing capacity that you carry around with you every moment of your life. You will look with new eyes at what an amazing miracle worker you are, and you will marvel at how simple it is to retake control over all aspects of your life. I read this book very carefully, taking notes as I went along, largely because I have so much respect for the man who created it. I can say with certainty that the contents of this powerful compendium have brought me to a whole new awareness of what I can do to circumvent the efforts of so many external factors that seem to conspire to keep me from living my life at the level of super health.

We were all meant to live at this super-health level. It is our original nature; it is the intent of the Divine force that created us. We are all walking pharmacies who are capable of producing whatever chemicals we need for perfect physical, emotional, and spiritual health. Yet we now live in a time when the children being born today have a shorter life expectancy than their parents. And this is a first in the entire history of our species.

We have come to a place where we are consistently looking outside of our perfect selves for solutions, ignoring our own Divine self-healing gifts. We have come to look everywhere but where the answers truly exist. *The doorway to perfect health opens inward.*

My friend and colleague Dr. Fabrizio Mancini has provided all of us with the ultimate guide for reversing this trend and putting us on a path of self-healing. As you read and study the contents of this remarkable book, keep in mind that when you come to trust in yourself, you are truly trusting in the very wisdom that is responsible for your creation. There is no greater power anywhere, and you are that power. I urge you to take the 21-day natural healing challenge that Fab offers and observe the transformation that you will experience. I have done it, and I have never felt better in my life.

I love this book, and I love this man who created it. Thank you, Fabrizio—*The Power of Self-Healing* is destined to become a classic, and I am honored that you asked me to write this brief Foreword for it. I celebrate every day because of all of the effort that you put into this monumental work, and I know millions of people will be celebrating as well.

— **Dr. Wayne W. Dyer**
Maui, Hawaii

INTRODUCTION

Most of us are no strangers to health problems, illness, or pain, but most of us wish we were. And most of us would love a new lease on life with the ability to live disease-free, have more energy, and enjoy greater well-being.

Is that possible, though? Is it too late to even try?

Yes, it *is* possible . . . and it's not too late.

But don't bother looking for answers in the rapidly changing and unfriendly "sick care" environment. They're not there.

The answers are within your own body. That's right. Your body has a built-in capacity to heal itself—a remarkable system of self-repair that goes on day in and day out—and improving its ability to heal is within your control.

Most people, however, don't fully grasp that the body has this incredible ability to heal itself, largely because traditional medicine has done little to maximize this potential, instead emphasizing that health comes from the *outside* in and not from the *inside* out. Did you know, for example, that many illnesses may eventually heal on their own? It's true!

I should take a moment here to introduce myself. I am a doctor of chiropractic and the president of Parker University in Dallas, Texas. Formerly known as Parker College of Chiropractic (of which I am also a graduate), the institution was founded by the late Dr. James

W. Parker, the man so many lovingly called "Dr. Jim." Parker College opened its doors in September 1982 with 27 students. Today, the university is the leading chiropractic school in the world. There are more than 6,000 Parker graduates practicing in all 50 states and living in 31 foreign countries.

I remember so clearly the day I received the phone call from the chairman of the board of Parker College. He told me that since Dr. Jim had passed on, the board felt that I was the right person to assume the leadership position. My heart skipped a beat. I was only 33 years old. I thought to myself, *What do I know about running such a huge institution?*

At the time, I had built a successful practice of Chiropractic Wellness in Texas. My wife, Alicia, was pregnant with our second child, and I was happy being in the office 27 hours a week and spending the rest of my time with my family. But as Alicia and I discussed the opportunity, I realized that I knew a lot more than I thought I did, as Dr. Jim had mentored me for ten years and was one of my closest friends. I was also aware of the challenges that the college would face without strong leadership and a clear vision. As a product of that educational system, I knew what could be done to improve it. I accepted the offer reluctantly and told the board members that if it didn't work out, a replacement should be found immediately. Once it was official, a reporter came to do a piece on me because, as I was told, I had become one of the youngest presidents of a college or university in the United States.

Twelve years later, I find myself loving every day as Parker's president. I realize the more I can contribute to the betterment of others, the more that *my* life is worth living.

You can't tell from reading my words on these pages, but I'm originally from Colombia and I have an accent. My family relocated from Colombia to Miami in 1978, after I had just turned 13 years old. When my parents announced our imminent departure to the U.S., it was traumatic news for my four brothers and me. Life in Colombia was our world—we had many friends and also played a lot of sports. It was scary to think about leaving all that behind. But my mother and father, who were very wise, put it like this: "Isn't it amazing that you can go to a whole different country, learn a whole different language, and pick up a whole different understanding of another culture? Isn't it amazing that you'll be able to explore *any* possibilities that are out there?" They were so right. You see, Colombia had provided us with a happy childhood, but the U.S. offered us the opportunity to grow and go beyond our comfort zone. My brothers and I felt much better about the move.

I can still recall my first day of school in Miami as if it were yesterday. It was frightening and unfamiliar. There was no such thing as "English as a Second Language" at the time, and very few students spoke Spanish at that school. Even though I was supposed to be in the seventh grade, they pushed me back to fifth because I didn't know a word of English.

I walked into the classroom and my teacher, Ms. Hill, said, "Okay, class. Let's welcome our new student. His name is Fabrizio." The whole class replied, "Hi, Fabrizio." Ms. Hill took my hand and sat me down next to a young girl named Maria, who was bilingual because her parents were Cuban. I sat next to her every day, and she translated what the teacher was saying. I had to spend two-and-a-half hours after class every day in order to understand the lessons. That was the beginning for me. Once school was out, my parents sent my brothers and me to a summer camp in Boston, Massachusetts, where nobody spoke Spanish . . . but that was where we really picked up a lot of the English language.

I bring up these challenges I faced as a young boy because there was a huge life lesson in all of it for me: sometimes we're going to be thrown into circumstances we don't expect—some monumental life change such as an illness, a new job, a lost job, a death, or a divorce, for instance—and we must respond optimistically. We must be resilient. I didn't expect to move out of the country; I didn't expect to learn a new language. But what I did know, even back then, was that I could do something positive about the situation. My parents always encouraged my brothers and me and told us that we could do, or become, anything we wanted. As we learned to speak English, for example, they'd remind us of the opportunities we were creating for ourselves in our lives and careers by being fluent in two languages.

Those early experiences profoundly shaped who I am, and how I think, today.

I think that sometimes we get stuck and severely limit ourselves. In other words, I mean that we become paralyzed by the circumstances we're thrown into rather than looking at a situation as an opportunity to grow and become a better person—a more powerful human being.

Responding to life's events in a positive way has been the greatest foundation in the life I've created for myself. Don't get me wrong. I've endured my share of suffering and negative experiences, including the heartbreaking loss of two family members. In fact, a friend once asked me, "With all that's happened, how can you be so happy and healthy?"

I shared with my friend that despite the hardships, I still felt immensely fortunate to have such an incredibly fulfilling, peaceful, joyful life. And every single day, I wake up and ask myself why others don't feel this way, too. The answer I constantly come up with is that most people don't think it's possible for them—they don't believe that they can do it or have it. They allow their negative perceptions and the opinions of others to interfere with their lives and dictate who they become or how they think and feel, rather than first turning inward and discovering all of that from within. In short, they just don't know how to maintain a positive, healthy outlook and view the journey through life with hope.

Your mind-set most certainly affects your well-being. And my purpose for writing this book is to share what I have learned after more than 20 years of studying and discovering exactly how to achieve your maximum potential in the most important area of your life: *your health*.

Until I was introduced to chiropractic, I had never made health a top priority. Chiropractic is a form of health care that emphasizes self-healing. It focuses on disorders of the musculoskeletal system and nervous system, and the effects of these disorders on one's health.

My background had been in conventional medicine; I was a pre-med student on my way to becoming a neurosurgeon. But I became fascinated by chiropractic, which taught me that the body is designed to heal itself, and that without proper health, we are limited in every area of our lives. But this book is not about chiropractic care—it is about the body's ability to fix itself.

There is a well-worn cliché that says: "If you don't have your health, you have nothing." Well, that's true—for everyone. If you're not taking care of yourself, this may impact the way in which you perform in your career. If you're not feeling well, maybe you don't feel like doing anything with your spouse or partner. If you have children and they want to play with you but you just don't feel up to it, you might push them away. Little by little they might start asking, "Why doesn't Mommy want to play with me?" or "Why doesn't Daddy want to play with me?" If you don't have your health, even all the money in the world has no value. If you don't have your health, you don't have much of anything.

Now I'm just not referring to physical well-being. I'm talking about physical, emotional, and spiritual health; and each of these areas are intricately woven together and form the heart of this book:

Part I: Physical Self-Healing. Unleashing your body's self-healing abilities starts with good nutrition and supplementation, physical activity, and positive lifestyle changes. In Part I, I'll empower you to make the necessary changes to support your body's inherent healing abilities.

Part II: Emotional Self-Healing. Negative thoughts and feelings can cause pain and illnesses that clear rapidly when you change those thoughts. The benefits enjoyed from emotional self-healing may include the following: relief from stress, deep relaxation, healing energy flow, increased and focused energy level, prevention of injury, relief from sore and aching muscles and joints, and enhanced confidence and well-being.

Part III: Spiritual Self-Healing. The majority us have a fixed idea that health is mostly physical and, to an extent, emotional, but good health encompasses more than that. It is also intensely spiritual, and I believe we are all spiritual beings.

Deepening your spiritual roots through faith or other practices, or simply feeling close to nature, has profound effects on healing. Spirituality provides meaning and comfort in times of illness so that the experience of a disease is better, which can promote healing. An illness may also help awaken your spirituality and help you achieve spiritual growth. And often, your spirituality can support and strengthen your capacity for self-healing in ways that border on the miraculous.

Self-healing occurs when the physical, emotional, and spiritual are aligned. When we're working every single day to make sure we nurture those three areas, then we can truly realize and achieve our self-healing potential. The human body has evolved to live well and fight off disease, provided we give it the nurturing it needs.

The word *doctor* stems from the Latin word *docere,* meaning "to teach." As a doctor of chiropractic, one of my most important jobs is to teach people how to keep themselves healthy and empower them to take responsibility for their own well-being. I always made sure that my patients never left my office without recognizing that they could only achieve their full potential—in their relationships, faith, life's work, and so forth—when they tapped into, and worked toward achieving, their ultimate health.

Using the guidelines and suggestions I lay out for you, you will not only help prevent disease from getting a foothold in the first place, but you will also help your body begin to heal from illnesses already in progress without resorting to drugs or surgery. This all comes together in the final part of the book:

Part IV: 21 Days to Self-Healing. I give you an innovative three-week program that focuses on how to improve the physical, emotional, and spiritual areas in your life and tap into your body's own healing potential through:

- Simple substitutions to your daily diet to stimulate your body's natural ability to rejuvenate and heal

- The latest breakthrough supplements that can strengthen the self-healing capacities of your body

- New insights into how physical activity floods your body with natural healing substances

- The latest nondrug, noninvasive technologies that can bring you back to optimal health

- The power of your mind and spirit to heal your body

I designed this program to get your body looking and feeling its best, according to what's healthy and realistic for you, so you can genuinely be at your best—inside and out. And what are some of the best surprises of a self-healed life? Take a look:

- Surges of energy that result from healthy living

- Renewed happiness and joy

- Newfound optimism

- An emotional and spiritual connection to your own well-being

- A life that feels more in focus

There are so many positive steps you can take toward self-healing, and I'm going to show you which ones are best. Granted, not all of them will resonate with you, or even work for your lifestyle, but I encourage you to try each step you can and use the ones that fit in with your way of being in the world. And don't even think beyond today! Make a choice to take one or two positive actions for your health each day from my 21-day plan. Do that every day, and you'll accumulate the rewards of health—rewards that will improve your odds against everything from heart disease, obesity, cancer, and diabetes to arthritis, allergies, colds, flu, and more.

My stance has always been that each and every one of us has been designed to be healthy. You have the power to be and stay healthy because healing comes from within. *The Power of Self-Healing* will help you live the life you were truly meant to live.

BODY HEAL THYSELF

I love to tell the story about the medical student who was taking a course on diseases. One morning after class, he said to his professor, "With all these diseases, I don't understand how anyone can survive." The teacher replied, "When you study how the body works, you'll wonder how anyone can get sick."

Our bodies were designed with the ability to make repairs and to even defend against illness or injury. We are, in truth, self-healing creatures. You've seen the proof many times yourself. If you nick yourself while shaving or scrape your knee, you can see the healing start almost immediately. Inside your body, specialized blood cells, called platelets, seal up the wound through clotting to stem the flow of blood. White blood cells are dispatched to the area to fight bacteria that might enter the body through the broken skin. And red blood cells arrive on the scene to nourish the healing tissue with oxygen. Over the next few days, the tiny wound scars over and finally disappears—thanks to the body's own natural team of "cellular paramedics."

And if you've ever broken a bone, you've experienced self-healing in action, too. After being in a cast for a few weeks, what happens to that bone? It heals itself with new, natural bone in quite an amazing process of repair. That's why when your doctor removes your cast and says, "You're as good as new!" he or she isn't kidding!

Likewise, a sprained ankle, pulled muscle, or a painful back will usually heal with rest. And while over-the-counter medicines will relieve the symptoms of a cold, it is your own healthy immune system that brings you back to health.

And just as miraculously, your body fights against cancer. Several times a day, a normal cell in the body might mutate into a cancerous one, but your body recognizes this and its natural defense mechanisms actually knock out that cancer cell. There is healing going on every single moment of our lives.

My Belief in Self-Healing

More than my profession, it was a personal experience that made me an advocate of self-healing. Many years ago, my father had colon surgery in Colombia because of some rectal bleeding. The surgeons removed part of his colon, and as we discovered later, this procedure was unnecessary.

When they sutured the small intestine to the rectum, it was not done properly and soon tore open. My dad developed peritonitis, an inflammation of the inner wall of the abdomen. At the time, my family made the decision to fly him from Colombia to a hospital in Miami, Florida. Due to the urgency of the situation, a team of doctors in Miami decided to operate on him immediately, within a few hours of his arrival. This saved his life.

My father spent the next 15 days in the intensive care unit, with a respirator and dialysis machine. Every single day was a victory in his struggle to live. He was later moved to a hospital room, and had to endure an open wound in his stomach that would not heal, along with an ileostomy bag. He had to relearn how to eat (starting with very small portions of food), and he also had to learn how to walk again. After six months as an inpatient, which included more surgeries, he was able to come home, where he continued his recovery with routine checkups at the hospital and another surgery in his stomach.

After two years of living like this, Dad's doctors were unable to close the wound in his stomach, as it kept opening up with every surgery. They later told my parents that an x-ray showed a black spot in his lung and referred them to an oncologist. After some tests, the oncologist informed us that he had detected lung cancer (stage IV), and it had already formed a metastasis in the other lung. The doctor also told us that my father had about three months left, but his desire to live was so strong that he survived an additional year and a half.

Throughout that period, he was only allowed to take painkillers; because of his open abdomen wound, he wouldn't benefit from chemotherapy or radiation. My father smoked and drank since he was a young man, but he'd given up both over the last 18 years of his life. I'm sure that the smoking and drinking played a part in damaging his lungs and liver. He also didn't exercise properly, and his diet wasn't the greatest either.

Sadly, for all of us, Dad passed away at the age of 64. We lost our father at a young age, and his early death was unnecessary. I still grieve to this day, mainly because my children and my brothers' children didn't have much time with their grandfather to share all the joys and experiences in their lives.

I tell this story often to help people recognize that we can make better choices, from our lifestyle habits to the types of treatment we choose. All of these choices have long-term consequences, good or bad. And when it comes to something like surgery, I want to know whether the doctor has exhausted every possibility before even considering going forward. Unless it's necessary because of an emergency, I've always encouraged my patients to visit at least three providers before making a decision. We need to find out whether surgery is needed, how soon it must be done, and if there are any other options.

The Power to Self-Heal

Each one of us is different in so many ways—physically, emotionally, and spiritually—and we all have unique needs when it comes to our health care. Ideally we should be treated based on our individuality, yet medical science prefers to treat the disease with standard protocols or treatments, rather than treat the whole person.

Of course, we are conditioned to run to the doctor after symptoms occur and get a prescription for a drug, which may or may not work. We want the symptom treated, and we ignore that perhaps the underlying cause should be treated. I believe, too, that we relegate most, if not all, of our decision-making authority to our medical doctors. All this does is foster dependence, and it undermines our personal responsibility for gaining and keeping our good health.

Dependence on third parties is not the best possible path to health and self-healing. It's up to us—as individuals—to be the keepers and protectors of our own health. Statistics prove my point: the health-care system affects only about 10 percent of our health outcome; the remaining 90 percent is determined by lifestyle choices, and how and where we live. Health-care providers have little control over those things, but we certainly do! And I am on a mission to help people everywhere realize that health and healing is within their own grasp.

Mainstream Medicine vs. Complementary Medicine

My opinion of Western, or mainstream, medicine is that it is effective for treating severe emergency conditions when the body's natural ability to heal itself has been damaged. But, it overfocuses on treating symptoms rather than the cause of the problem. Symptoms are the body's way of telling us it needs help; they shouldn't be masked or suppressed. They should lead us to the cause so it can be alleviated.

Western medicine also tends to zero in on a distinct object of disease—be it a gallbladder, a germ, or even a gene—instead of restoring harmony in the whole person. Medical treatments, especially for the degenerative diseases of age, generally help people get along by fixing their hearts, replacing joints, or medicating pain, but don't do much to help heal any underlying damage.

Other systems of healing, ancient or modern, do it differently. They view sickness in a holistic way and the body as an entire entity—in balance or imbalance—with every part of your life affecting every other part. For example, if you're depressed, the depression will interfere with your physical being; and a problem with your physical being, such as poor nutrition, can create depression. Even a problem in your environment, such as living around toxic chemicals, can harm your body and mind. All of these factors must be taken into consideration for self-healing to occur.

I'm sure you've heard other healing approaches referred to as "alternative" or "complementary" medicine. In many parts of the world, conventional medicine is considered a minority approach and might be considered alternative or complementary by Oriental, African, Ayurvedic, Native American, and other healers!

Thankfully, Western medicine is opening its arms to all forms of treatment. More doctors are now convincing their patients to follow diets and take nutritional supplements. There is more interest in giving patients options in care that were formerly dismissed by many Western-trained doctors. When I have something amiss in my own health, I turn to multiple experts, including nutritionists, chiropractors, naturopaths, and of course, medical doctors. I am among the more than one in three Americans who uses some form of non-Western medicine, according to the National Center for Complementary and Alternative Medicine, and that number is rising.

I applaud this trend. Medical doctors, nurses, chiropractors, naturopaths, and other healers can certainly play a pivotal role in your health. The treatments they advise can stimulate the healing potential that is already within you. And if you fervently believe in your healer, science tells us that the results will be much better. There are far too many people who are diagnosed with life-threatening illnesses and automatically think they are doomed. You cannot think in this way. Very often, it isn't just the treatment or the healer that is doing the healing, but your trust in them.

Self-Care: The Heart of Healing

Fortunately, many people are asking: Is there a better way to stay healthy? Is there a better way to get healthy? Isn't there something better out there? The answers are yes, yes, and yes. Throughout the following chapters, you'll come to realize that your health comes from within; it does not come from the outside. Once this concept sinks in, you'll want to make self-healing an operating principle in your life.

There are so many simple lifestyle options to help your body self-heal. Here are a few examples:

— *Exercise is self-healing.* Imagine sitting indoors on a nice day watching television. But you also feel tired, maybe even depressed. So you get up, turn off the TV, and go for a walk. It might be hard at first, but the longer you walk, the better and more energized you start to feel. Mood-lifting chemicals in your brain start to circulate. Your heart strengthens. Your metabolism revs up. And these effects continue for at least 48 hours afterward. You have actually begun to self-heal!

— *Sleep is self-healing.* A good night's sleep helps your body regenerate. When you wake up in the morning, you'll feel refreshed.

— *A healthy body weight is self-healing.* If you're overweight, changing your diet habits and losing excess pounds will immediately improve your health. You may reduce (or no longer need) your blood-pressure or diabetes medication. Your joints may heal, and your heart function will improve—all by simply changing your nutrition and physical activity!

— *Hugs are self-healing.* Anyone who knows me knows that I believe in hugs. Have you ever had anyone say to you, "Hey, do you need a hug?" Then they hug you, and you just feel better. There's power in a hug. Science has verified that the simple act of reaching out and hugging another person slows heart rate, reduces blood pressure, and even accelerates recovery from an illness. All that in a simple hug!

By these few examples, I believe you can see that we all have the power to make self-healing easier or harder by our actions. And what about miracles? Yes, they can and do occur. But in general, when an illness is healed, the body is the healer, and that is the real miracle.

Self-Healing Leads to Health and Wealth

Most of us today are looking for ways to improve our financial situation, but the answer isn't necessarily in working harder or longer. The answer is in taking better care of ourselves and our family. Some colleagues of mine put together an impressive piece of data on this issue. They calculate that if you make enough of a lifestyle change to reduce health risks by 50 percent, you can save up to $1,000,000 over a 35-year period.

A study published in the journal *Health Affairs* states that the average health-care cost per American—every man, woman, and child in the United States—is $6,280 a year. That is a startling statistic—more than $25,000 per year for a family of four. Imagine how much wealthier you'd be if you could save that much each year—or even half that amount. Take a look:

- Present cost of health care for a family of four:
  $6,280 x 4 = $25,120

- Savings resulting from a self-healing lifestyle:
  $25,120 / 2 = $12,560

- Monthly savings to invest:
  $12,560 / 12 = $1,047

A 30-year-old who stays well and adopts healthy habits can theoretically (using averages) save more than $1,000,000 by the time he or she is 65. And that million dollars is just a bonus to the fact that they will enjoy a life of emotional, physical, and social wealth far beyond the financial benefit.

Adapted from *Discover Wellness* by Dr. Bob Hoffman and Dr. Jason A. Deitch. Used with permission.

What Exactly Is Self-Healing?

In 2004, a friend of mine, Becky, was diagnosed with chronic fibromyalgia. This condition is believed to be activated by changes in the central nervous system that heighten sensitivity to touch and temperature. Becky is a 52-year-old, strong, and petite woman. An officer in the military, she was diagnosed with this condition six months prior to being deployed to Iraq. For four years, she commanded at the strategic levels of the U.S. Army, but she also endured chronic pain the entire time. Deep and debilitating aches permeated every muscle, tendon, and ligament in her body.

During the next four years, doctors had prescribed more than 17 different prescriptions to help manage her symptoms. "Everything hurt, and I was deeply unhappy," Becky told me. "I couldn't perform to the level my soldiers deserved. That's when I decided I wasn't going to live like this for the rest of my life."

Becky retired from her stressful military career, changed her lifestyle, and focused on recovering her health. Over 18 months, she switched to a natural foods diet, practiced various forms of detoxification, received regular massages and chiropractic adjustments, and underwent acupuncture. What resulted was nothing short of miraculous: Becky no longer had to take prescription drugs. Today, she lives with much less pain and has a wonderful quality of life. She says, "Self-healing? I'm living proof that it can be done!"

As Becky's story so wonderfully demonstrates, if we give our bodies what they need, they will function properly and will often heal on their own.

10 Steps to Achieving Wealth Through Health

1. Stay well and fully fund a "health savings account" as an additional retirement investment vehicle. This is a tax-exempt account that is paired with a high deductible health plan. It's used to pay routine medical expenses, while the health plan pays for the costs of major medical events and chronic medical care.

2. Stay well and save the money that you would be paying for pharmaceutical co-payments. The average co-payment is $15 to $30 per month, and often people are paying much more. Put that money into your health savings account or an IRA, or invest it. Over time, that money will grow with compound interest.

3. Get a part-time job exercising for money. Teach a fitness class at your local gym or rec center. You have to exercise anyway, so why not get paid for it?

4. Redirect the money you spend on things that are destructive to your health into things that are constructive to your health. On average, a pack of cigarettes costs $3.80, so a pack-a-day habit would set you back more than $100 a month. Stop smoking and invest the money *and* stay well. How about investing the money you spend on alcohol? Cable TV? Bar night? You can find $25 to $100 a month that you are presently spending on harming your health and instead invest it for your future—while kicking bad habits!

5. Many employers have arrangements with their local fitness centers. If your employer is willing to subsidize you, take the money you would spend on a membership and invest it while staying well.

6. Many employers offer wellness programs such as smoking cessation, weight loss, and stress management, and even offer incentives to participate, because it is in both of your interests for you to stay well. Take advantage of any incentives your employer is offering. Take the money you would otherwise spend yourself, and invest it.

7. Stop spending money on fast food and prepare fresh, wholesome meals at home. You should also bring healthy meals to work. It will be healthier for you and save you thousands of dollars over time.

8. When you feel better, you will save thousands on over-the-counter medications that are just masking your symptoms anyway. Stay healthier by not living on unnecessary medication, and invest the money for your future.

9. Think about your performance at work. If you felt better and performed better, could you make more money? Would you have the energy to get a part-time job or turn a hobby into a home-based business?

10. If you have a preexisting condition and try to change your health insurance, unless you work for a big company, your condition can cost you thousands of dollars in increased premiums—even if it's only a minor condition. Staying well will prevent you from paying these increased premiums. Invest the savings for your financial future.

Adapted from *Discover Wellness* by Dr. Bob Hoffman and Dr. Jason A. Deitch. Used with permission.

How the Body Self-Heals

In the chiropractic profession, we emphasize *innate intelligence.* It simply means that "the power that made the body, heals the body." Benjamin Franklin put it this way: "God heals and the doctor takes the fee." Other disciplines refer to innate intelligence as a *life force.* Whatever the title, it endows the body with healing power, as long as we provide positive health practices such as diet, exercise, and natural remedies.

Innate intelligence can be a difficult concept for some to grasp. The important thing to know is that as long as you believe you're connected with, and created by, something greater than yourself, then you can easily recognize that everything you need to be healthy is already within you. There is never a moment when this intelligence or life force is not acting at its utmost to provide you with a more enriched living experience. But it's up to you, through your behavior, actions, and choices, to support that healing intelligence.

Is the concept of innate intelligence something testable? Not until quite recently. Cutting-edge research into communication among cells is validating the guiding force of innate intelligence. We now know how innate intelligence activates something called "cell signaling." This refers to how cells interact with, and "talk" to, other cells using various biochemical signals.

For example, let's return to the example of nicking your skin. As I described earlier, the body does so many miraculous things, all working in concert, to bring healing. Blood vessels dilate to deliver oxygen, nutrients, and other healing substances to the wound. Bacteria and germs are attacked, and the skin is repaired and rebuilt. How is all this orchestrated? It is the innate intelligence at work, controlling all the signals among cells to effect healing.

We know too that bad choices can block this process and interrupt cellular communication. Take cigarette smoking, for example. Studies show that smoking delays the delivery of healing substances to wounds, and healing is slowed. Smoke also causes the body to form too much scar tissue.

Improper cell signaling is at the root of many diseases, including cancer, diabetes, and arthritis, to name just a few. Scientists are now looking at the body as a huge communications network, and those of us in the natural healing fields believe that an innate intelligence is at the helm, activating self-healing.

One reason I'm so faithful to my profession is because it introduced me to innate intelligence. And when you tap into that intelligence, I promise you that it's the greatest support you can ever imagine.

The body is designed perfectly to function perfectly. It contains infinite wisdom and vast resources that can, given the right conditions, conquer illness, extend life, and perform miracles. Whenever a patient would say, "Dr. Mancini, you're the greatest—you healed me," I'd always reply, "I didn't heal you. I want you to thank yourself because *you* are giving your body what it needs to heal itself."

The greatest miracle on Earth is the human body. It is stronger and wiser than you probably realize. And improving its ability to heal is within your control. Start believing in your innate ability to heal, give your body the right nutrients, provide your body with self-repair tools, remove all negative obstacles and interferences to the process . . . and your body will heal. Don't you think it's time to unlock your self-healing powers?

HEALING
VERSUS CURING

We use the words *heal* and *cure* interchangeably, but do they mean the same thing? Not exactly. They are subtly different in meaning, and I'll explain why.

As I've emphasized, healing comes from within. It's the process by which the body, mind, and spirit work in concert so that we become whole again. Curing is when we are completely freed from illness or injury.

In curing, we depend on the expertise of a practitioner (such as a doctor) to control the course of the disease; in healing, we depend on our own inner resources.

Someone might be healed, but not cured. Another person might be cured, but not healed. There are many people who are "cured" but don't feel like they are living a life full of meaning. In reality, they aren't healed. Still others might be healed and cured.

Consider the example of some cancer patients. Studies have shown that cancer patients live longer if their quality of life is better—that is, they adhere to a nutritious diet, they exercise to relieve stress, they're surrounded by supportive friends and family, and they have a spiritual foundation on which to lean. These are all parts of a healing lifestyle. So healing, because it positively affects quality of life, is associated with living longer. And in cancer survivors, healing has been known to prevent the recurrence of cancer—curing it, in other words.

I'm not hairsplitting these concepts; I'm just pointing out their subtle distinctions. To further illustrate these distinctions, I'll share the story of Carlos, who was treated by my dear friend, Dr. John F. Demartini, D.C.

Healed

Carlos was an aspiring young actor who had been injured in a serious car accident that severed his spinal cord. When Carlos appeared at Dr. Demartini's office in Houston, Texas, he was strapped very carefully into a special quadriplegic wheelchair. His head was harnessed, and his body was paralyzed from the neck down.

His eyes were cast downward and his mother said that he was feeling hopeless, depressed, and—yes, sadly—suicidal. Carlos's inner dream had been to become a great actor, performing in theater and movies. He wanted to be on Broadway and dance in musicals. But there he was in a quadriplegic wheelchair.

Dr. Demartini looked at him and said, "Carlos! What are you thinking and feeling inside? Talk to me!"

"I just want to walk again," he replied. "I want to dance and act again. I don't want to live if I have to remain like this."

"Carlos, if you have a determined will to live, if you have a strong desire to return to greater function, and if you believe in the possibility of having some kind of recovery, then and only then will you have the necessary elements with which to achieve success. And I will help you get there. It's essential that you have some meaningful and inspiring vision to work toward. Because if you don't have a will to live, then you're already defeated. Do you truly have the necessary desire to overcome your potential challenges and obstacles? I need to have your complete commitment. I want to make sure you have something driving you to success far beyond the ordinary."

Carlos made his decision immediately and with enthusiasm. "Yes, I want to do it! I want to walk, dance, and act again!"

Dr. Demartini examined Carlos's spine, reviewed his huge stack of radiographs, pored over his mountain of previous test results, and formulated a treatment plan. He worked with Carlos daily. During one treatment, Dr. Demartini decided to adjust a certain single vertebra that had been severely displaced. On the night following this adjustment, Carlos began to feel his toes for the first time since the accident.

The next day, Dr. Demartini adjusted him again, and Carlos was able to partially control his own bladder. He adjusted Carlos almost every day, and over the next six months, not only was Carlos able to move his toes, feet, and legs, and regain some control over his bowel, but he was also starting to move his hands and torso. His newly enabled upper-torso movement enhanced his ability to breathe independently. In fact, Carlos's adjustments were changing his entire physiology.

Then, after about nine months of steady chiropractic care, Carlos experienced a major psychological breakthrough. He announced confidently: "Next week, I'm going to walk for you!"

At that moment, Dr. Demartini was taken aback and didn't quite know how to respond. A part of him was thinking it would be a stretch, yet he couldn't say that. Instead, he replied, "Great! That's the spirit and determination of a champion!"

Several days later, Carlos came in for his treatment. He eased himself off the table, unassisted, and with the help of gravity, he swung into his wheelchair. Then, with no assistance but the use of his own hands and arms, he carefully leaned forward and grabbed the edge of the countertop. Carlos slowly "walked" his bottom to the front edge of the wheelchair and began to pull himself up. With shaking legs, he gradually leaned forward until he was completely upright. Then Carlos turned toward Dr. Demartini and attempted a few faltering steps. Within moments, he started a slow-motion fall into the doctor's waiting arms. These were the first steps Carlos had attempted since his near-fatal car crash.

Over the next few months, Carlos developed the ability to hobble, hunched over, with a cane. Sometimes he would even take his cane under his arm, stand erect, and walk very slowly. His original doctors said he would remain paralyzed forever—his case was hopeless. And at one time, even Carlos believed it and wanted to kill himself. But all that eventually changed. The only people who became hopeful, and remained that way, were Carlos and Dr. Demartini.

Was Carlos cured? No, he never fully recovered enough to regain his ability to act or dance. Was he healed? Definitely. His desire and determination gave him his life back. Today, Carlos is a drama teacher, fulfilling his dreams and goals through the lives of his students. To me, that is healing in every sense of the word.

The Three Levels of Healing

As the story of Carlos illustrates, healing is much more than just recovering health. It's a way of living that imbues life with energy and purpose to get us through difficult times. And how exactly do we get to that point? The answer is by tending to ourselves at each of the three levels of healing.

First there is the *physical level,* and this is what we usually focus on. Healing definitely takes place physically, as when a bone mends or a wound heals. Healing happens, too, when we eat properly, take supplements, exercise, and follow our healer's recommendations for treatment.

Second is the *emotional level,* which begins with our thinking. Thinking leads to emotions, and the two are intertwined. If we have a negative mind-set, this triggers negative emotions such as fear, sadness, frustration, or anxiety. Negativity, in turn, can harm our health and thwart the healing process, because the mind has control over what we experience physically and emotionally.

The *spiritual level* is third, as we relate in some meaningful way to what we hold sacred. Spirituality, whether experienced through the practice of one's faith or through the appreciation of nature, gives life a deep sense of meaning and purpose, and a connection to something greater than ourselves. When I feel in spiritual balance, for example, I can look at a mountaintop, a sunset, or a wave cresting in the ocean and appreciate its profound beauty. Or my sense of purpose might call me to ask, *What can I do for others?* For many of us, spirituality puts us in touch with the divine—perhaps through prayer, worship, meditation, or simply a peace that is within or around us.

Three Levels, Working Together

We often talk about these three levels of healing as distinct realities. Yet when it comes to health, they are not separate. Imagine walking into the supermarket and picking up a bag of flour, a box of sugar, some eggs, butter, and frosting. These are separate items, but once you combine them to make a cake, they're fused into a single dish. You can still distinguish the frosting from the cake, but all of the parts have come together. And the contribution of each ingredient is essential to the quality of the cake. So it is with each level of healing. If one is missing, you aren't really whole, and your well-being is not all it could be.

Healing can even be experienced when someone is dying. A good example of this is the story of a 10-year-old named Cheryl Jean. For the last six years of her life, she fought leukemia. She never gave up, even in her last breath. She cherished every second of every day and still managed to smile at everyone she met, although her body and insides were often screaming in pain. This little girl displaced her own personal turmoil by redirecting her attention to helping others feel better. These are spiritual lessons from which we can all benefit: "Cherish every moment," and "Consider others first."

Cheryl Jean wanted to be home in her own bed with her own teddy bears on her last night on Earth. She asked Dr. Steven J. Pollack, D.C., who was part of her medical-care team, to be there with her and her family. Dr. Pollack later told me, "Our eyes locked, and I knew she had come to peace." Her body was no longer in pain, she was free emotionally, and her being had found spiritual peace. She was healed, though not cured.

Maybe you've experienced this with someone you love who was terminally ill. Maybe that person could not be cured of a physical disease, but he or she made spiritual peace with the divine, however defined—and was in effect, healed. I believe that we can always be healed, even if we might not be cured in our bodies.

Healing, Curing, and Chronic Disease

Maybe right now you're dealing with a chronic disease such as cancer or diabetes. Chronic disease is tough—for the patient, as well as for the family and other loved ones. Feelings of grief, fear, regret, and anger can hang over you like a heavy cloud. A lot of people want to pretend the cloud isn't there. They've heard or have been told that they should "stay positive." Well, what if you don't feel like staying positive? Forcing positivity is just as harmful as being negative; it puts you under additional stress that will counter healing. Go with, and work through, all emotions or else you'll block healing energy.

Joseph's story exemplifies these truths.

The oncologist threw numbers at Joseph about life expectancy: one year, 18 months at best. As he listened to the grim prognosis, he didn't just go deaf; he went numb. This was in April 2004. For months, Joseph, age 56, had been experiencing torturous pain throughout his body. It was virtually impossible for him to sit in a chair. He couldn't sleep for more than several minutes at a time. He was in and out of the bathroom, urinating on the hour, every hour. He hobbled like a horse with three legs and hoped no one would notice. His weight dropped quickly. His eyes sunk back into his face, and his complexion turned ghostly. The pain became a part of him, inhabiting his body like an unwelcome visitor who refused to leave.

Prior to seeing the oncologist, Joseph had a prostate-specific antigen (PSA) test. This test measures levels of a protein produced by the prostate gland and is used to detect disease. He learned that his PSA test result was 335.

He asked, "What's normal?"

"Four or under," the doctor replied.

"Shouldn't I be dead?" Joseph asked. The doctor told him that there may have been a mix-up in the lab and ordered another PSA. After it came back two weeks later, Joseph's test results were 435.

As it turned out, 90 percent of his prostate was saturated with cancer cells, and he was referred to cancer treatment. Joseph was devastated as he listened to his diagnosis: "You have stage IV metastatic prostate cancer that has gone to the bone. Cancer cells have pushed their way into your pelvis, ribs, shoulder blades, and lymph glands."

There was, of course, the horrible shock of the diagnosis, followed by depression, anger, and disbelief—all natural, understandable emotions that had to be experienced and worked through. Everything Joseph had learned to identify as himself had changed: his physical appearance, lifestyle, relationships, and all the other details that make up a person's life. He knew that things would never be the same.

After facing the diagnosis of cancer, Joseph eventually came to grips with it and asked himself, *What must I do to get through this?*

He persevered in his treatments, which over time included grueling, painful bouts of radiation, chemotherapy, and surgery. Regardless, he was determined to maintain a somewhat normal life by continuing to do what he enjoyed. He stayed active and went to work, knowing that activity would build his energy reserves. In the middle of this, he even fell in love and got married. In short, *he kept on living*—and living with the expectation of positive results, a belief that is a key ingredient in healing. And through it all, he accepted his disease.

Whether or not Joseph was able to change the course of his disease, he unquestionably altered his experience of it. Healing occurred when he faced the reality of whatever confronted him while continuing to put his energy into living a full life. Researchers investigating mind-body health believe that if we transform the experience of an illness, we may also affect the course of the disease. And so it was in the case of Joseph: an 18-months-to-live prognosis turned into seven years and counting. I see that as an inspiring example of self-healing.

Have you ever wondered what keeps a person going, sometimes far longer than expected, whether a 56-year-old fighting cancer or a 45-year-old recovering from a heart attack? I believe that at least part of the answer lies in the fundamental differences between healing and curing.

You and I are going to get sick; that's just a reality. I've known people who are actually thankful for a health crisis because it was a wake-up call that forced them to make significant lifestyle changes—physically, emotionally, and even spiritually. Although I'd rather not have to wait for a wake-up call, I do believe that illness and disease can teach us things about ourselves that can improve our lives and help us set priorities for what really matters.

Know That You Are Unique

Almost every health-care profession and discipline uses "treatment protocols," standardized step-by-step instructions on the techniques and procedures involved in a care plan. Protocols are helpful because in many cases they do improve a patient's outcome.

As I delved more into healing-related issues, the more I came to believe that protocols, including those in my own profession, approach health problems in a simplistic way, as if the body has only one way of reacting. Let's say you were diagnosed with some form of cancer, for example. You might assume that your treatment was chosen because of your unique situation—say a chemotherapy regimen of several drugs tailored for you. In actuality, though, it might be a standard protocol given to many people with the same type of cancer. This "one size fits all" approach might work well if superior results were always the outcome, but sadly, this is not always the case. I read a study of women with breast cancer, all age 50 or older, who also had cancer present in their lymph nodes. The standard chemotherapy protocol given increased ten-year survival rate by only 3 percent.

The answer is not to abolish treatment protocols; that would be foolish. In my way of thinking, the answer is to seek out, and add in, more enlightened paradigms—not necessarily protocols—that truly tailor treatment to the individual. Those treatments could be nutritional, emotional, spiritual, and medical, as long as they can be customized.

A Sense of Hope

Hope is defined in most dictionaries as a "desire accompanied by expectation of, or belief in, fulfillment." It has long been an intriguing concept in health care. Ill patients who believe they can get better often do. In my work as president of Parker University, I've met thousands of healers, listened to their stories, and marveled at their ability to offer hope and healing to their patients. Through their experiences, I've learn firsthand that hope plays a decisive role in healing.

Karla, for example, was a very sick young woman. She was legally blind, suffered from persistent nausea, and had endured constant headaches for almost seven months. She also suffered out-of-control diabetes that was slowly killing her. Her blood-sugar monitor routinely registered "high," which meant that it was above the top-listed reading of 600. She was on two different medications for headaches and was taking metoclopramide (Reglan) for nausea, a medicine given to chemotherapy patients.

Karla had sustained kidney damage due to her diabetes and was only filtering at a rate of 50 percent. She was told that more than 1,100 micro-units of protein were spilling over into her urine every day. A normal quantity is under 200.

But probably the worst condition from which she suffered was hopelessness. Karla had tried, and been through, all the conventional means of health care, and yet she was dying. On the advice of her parents, she went to see Dr. Bill Hannouche, D.C.

Dr. Hannouche asked Karla, "Do you expect to improve, stay the same, or get worse if you stay with your current medical treatment?"

"I'm getting worse," she admitted.

"Would you give chiropractic a try?

She hesitated. "What's involved?"

"It's noninvasive, requires no drugs, and there's only one side effect: improved health," he replied.

Karla agreed, but considered it a last resort.

Three weeks after Karla started regular chiropractic adjustments, she was completely off her headache medicine. After two more weeks, she was off Reglan.

Dr. Hannouche made sure she took a blood-sugar reading prior to her adjustment and then immediately afterward. It would routinely drop 50 to 60 points. Eventually, when she took her own readings, they never registered more than 300 points, and the numbers kept improving. Also, Karla's kidney function improved to 60 percent with her protein levels still dropping.

Additionally, the last time she went to have her eyes checked, her vision was blurring because her prescription glasses had become too strong for her improving eyesight. Her ophthalmologist documented the improvement.

Dr. Hannouche told me: "Seeing these health changes was, of course, wonderful, but seeing the look of purpose, hope, and life in Karla's eyes was the ultimate outcome."

Recently, I read a fascinating study conducted on the healing power of hope. In 2005, researchers at the School of Nursing at McGill University in Canada discovered that if someone has enough hope as Karla had, they may "will" a change in the course of the disease in the body. This study examined eight stroke survivors, each on the road to healing, and asked them three questions: "What does hope mean to you? Has your sense of hope changed since you had your stroke? What are you hoping for now?"

I was fascinated by the findings that emerged. The first was that "storytelling" has profound healing power. When you tell your story about your disease and its impact on your life, it lets you express your fear, anxiety, uncertainty—and your hope. One young man, only 19 years old, told his story like this: "It was terrifying, very terrifying. I knew something terrible was happening. I have no idea what caused it. I fell down on the floor. My whole left side was paralyzed. I was afraid. I saw my whole life in front of my eyes. My head was down and I couldn't look up."

The survivors also identified a hopeful attitude as a force in healing. As one person said, "As long as there is life, there is hope. I still have life. I'm still optimistic that I'll get better."

All eight people talked about the spiritual dimension of hope. They defined it as "a sense of relatedness and connectedness with others, nature, and God." Or as another survivor put it: "Hope is like a clear blue sky and bright sun; it warms you—it is beautiful."

The final theme to emerge was "self-healing." The participants believed they had the power to heal themselves in three important ways. The first was self-awareness: listening to the body and tending to its needs. As the 19-year-old said, "I realize that in the future when I'm feeling tired, maybe I shouldn't push myself as I do now. Maybe I'll take things a little more easily and relax when I'm tired. I saw what can happen if you push yourself too hard."

The second way revolved around adopting a positive outlook on the future. "I'm okay, but [the stroke] has made me realize that I need to think about the future differently," said one woman. "Not just my goals. There are other things to think about, including my son. I have new priorities." And the third way toward achieving healing was letting go of the past. One participant realized that to continue to heal, she would have to let go of long-held destructive behaviors. "I've let go of everything that isn't necessary."*

Let Hope Heal You

Hope is a self-healing inner strength. To activate it, tell your story, listen to your body, adopt an optimistic view, and let go of what no longer serves you. Staying hopeful will help you recapture your purpose, establish a sense of the future, and open up to joy, despite the presence of an illness.

Yes, life is often difficult and painful. But this reality doesn't describe all of life, and it doesn't describe how we respond to trials and challenges. The sun comes up after a dark night. A hug, a smile, or a touch from a friend touches the heart. As the poet Robert Frost once said, "I always entertain great hopes."

So I say to you: *Stay hopeful!*

---

*For more on this fascinating study, read: Arnaert, A., et al. 2005. Stroke patients in the acute care phase: role of hope in self-healing. Holistic Nursing Practice 20:137–146.

Healing is a process that goes on continually. You don't just get sick, heal from it, and then the healing is over. You are always healing, at all three levels, if you stay focused on what is best for your body, mind, and spirit. Healing is a never-ending journey.

And now, if you're ready, I invite you to take that journey with me . . . into the amazing, often miraculous world of self-healing.

PART I

PHYSICAL SELF-HEALING

Your health can be different—it really can—if you take self-healing in small steps. One step is proper diet; another is regular exercise. The scientific literature abounds with research proving that diet and exercise are self-healing. But what exactly do you need to do? What should you eat? How should you exercise to self-heal? In Part I, I answer these questions and more. I'm starting with physical self-healing because it will give you the energy, focus, and desire to be happier and healthier at every level of healing.

CHAPTER ONE

SELF-HEALING FOODS

In 2002, Phil, a student at Parker University in Dallas, Texas, heard the three words no one wants to hear: "You have cancer."

Understandably, Phil was crushed, filled with hopelessness and despair. In an instant, his world shattered and he sunk into a deep depression. His focus turned inward, and he was unable to process much of the information that immediately followed his diagnosis. Even when people spoke to him, their words sounded garbled and muffled, as if they weren't real. He was overcome by his emotions.

"I became infuriated with the current health-care system," Phil said, "believing it had failed me. I felt like a victim, but I also knew that no amount of feeling sorry for myself would restore my health or help me in any way. I channeled those emotions and decided to do something; after all, this is who I am: a person of solutions and action."

Phil was diagnosed with non-Hodgkin's lymphoma, a type of cancer that attacks the body's lymphatic system and is estimated to be the sixth-most-common cancer in the U.S.

In our bodies, we have a second circulation system called the lymphatic system. It is made up of channels through which white blood cells called lymphocytes travel. Lymphocytes patrol the body, looking for foreign invaders that cause disease. The system is also made up of lymph nodes, small clusters of bean-shaped tissue that house lymphocytes; as well as organs such as the spleen, thymus, and tonsils. It is a very elaborate system—one we should all appreciate—as it is designed to help the body self-heal. An indication of non-Hodgkin's lymphoma is a painless swelling of a lymph node, and it must be checked out immediately.

At the time of his diagnosis, Phil was serving his final years as a Marine flight instructor for advanced tactical jet training. "I'm not a quitter, and I won't go down without a fight" was his attitude. He had overcome many challenges in life, such as landing on an aircraft carrier at night, and he also graduated with honors from naval flight school to become an F/A-18 Marine fighter pilot. Phil's philosophy was this: "Obstacles in life are part of spiritual growth and opportunity, and this is no different."

Courageously, Phil decided to look beyond Western medicine for treatment and began searching for a doctor who specialized in nutritional treatments for cancer. He found a doctor of osteopathic medicine (D.O.) who practiced with a team of three naturopaths in Tulsa, Oklahoma. Their practice was based on the huge amount of research and clinical evidence indicating that a plant-based diet can slow, or reverse, tumor growth and can also bolster the body's natural resistance to disease. Feeling hopeful, Phil made an appointment.

The treatment that he began was largely based on a raw-foods diet and large quantities of vitamins, minerals, and supplemental enzymes. Enzymes are a type of protein made by the body and also found in foods. They act as catalysts that either initiate chemical reactions or accelerate ones already in process. Many enzymes work by breaking down matter. Digestive enzymes are a good example, as they help break down food into smaller components. Overall, the body calls on enzymes to help fight disease, inflammation, and aging. Enzymes are involved in self-healing, too; they help the body repair itself after an injury or disease.

Many doctors and other health-care practitioners believe that a shortfall of enzymes in the body initiates disease. The underlying premise is that natural plant enzymes from fruit and vegetables help remove undigested proteins, carbohydrates, and fats—collectively known as "floating immune complexes" (FICs)—from the body. Detailed in research since 1982 in many peer-reviewed journals, FICs suppress normal immune function and coat cells with a sticky mucous coating. This congests the cells, confusing normal communication between them and the immune system—a process that sets the stage for disease. And the older we get, the more FICs our bodies generate.

Phil adhered strictly to the prescribed enzyme-rich diet. It consisted of raw organic produce (often juices), whole grains, nuts, beans, some fish, and small amounts of protein; but no meat, refined sugars, or processed foods. He faithfully took his enzyme supplements.

"It was socially restrictive and time-consuming, but I believed that my life depended on it," Phil said.

And sure enough, it did. Today, Phil is cancer-free. He attributes his healing to this natural treatment.

Obviously, not every experience like Phil's leads to such miracles. But I still wonder: can we, by making a single important decision, like changing our diet, spark a series of events leading to self-healing?

I think the answer is yes. By making decisions to alter our diet or make more healthful choices, we have greater potential for self-healing. I hear stories like Phil's all the time, and they aren't anecdotal. The scientific research is loaded with proof of how proper nutrition can heal. There are thousands of studies, for example, showing that a diet heavy in fruits and vegetables protects against heart disease and cancer. Maybe we really don't need to throw so many pills and drugs at a disease, just more fruits and vegetables!

Even today, there are people in other parts of the world who emphasize natural foods. One of these places is in the Himalayas, home to some of the longest-living humans: the Hunza, many of whom live to be 100 years old or more and maintain excellent health throughout their life span. Members of the Hunza tribe don't get cancer or have hereditary illnesses. There are *no known cases of obesity,* either. Many believe that the Hunza civilization was the inspiration for the fictional Shangri-la in James Hilton's novel *Lost Horizon,* since its people are famous for their health and longevity—an important theme in the book.

How have the Hunza managed to live such long, healthy lives with so little disease? The answer isn't complicated: their diet consists mainly of fresh fruits and vegetables and whole grains; and it's low in animal fats. They don't know what it means to eat processed or fast foods—the stuff that's partly responsible for making us in the Western world sick.

True, you're not a Hunza, and you don't live in a locale isolated from fattening, processed foods, and other disease-provoking temptations. But here's what you can do: eat more whole foods, including fruits, vegetables, and lean proteins, all of which promote self-healing.

More than anything else in the physical realm, what you eat tells your body how healthy you want to be. Proper nutrition is the essential foundation for healing. It has a direct impact on every organ and function in your body. Simply put, when you eat well, you feel well.

The Strengtheners

All whole foods are self-healing, but I've zeroed in on 25 foods that have special powers. I've compiled this list after consulting nutrition experts and reading hundreds of studies. I call these foods the *strengtheners.* All of them fight disease, promote a strong immune system, and provide nutrients you need to feel great. Try to include as many as possible in your diet. You have 21 opportunities every week (seven breakfasts, lunches, and dinners), plus snacks, to do this.

1. Apples

I'm sure you've heard the wise old saying, "An apple a day keeps the doctor away." There's a reason these "old sayings" stick around:

there's more than a nugget of truth in them, and apples are a great example. They're a powerhouse of healing nutrition. Apples:

- Are high in fiber for a healthy digestive system
- Reduce the risk of stroke and chances of dying of a heart attack
- Help prevent prostate, liver, and lung cancer because they're high in catechins, a disease-fighting phytochemical

So apples? Yes—enjoy one a day for great health.

2. Artichokes

This humble vegetable is a treasure trove of natural compounds that protect the body in numerous ways. Artichokes:

- Protect the liver against toxic build-up
- Reduce levels of LDL ("bad") cholesterol, because they are rich in an antioxidant called luteolin
- Provide a source of satisfying fiber

Boil these vegetables and dip their leaves in low-calorie salad dressing for a great side dish or snack.

3. Avocados

Avocados have suffered from a bad reputation, though undeserved. They're thought to be fattening and, therefore, should be avoided at all costs. Not true, so let me set the record straight. Avocados are an amazing source of superior nutrition. Technically, the avocado is a mixture of protein, fat, and carbohydrate, making it a near-perfect food. As for the fat in this food, it's heart-healthy monounsaturated. There's more. Avocados are:

- High in several self-healing nutrients: fiber, vitamin E, folic acid, and potassium

- The number one source of beta-sitosterol, a natural substance that helps reduce total cholesterol

- Loaded with the powerful antioxidant glutathione (more than three times the amount found in other fruits), which helps the body get rid of cancer-causing substances

You'll definitely want to make avocados part of your diet. Enjoy them in salads or mashed as a sandwich spread.

4. Beets

You've probably seen beets on salad bars. If so, load up! They're one of the most nutritionally important veggies you can eat—high in fiber and antioxidants. Beets:

- Are loaded with folic acid, an important B vitamin that protects against heart disease and cancer. One serving (one beet or a cup of sliced beets) provides more than a third of your daily requirement for folic acid.

- Contain an antioxidant called betanin. It appears to help prevent the formation of LDL cholesterol, according to a study published in 2001 in the *Journal of Agricultural Food Chemistry*. Betanin is well absorbed by the body when obtained through beet juice.

You can roast beets, serve them from a can, or juice them. They're great on salads or as a side dish in place of your usual baked potato.

5. Blueberries

Blueberries are a recognized superfood, known to help prevent everything from dementia to heart disease. They:

- Combat damage to cellular membranes, thanks to the purple-red pigments, or anthocyanins, they contain. This action helps combat aging.

- Help your brain produce dopamine, a neurotransmitter involved in memory, coordination, and feelings of well-being. The levels of dopamine in the brain decline as you age.

- Reduce inflammation, a process that might harm brain tissue over time.

- May prevent the growth of breast cancer cells (an effect seen in test-tube studies).

Enjoy blueberries raw, over cereals, in yogurt, or as an ingredient in smoothies.

6. Broccoli

If I had to eat just one vegetable, I'd choose broccoli. And it is, in fact, my favorite vegetable—and supremely self-healing. Broccoli is:

- Rich in sulforaphane and indole-3-carbinol, two powerful cancer-fighting substances

- High in potassium to help normalize blood pressure

- Rich in fiber for a healthy digestive system

- High in heart-protective folic acid

- Loaded with vitamin C and beta-carotene, both of which strengthen the immune system

There's just so much nutrient power in this vegetable that you really should try to eat it several times a week, whether raw or cooked.

7. Cherries

Cherries make great garnishes on ice-cream sundaes, but they do so much more—and I'm talking about fresh cherries, not the red-dye-bottled variety. Cherries:

- Provide a natural substance called perillyl alcohol, which has an unusual ability to kill cancer cells while sparing healthy cells. In animal studies, perillyl alcohol shrank pancreatic, breast, and liver tumors.

- Are high in melatonin, a hormone that helps normalize sleep cycles. Melatonin also acts like an antioxidant that protects cell membranes from damage.

The best way to eat cherries is raw, as a snack or dessert.

8. Chicory

Toss some chicory in your salads. This cousin of endive and escarole has more vitamin A than any other salad green. Just a quarter cup of raw chicory greens provides all you need daily. Vitamin A is another potent self-healer, vital for a healthy immune system and protecting your vision. Most of the vitamin A in chicory comes from beta-carotene. This is a cancer-fighting carotenoid that your body converts to vitamin A.

9. Coconut Oil

For years, we've been cautioned to avoid tropical oils because they're high in artery-clogging saturated fats. But often yesterday's nutritional bad guy is today's nutritional hero, and that's the case with coconut oil. It has immune-stimulating properties, thanks to lauric acid, a fatty acid in the oil. Lauric acid fights viruses and bacteria in the body. Like most oils, coconut oil is high in calories, so don't overdo it. A teaspoon or two a day is all you need.

10. Cranberries

This Thanksgiving dinner staple doubles as a natural remedy for many ailments. One of the most common is urinary infections. Cranberries work by keeping harmful bacteria from sticking to the lining of the urinary tract. The active ingredient in cranberries is a group of phytochemicals called proanthocyanins. If you suffer from recurrent bladder infections, try drinking about eight ounces of cranberry juice that contains at least 27 percent juice. This recommendation is based on a study published in the *Journal of the American Medical Association (JAMA)*.

The self-healing power of these little gems doesn't end there. Cranberries contain more "phenols" than red grapes and 18 other fruits, according to a study in the *Journal of Agriculture and Food Chemistry* in 2001. Phenols are plant chemicals that help prevent the formation of LDL cholesterol in the arteries.

11. Flaxseeds

These tiny seeds are one of the few plant sources of the healing fats—omega-3 fatty acids. Omega-3s are wonder workers: they help decrease rates of heart disease, stroke, and depression. Flaxseeds also contain lignans. These are phytoestrogens, plant estrogens that mimic the positive effects of estrogen in your body. A clinical trial found that postmenopausal women who ate about five to six tablespoons of ground flaxseeds each day for three months reduced their total cholesterol by about 6 percent. The findings were published in the *Journal of Endocrinology and Metabolism*. Easy ways to eat flaxseeds are to sprinkle a few tablespoons on your cereal in the morning or include them in a smoothie. You can also use them in baked goods.

12. Garlic

Many people try to avoid garlic (or a lot of it) because it does stink up the breath, but locked in those small cloves is tremendous healing power. Garlic has been found in lots of studies to:

- Help fight cancer
- Lower LDL cholesterol
- Reduce blood pressure
- Fight infection (including harmful bacteria and fungal organisms)

Use garlic to spice up fish, chicken, and lean beef dishes; or over vegetables, such as broccoli, green beans, and baked potatoes.

13. Kale

Kale is a newer self-healer on the block. This leafy green has the second-highest antioxidant concentration of any vegetable. Kale:

- Is packed with lutein, an antioxidant that protects your eyes and fights heart disease
- Is loaded with cancer-fighting sulfur compounds such as sulforaphane

Kale has a slightly bitter flavor, so you may want to season it with garlic or use it in soups or stews with other veggies to compensate. You can also buy kale chips at health-food stores. They're a delicious replacement for fattening potato chips.

14. Legumes

When I say *legumes,* I'm talking about beans, peas, and lentils—foods high in fiber-rich carbohydrates and protein. Legumes:

- Help normalize cholesterol
- Contribute to a healthy digestive system
- Contain various self-healing nutrients, including the B vitamins, folic acid, thiamin, riboflavin, and niacin

One of my favorite legumes is yellow split peas, a veggie common in my native Colombian cuisine. This legume is loaded with genistein, a phytochemical that may protect against heart disease by preventing the clogging of arteries. Like their other legume cousins, yellow split peas are full of fiber.

Beans and legumes are so versatile. Enjoy them in salads, soups, as part of dips—or as a side dish or main dish if you're a vegetarian.

15. Nuts

It's easy to overindulge on nuts because they're so tasty, but you only need a small portion to get their big nutritional dividends. All nuts are significant sources of healing nutrients, although almonds and walnuts are my favorites. Two ounces of almonds (about 48 nuts), for example, provide more than 50 percent of your daily requirement for magnesium, a heart-healthy mineral. Almonds are great sources of vitamin E, fiber, and monounsaturated fat—all heart protective, too. A small study published in *Circulation* found that after eating about two-and-a-half ounces a day for two months, participants significantly lowered their total cholesterol and lowered several other risk factors for heart disease as well.

Walnuts provide two essential fatty acids that are good for your heart: linoleic and linolenic fatty acid. Linoleic acid may slash the risk of having a stroke, and linolenic acid helps prevent heart disease, as stated in a study published in 2001 by the *American Journal of Clinical Nutrition.* In addition to these attributes, walnuts are high in fiber and antioxidants.

Sprinkle chopped almonds or walnuts on your cereal or salads, blend them in smoothies, or simply enjoy them as between-meal snacks.

16. Olive Oil

Being of Italian descent on my father's side, I feel like it's mandatory to use olive oil, and I love it on salads and in pasta dishes. Unlike most oils, olive oil is packed with plenty of heart-healthy monounsaturated fat, as well as antioxidants. It really is one of the healthiest oils you can use. Olive oil:

- Reduces blood pressure
- Protects against heart disease
- Reduces risk of ovarian cancer

Even though it's a beneficial fat, olive oil is rather high in calories—more than 100 calories in one tablespoon—but you don't need a lot to take advantage of its self-healing powers.

17. Onions

I'm always amazed when people order salads or sandwiches and say, "No onions, please!" If they only knew about the incredible self-healing power of onions. Onions:

- Help prevent arteries from clogging
- Contain beneficial compounds that prevent the formation of dangerous blood clots, which can lead to heart attacks
- Are high in saponins, which prevent cancer cells from multiplying
- Are rich in allylic sulfides, which usher carcinogens from the body, decrease tumor production, and fortify your immune system
- Are high in quercetin, another anti-cancer phytochemical

Once you understand how healthy onions are, I hope you'll consider keeping them on your plate!

18. Oranges

Oranges are best known for their vitamin C content, an immune-boosting vitamin. But oranges (and other citrus fruits) are also loaded with an array of self-healing properties. Oranges:

- Contain hesperin, a natural compound (a flavonoid) that protects against cancer, heart disease, infections, asthma, and inflammation
- Are high in beta-cryptoxanthin, a pigment that shows promise for preventing heart disease

- Are packed with pectin, known to help lower cholesterol
- Are full of two heart-healthy nutrients: potassium, which helps control blood pressure; and folic acid, a B vitamin known to lower levels of homocysteine in the blood (homocysteine is a harmful protein that has been linked to heart disease)

Help yourself to at least one citrus fruit daily to reap all these self-healing benefits.

19. Red Bell Peppers

Red bell peppers have the highest antioxidant activity of the most common vegetables (broccoli was second), says a Cornell University study. This means that antioxidants in red peppers are highly effective at protecting cells from damage. In other research, antioxidants from red peppers, cabbage, and spinach have been found to stop the spread of liver cancer cells cultured in lab dishes.

Use red bell peppers on salads every chance you get, or stuff them with low-fat meat and brown rice as part of your self-healing meals.

20. Salmon

I love salmon for its taste, but it also tops the fish list for its impressive résumé of healing benefits. Salmon is loaded with omega-3 fats, known to combat heart disease, cancer, dementia, depression, and even obesity. Salmon is also:

- High in easily digested protein to help the body repair
- A great source of health-protective vitamin D
- Rich in the antioxidant mineral selenium, which protects cells and helps the body build new protein

Ask for wild salmon at your grocery store, as it contains fewer toxins than the farmed variety.

21. Sweet Potatoes

Full disclosure: I had never eaten a sweet potato until I started researching self-healing foods, but now I'm believer in their power to bring us great health. Ounce for ounce, the sweet potato is one of the most nutritious vegetables around. Sweet potatoes are:

- Loaded with beta-carotene, which converts to vitamin A in the body
- A good source of cholesterol-lowering fiber
- High in vitamin C, vitamin E, and the B vitamin thiamin
- A slow-digesting carbohydrate that helps regulate blood sugar

Although sweet, these spuds are not at all high in calories. A medium-sized sweet potato (about the size of your fist) supplies a mere 120 calories.

22. Tea

All varieties of tea are healing; this has been known for eons. Green tea, in particular, has been found to inhibit breast, digestive, and lung cancers. The catechins in tea are responsible for the protective effect. A 2002 study in the *American Journal of Clinical Nutrition* found that Dutch citizens who drank 1½ cups of black tea daily were less likely to die of a heart attack than non–tea drinkers. Tea is also a bone-builder. A study published in the *Archives of Internal Medicine* found that people who consume two or more cups of tea (green, black, or oolong) daily for six to ten years had stronger bones than people who were non–tea drinkers.

Most people don't realize this, but black and green teas are made from the same plant; they're just processed differently and contain a different mix of antioxidants. That's why it's a good idea to drink both types (perhaps on alternating days) to get the greatest health benefits.

23. Tomatoes

Pass me the spaghetti sauce, salsa, and the tomatoes—please! All are terrific sources of lycopene, a carotenoid that works as an antioxidant. Known mostly for its protective power against prostate cancer, lycopene may also help fight cancers of the colon, bladder, and pancreas.

24. Watercress

Watercress is coming into its own as a powerhouse veggie, as compounds in this vegetable can actually detoxify nicotine, according to a clinical trial published in *Cancer Epidemiology, Biomarkers & Prevention.* Watercress is also a key source of a very powerful anticancer substance with a hard-to-pronounce name: beta-phenylethyl isothiocyanate (PEITC). If you have high levels of PEITC in your blood, your body may be able to zap carcinogens before they can start damaging cells.

Watercress is wonderful on sandwiches and as part of soups.

25. Yogurt and Other Fermented Foods

Did you know that most of your immune function is centered in the gastrointestinal tract? It's true, so a healthy digestive system means a healthy immune system. Adding yogurt, kefir, and fermented vegetables (such as sauerkraut) will help bolster both systems. All these foods contain beneficial bacteria called probiotics, which go to work against everything from colds to cancer to obesity.

My favorite source of probiotics is Greek yogurt. It's higher in protein and lower in sugar than regular yogurt. Plus, it's much creamier and can be used to replace high-fat foods such as sour cream or cream in recipes, or as a condiment.

Nutrition, Disease, and Self-Healing

*"Eating a diet of processed foods
is proven to raise cancer risk in women."*
— **World Cancer Research Fund**

*"Women who ate approximately 1 slice of processed
meat 2 to 3 times a week for a decade were 50 percent
more likely to develop colon cancer."*
— **Michigan State University study**

*"Just one extra serving of fruits or vegetables
a day may reduce the risk of developing cancer."*
— **Reuters, April 17, 2007**

*"Blueberries cut the risk of colon cancer
57 percent, and also lower cholesterol."*
— **Rutgers University and USDA study**

*"People who ate cabbage and sauerkraut more than 3 times
a week were 72 percent less likely to develop breast cancer."*
— **Michigan State University study**

*"Eating broccoli and tomatoes together is more effective
in fighting prostate cancer than eating either alone."*
— **University of Illinois study**

"Research shows that refined sugar helps cancer cells proliferate."
— **UCLA's Jonsson Comprehensive Cancer Center**

*"70 percent of children 12 to 13 years old already have
the beginning stages of hardening of the arteries."*
— **Bogalusa Heart Study**

Commit to a Self-Healing Diet

There's no denying that food is medicine. Every day you should eat foods that are good for you. This includes not only the specific foods I've mentioned here, but any whole, natural foods: other vegetables, fruits, lean meats, low-fat dairy foods, and whole grains. Eat the right foods, and you'll start feeling better and healthier in only a few days—and you'll rarely get sick.

Let me give you some practical pointers and additional guidelines to help make this happen.

Make Time for Breakfast

Breakfast helps fuel your body for the day and revs up your metabolism—your body's food-to-fuel process. Good breakfast choices include eggs, a high-fiber hot or cold cereal, or yogurt. Add to these a fresh fruit, particularly a cup of berries, a citrus fruit, or an apple. With your cereal, have some low-fat milk or a non-dairy milk such as unsweetened almond, coconut, or rice milk.

Prepare Self-Healing Lunches and Dinners

Each week, aim to eat seven plant-based meals and seven lean-protein-based meals. Your vegetable meals might look like this:

- A large salad made with dark greens, several different colors of vegetables, and ½ cup of beans (pinto, kidney, black, white, red, garbanzo, navy beans, or lentils); use a tablespoon or two of olive or flaxseed oil as a dressing

- A large plate of raw or steamed vegetables (again, shoot for several colors of vegetables)

- A large bowl of vegetable soup

For your protein-based meals, I recommend fish, chicken, or turkey with a vegetable side dish. Your body is under constant renewal, and in fact must replace about 2.6 ounces of muscle each day. Ample protein is required to help the body do this task.

Add in Whole Grains

Include up to 1½ cups a day of cooked whole grains, such as oatmeal, brown rice, or bulgur wheat, among others. These foods fuel and energize your body; plus, they're high in fiber. Whole grains have also been linked to reduced tummy fat.

If you've been diagnosed with a wheat allergy, you may have to avoid grains containing gluten. Substitute offending grains with gluten-free swaps.

Enjoy Self-Healing Snacks

For snacking, shoot for two to three pieces of fresh fruit a day. Raw nuts, especially almonds and walnuts, also make great snacks. If you're trying to lose weight, limit the nuts to two handfuls a week and limit fruit to two low-sugar fruits a day. Low-sugar fruits include berries, Granny Smith apples, and citrus fruits.

Incorporate Healing Fats

Play down saturated fats in your diet by eating less butter, cream, cheese, and other fat-laden dairy products. Cut back on fatty meats and skin-on poultry, too. Avoid trans fats (margarine, vegetable shortening, and products with them).

Use olive oil and coconut oil for cooking and salads. Enjoy other healthy fats such as avocados and nuts. Increase your intake of healing omega-3 fats by eating salmon (preferably fresh or frozen wild), sardines packed in water, tuna, cod, halibut, herring, flaxseeds, and walnuts.

Fiber Up

I'm generally not a fan of counting calories or carbs, but I do believe in counting grams of fiber. Work on boosting your fiber intake to 35 to 40 grams a day. Do this by eating more beans and legumes, fruits, vegetables, and whole grains. High-fiber cold cereals such as All-Bran or Fiber One help, too.

Gravitate Toward Organic

Is organic the way to go? I say yes! I once read how organically grown and fed livestock is healthier and tends to live longer, which made me wonder if humans would see the same results if we went 100 percent organic. My wife and I soon decided to switch to mostly organic food, and the health impact we've experienced has been profound. I feel much more energetic, and I don't need as much sleep. I rarely get sick, even though I travel frequently. A lot of people have also commented that I look healthier and younger.

Science backs up the merits of going organic. A study published in the *Journal of Alternative and Complementary Medicine* reveals that our food quality has declined dramatically in the past 60 years in the following ways:

- 32 percent less iron
- 29 percent less calcium
- 21 percent less magnesium

Organic food, by contrast has 21 percent more magnesium, 27 percent more vitamin E, and 21 percent more iron. It is also much lower in nitrates, a harmful toxin. I rest my case: organic food is healing.

Establish Regular Meal Intervals

Don't skip meals or avoid eating. It's best to have three main meals with some healthy snacks in between to help from getting famished. Nourish your body regularly to support its healing ability.

Water Your Body

Water is a powerful self-healer. Drinking enough water daily can protect against kidney stones, urinary tract cancers, and colon cancer. Drink eight to ten glasses of pure water a day.

Drink Alcohol in Moderation

Alcohol has tons of calories, and when consumed in excess, it can cause damage to just about every organ in the body. If you drink, do so moderately. This means up to one alcoholic beverage a day for women and two for men.

Use Portion Control

Watching how much you eat is as important as what you eat. Here's a look at some typical daily serving sizes for self-healing:

- *Non-starchy vegetables (broccoli, cauliflower, kale, spinach and other greens, salad vegetables, and so forth):* Enjoy unlimited quantities. Have veggies raw whenever feasible.

- *Starchy vegetables (legumes, sweet potatoes, yams, winter squash):* One serving daily. One serving equals a medium potato, one cup of mashed vegetables, or ½ cup of legumes.

- *Fresh fruits:* Two to three pieces or servings a day. For berries or chopped fresh fruit, one serving equals one cup.

- *Lean proteins:* 8 to 12 ounces daily; 4 ounces equals the size of a deck of cards. Enjoy up to four eggs weekly.

- *Whole grains:* Up to 1½ cups of cooked servings daily.

- *Yogurt, dairy, and non-dairy milks:* One to two one-cup servings daily.

- *Healing fats:* One to two tablespoons daily.

My 21-Day Self-Healing Diet, beginning in Chapter 12, will show you how to put these principles into daily action.

Treat Yourself

We all deserve a treat, so go ahead and indulge once in a while. Just watch your serving sizes and the number of treats you allow yourself.

As I do, I hope you take advantage of what these foods can do for your health. Enjoy this part of your self-healing journey . . . and know that it is only the beginning!

The next chapter is about kicking out certain substances from your diet. I call these substances *anti-healers*. They include sugars, chemicals, and nutritionally bankrupt additives. Eating this stuff can contribute to heart disease, cancer, diabetes, obesity, and a host of other disorders. Don't worry: It's easy to sweep these things out of your diet. And when you do, the benefits will be life changing.

CHAPTER TWO

ANTI-HEALERS

More than ever, I believe that we've become increasingly concerned about what's in the 1,500 pounds of food each of us eats every year. We're enjoying more lean meats, vegetables, and fruits—and trying to cut back on fattening stuff like desserts and fried foods. All of this is certainly a step in the right direction, but many of us still have a long way to go.

Our misconceptions run rampant, too. Some people still think margarine is much better than butter (it's not—margarine is high in nasty, artery-clogging trans fats), so they'll use twice as much. Or they think granola bars are a healthy snack, when they're actually processed foods, loaded with fat and sugar.

The Suppressors

Any dietary problem can turn into a health problem. What I'd like to do in this chapter is look at what I call the *suppressors,* foods that negate self-healing. They can make an unexpected appearance in your lifestyle, and you might not even be aware of them. Fortunately, I don't have a long list, so a few little tweaks will obliterate suppressors from your diet.

Added Sugar

Ever wondered why you get cold sores or canker sores after eating candy or sweets? The reason is this: sugar is an "immunosuppressant." It interferes with the activity of immune-boosting lymphocytes. Your natural defenses go down—and you get infections.

Imagine 150 bags of sugar piled up in your garage. That's how much sugar the average person consumes in a year! This means many of us are suppressing our immune systems by eating too much sugar. I believe that if we stopped eating such large amounts, we'd see a major decrease in colds, flu, and other infections.

You may have heard that sugar feeds cancer cells. There is evidence for this, but here is actually what happens: A diet high in sugar and refined foods makes blood sugar, or glucose, spike really high. This spike increases insulin production in the body (insulin helps your cells store and use glucose). A blood chemistry marked by chronically elevated glucose and elevated insulin sets the stage for cancer and its spread. Cancer cells are studded with insulin receptors. Receptors operate like door locks. Once insulin gets to the receptor, it acts like a key and unlocks the receptors on the cell wall. The cell opens up and lets insulin in the cancer cell, where it stimulates the division of the cell.

Can you circumvent this process? Yes—in the following ways: avoiding refined sugars and flours, exercising regularly, cutting back on alcohol, reducing stress, and taking certain nutritional supplements (more on supplements in the next chapter).

Sugar in all its various forms, including corn syrup, contributes to obesity and therefore to a whole range of related problems such as high blood pressure, heart disease, diabetes, and depression. We don't really need sugar to live.

How about you? Are you consuming too much sugar? Take the following brief sugar assessment to find out. Select the answer that best describes you.

Sugar Assessment

1. How often do you get cravings for sugar?

    a. Rarely/never

    b. A few times a week

    c. Daily

2. Estimate how many teaspoons of sugar you add to food (in tea, coffee, cereals, and so forth) each day:

    a. 0–4

    b. 5–10

    c. More than 10

3. How often do you drink sugar-containing drinks (sodas, juice drinks, punches, cocktail mixers, liqueurs, and so forth)?

    a. Rarely/never

    b. A few times a week

    c. Daily

4. How often do you drink sports or energy drinks?

    a. Rarely/never

    b. A few times a week

    c. Daily

5. How often do you eat sweets and desserts?

    a.   Rarely/never

    b.   A few times a week

    c.   Daily

If most of your circled answers are B's and C's, then I suggest that you gradually cut back on sugar. It usually takes between two and five days to "withdraw" from a sugar dependence. You may even lose your sweet tooth altogether over time. Here are some pointers in cutting down on your consumption:

- If you use sugar in hot drinks, gradually cut back on the amount until you can cut it out completely.

- Stop drinking beverages that contain sugar, including soft drinks, certain juice drinks, and punches. A 20-ounce bottle of soda can contain 16½ teaspoons of sugar! Get in the habit of drinking more water. Jazz it up with lemon or a cucumber slice.

- Instead of spreading sugary jam or jelly on your toast, make the switch to a no-sugar-added or all-fruit jam, a sliced banana, or fat-free cream cheese.

- Be aware that many foods you're eating may be filled with added sugar. Some examples are breakfast cereals, cereal bars, and baked beans.

- Become a sugar detective. Read labels, looking for added sugar. If sugar is listed as one of the top ingredients, then the product contains a high amount. Sugar also goes by other names: corn syrup, high-fructose corn syrup, invert sugar, fructose, dextrose, maltose, glucose, or any word with "ose" in it.

- Definitely avoid products that contain high-fructose corn syrup. It is a particularly nasty sweetener that has been implicated in heart disease, diabetes, and obesity.

- When you crave something sweet, reach for fruit such as a banana, watermelon, a peach, or strawberries.

- You can usually cut back on sugar in recipes by one-third to one-half. Try substituting applesauce or fruit puree for some of the sugar.

Additives

It's simply not enough to buy healthy, high-quality food; it's also important that your food be free of harmful additives.

Broadly defined, food additives are substances that do not occur naturally in food. They may be "direct" additives that are introduced intentionally into foods to enhance flavor, improve texture, or prevent spoilage. Others are "indirect" additives; these include pollutants that come into contact with food from the environment, during growing, processing, or packaging.

The average American takes in about five pounds of additives a year through processed foods. Additives and artificial ingredients add little or no nutritional value to foods and can pose a threat to your health. Try to eat additive-, preservative-, and chemical-free foods whenever possible.

In the following chart, I've listed my "Additive Hit List"—the most harmful additives known today. You'll see that a majority are linked to cancer in animals. Yes, I know you're not a lab rat, but when an additive causes cancer in animals, it may cause cancer in humans, too.

My Additive Hit List			
Additive	**Commercial Use**	**Sources**	**Health Implications**
Acesulfame-K	Artificial sweetener	Baked goods, chewing gum, gelatin desserts, diet sodas	Animal studies suggest a link to cancer and negative effects on the thyroid gland
Aspartame	Artificial sweetener	"Diet" foods, including soft drinks, drink mixes, gelatin desserts, low-calorie frozen desserts	Animal and human studies hint that lifelong consumption may increase the risk of cancer; and might cause altered brain function
Blue 2	Artificial coloring	Pet food, beverages, candy	May cause brain cancer in male rats
Butylated hydro-xyanisole (BHA)	Antioxidant used to retard rancidity in fats, oils, and oil-containing foods	Cereals, chewing gum, potato chips, vegetable oil	The U.S. Department of Health and Human services considers BHA to be "reasonably anticipated to be a human carcinogen," even though the FDA still allows it to be used in foods.
Caramel coloring	Food coloring	Colas, baked goods, precooked meats, soy and Worcestershire sauces, chocolate-flavored products, beer	Contains certain contaminants that cause cancer in lab animals

My Additive Hit List			
Additive	**Commercial Use**	**Sources**	**Health Implications**
Olestra	Fat substitute	Some brands of light potato chips	Causes diarrhea and loose stools, abdominal cramps, flatulence, and other adverse effects; reduces the body's ability to absorb fat-soluble, cancer-preventing carotenoids (such as beta-carotene and lycopene) from fruits and vegetables.
Potassium bromate	Flour improver	White flour, bread, and rolls	May cause cancer in animals (look for "bromate-free" bread)
Propyl gallate	Antioxidant preservative	Vegetable oil, meat products, potato sticks, chicken soup base, chewing gum	May cause cancer in animals
Red 3	Artificial coloring	Cake icing, fruit roll-ups, chewing gum	May cause thyroid cancer in rats
Saccharin	Artificial sweetener	Diet, no-sugar-added products, soft drinks, sweetener packets	May cause bladder cancer in mice and in female rats, and other cancers in both rats and mice

My Additive Hit List			
Additive	**Commercial Use**	**Sources**	**Health Implications**
Sodium nitrite, sodium nitrate	Preservative, coloring, flavoring	Bacon, ham, frankfurters, luncheon meats, smoked fish, corned beef	Linked to various cancers in humans
Trans fats	Fat, oil, shortening	Stick margarine, vegetable shortening, crackers, fried restaurant foods, baked goods, icing, microwave popcorn	Promote heart disease
Yellow 5	Artificial coloring	Gelatin dessert, candy, pet food, baked goods	Yellow 5 is a potential allergen that in susceptible people may cause hives, a runny or stuffy nose, and occasionally, severe breathing difficulties. It may be contaminated with cancer-causing substances
Yellow 6	Artificial coloring	Beverages, candy, baked goods	May cause tumors of the adrenal gland and kidney in animals; may cause severe allergic reactions in some people

Additive Quiz

Are you ingesting too many additives? Find out with the following questionnaire. Choose the response that best fits your dietary pattern.

1. How often do you use artificial sweeteners in your food?

    a. Rarely/never

    b. A few times a week

    c. Daily

2. Are most of the fruits, vegetables, and meat you buy organically grown or raised?

    a. Yes

    b. Some of them

    c. No, or I don't know

3. How often do you eat processed meats, such as bacon, cold cuts, hot dogs, and pepperoni?

    a. Rarely/never

    b. A few times a week

    c. Daily

4. How often do you eat processed foods, such as potato chips, popcorn, cookies, pastries, and fast food?

    a. Rarely/never

    b. A few times a week

    c. Daily

5. How often do you eat commercially baked goods such as rolls, pizza dough, breads, and other foods that you have not made yourself from scratch?

    a.   Rarely/never

    b.   A few times a week

    c.   Daily

Responses of mostly B's and C's are red flags. You may be consuming too many anti-healing substances. To remedy this:

- Gradually wean yourself off artificial sweeteners. Try a more natural, calorie-free sweetener such as stevia. Or go with sweeteners such as agave syrup or coconut nectar. Neither raises your blood sugar in the way that regular sugar does.

- Populate your diet with high-fiber foods, such as fruits, vegetables, legumes, and whole grains. High-fiber foods speed through your digestive tract, picking up additives and preventing your body from absorbing them.

- Cut back on foods that come out of boxes, cans, or other packages.

- Read food labels, and try to avoid foods containing additives on my Additive Hit List.

Food Allergens and Sensitivities

Our immune system stays on high alert. It recognizes when an unfriendly substance is present in the body. When it meets such a substance, the immune system makes protective antibodies or churns out other chemicals to fight it. In susceptible people, the immune system goes a bit overboard. It considers everyday foods or food particles, such as wheat or milk, as unfriendly and tries to fight them off. The result is an allergic reaction that might show up as hives, sneezing, watery eyes, coughing, congestion, diarrhea, vomiting, bloating, or stomach aches. Though rare, other reactions might be fatigue, headache, or mood swings. Substances that seem to trigger these reactions the most are wheat, milk, eggs, certain nuts, corn, soy, yeast, and chocolate. Certain food additives are common offenders, too.

Healing a Food Allergy

Genevieve, a student at Parker University, told me that she had lived with food allergies her entire life, especially an allergy to nuts. In the last few years, she's been experiencing mild reactions to even raw fruits and vegetables—the very foods that are supposed to keep us well.

On the advice of her father, who is a chiropractor and a food-allergy expert, Genevieve eliminated foods containing gluten from her diet. Gluten is a protein found in wheat, rye, spelt, and some other grains. Normally, it's easy to digest, but for people with celiac disease, the body perceives gluten as a foreign invader and responds with a full-blown allergic response. Immediate symptoms include bloating, diarrhea, abdominal swelling, and pain. Longer-lasting symptoms include gastrointestinal disturbances, skin disorders, weight loss, anemia, muscle pain, fatigue, and behavior changes. Over time, untreated celiac disease can lead to worse complications and may increase a person's risk of disease, such as gastrointestinal cancer.

Within two months of eating a gluten-free diet, Genevieve eased raw fruits and vegetables back into her diet. Her face looked less puffy, especially beneath her eyes. Most striking was the diet's positive effect on her digestion and energy levels. If she cheated and ate something with gluten, her symptoms returned with a vengeance.

"I thought I'd have a difficult time giving up gluten because I craved pasta," Genevieve said. "I bought rice pasta as a substitute, and it fills the bill. This has definitely been a life-changing diet plan for me. I'm now gluten-free not because someone told me I should be, but because my body is begging me to be. I'm finally in tune with what my body wants and needs in order to function at its optimal innate health."

Food allergy pops up in only 1 to 2 percent of Americans, whereas food intolerance occurs in up to *a whopping 70 percent of our population!* Where a food allergy is an abnormal reaction to certain food proteins, a food intolerance is a delayed, negative reaction to a substance usually due to insufficient levels of a specific enzyme.

There are four main types of food intolerances: lactose, gluten, fructose, and histamine. In lactose intolerance, a person has a hard time digesting the lactose (a milk sugar) in milk or milk products. It is caused by a deficiency in the enzyme lactase. Lactose therefore goes undigested and enters the intestines. Bacteria process the sugar and release gas. This leads to bloating, abdominal pain, and diarrhea.

A gluten intolerance means the body has a hard time digesting or breaking down gluten. The condition can range from a mild sensitivity to gluten to full-blown celiac disease (which is recognized as a true food allergy).

A fructose intolerance is a sensitivity to fructose, the natural sugar found in fruits, nuts, and honey. It's frequently added to sweetened beverages such as sodas, sports drinks, fruit punches, bottled tea and coffee drinks, and flavored waters (often in the form of high-fructose corn syrup).

This intolerance can be mild or serious. The more serious form is known as "hereditary fructose intolerance" and is a rare genetic disorder. With this condition, people lack an enzyme that breaks down fructose during digestion. Hereditary fructose intolerance can lead to liver and kidney damage. Fortunately though, it can be identified and diagnosed at a young age. The other, milder form is called "fructose malabsorption." It means you have trouble digesting fructose. Among the symptoms are bloating, abdominal cramps, gas, and diarrhea, but not kidney and liver damage.

A lesser known food intolerance is histamine intolerance. This is a condition in which an enzyme called diamine oxidase (DAO) is faulty and unable to adequately break down histamines in foods. Foods such as pizza, beer, red wine, cured and smoked meats and fish, and many types of cheeses and nuts are high in histamine. When the body can't degrade histamine, allergy-type symptoms flare up.

How can you tell the difference between a food allergy and a food intolerance? Here's a quiz to help you find out.

Allergy or Intolerance?

Ask yourself whether you experience any of these reactions soon after eating certain foods:

- Itching or tingling in and around your mouth
- Swelling in the mouth or a "narrowing" or "closing" feeling in your throat
- Rashes, blotches, or redness on your skin
- Irritated or runny eyes, or runny nose
- Wheezing or difficulty breathing
- Feeling acutely sick or even vomiting

If you answered yes to even one of the above, you may well have a food allergy to a certain food or foods.

Next, ask yourself whether you experience any of these reactions awhile after eating foods:

- Bloating or pain in your stomach or abdomen
- A rumbling abdomen—perhaps accompanied by gas
- Constipation or diarrhea
- Tiredness or lethargy
- Headache or migraine

One or more "yes" responses may—but only may—indicate a food intolerance. Understand that occasional reactions to foods are natural. Maybe you ate too much, which may lead to indigestion. Or perhaps something just didn't agree with you. Neither would be true food intolerances. But obviously, if you're in pain or have persistent symptoms, see your doctor at once.

Your doctor may refer you to an allergist. If so, you'll be asked to keep a food diary, in which you write down everything you eat and how you respond to it. You have to be very specific. Writing down "Caesar salad," for example, isn't helpful. You must record what's in the salad and the dressing—croutons, eggs, anchovies, everything. From there, you'll probably undergo an allergy test. If you have true sensitivities, you'll have to eliminate the offenders and add in certain self-healing foods and supplements. A food allergy isn't curable; you simply must avoid that food.

In the next chapter, we'll talk about supplements. I'm a big advocate of taking nutritional supplements. It's something I do every day without fail. There's a lot of confusion out there regarding what works and what doesn't. I'm going to help clear it up for you by talking about which supplements truly support your body's self-healing potential. Let's go there now.

CHAPTER THREE

SELF-HEALING SUPPLEMENTS

I'd like to introduce you to Dr. Skip S., a friend of mine whose self-healing story can be described only as miraculous. On a March day in 2005, Skip and his wife, Judy, had full-body MRIs while on vacation in Phoenix, Arizona, just to see, really, that they were as healthy as they felt. MRIs are increasingly used to detect many different conditions in the body, even to confirm that nothing is wrong.

But what happened next stunned them. Skip's MRI revealed a mass lurking in his upper-right lung and several comma-shaped masses that dotted both lungs. Doctors said the masses looked "unfriendly" and should be biopsied. The potential culprit was lung cancer.

"To say I was terrified is to understate the case. My mental anguish was off the charts," Skip told me. "I had visions of having only one lung and lugging around an oxygen tank for the rest of my life. I was so afraid of dying, of leaving my family without a dad."

Skip talked to his friend Beverly about the terrifying situation. Beverly had beaten colon cancer and had been cancer-free for six years. She recommended a natural glutathione supplement called Immunocal. It comes in powder form and contains the building blocks the body needs to make its own glutathione. Your life depends on glutathione. Without it, your cells would disintegrate from unrestrained free-radical attack; and your body would have a hard time resisting bacteria, viruses, and cancer. Your liver would not be able to rid the body of toxins.

Skip started taking the supplement right away. He also did some mind-body work. He spoke positive affirmations and did visualizations, all centered on producing a miraculous healing.

In the meantime, Skip sought other medical opinions and had further tests. He underwent a pulmonary examination, a CT scan, and a PET scan. In between the tests, he met with four different physicians, including two certified radiologists who specialized in reading soft-tissue pathology. All four doctors concurred with the original findings: the masses looked suspicious and should be biopsied. They reasonably believed that things looked bleak for Skip.

Skip's first biopsy was scheduled for April 25, 2005. A CT scan was performed first so that the doctor would know where to insert the needle for the biopsy. After the radiologist read the CT radiograph, the doctor walked into the room and said, "I've got good news for you. We're not going to do a biopsy today. The mass has shrunk by 50 percent."

Skip's next CT was three months later. He was still taking the supplement and doing his mind-body work. This time, the mass had shrunk to the size of the fingernail on his little finger. The other lesions had disappeared completely. The doctor announced, "You're out of the woods."

Skip's last CT was in December 2008. By then, there were no lesions on either lung. Today, the doctors shake their heads in amazement and tell Skip that they don't know what he's doing, but he shouldn't let up!

Was it the supplement that helped him? Was it the mind-body work? I don't know. After all, no supplement has ever been found to "cure" cancer, or any disease for that matter, unless you have been diagnosed with a vitamin or mineral deficiency. Or, it could have been the placebo effect at work. Research has long shown that placebos sometimes work as well as if someone had taken the actual medicine or received a specific treatment, particularly if the patient believes that the treatment will work.

And absolutely, positive thoughts and attitudes can push us toward healing. No one knows how many people self-heal with little or no medical treatment from seemingly invasive or incurable cancers, and other life-threatening diseases. Documented cases are rare.

Back to supplements: One of my basic strategies for self-healing includes the use of nutritional supplements. I believe we cannot be healthy without them. And I believe that we cannot get all our nutritional needs met by simply eating a good diet. There are too many variables in our diets today, regardless of how many healthy foods we consume. Fields where food is grown have been depleted of nutrients, for example, and we don't know whether our fruits and vegetables were picked ripe, too ripe, or not ripe enough. All of these factors affect the nutrient quality of food.

Every morning, I fix myself a shake, and I sneak a lot of great nutrients into it, including essential fatty acids, a high-quality protein blend, fiber, berries, and a greens mixture. I also take my morning supplements with my shake. I strongly believe that this regimen helps maintain my health at peak levels.

Could you possibly not need supplements and eat a diet that might be raw or fully organic, or from your own garden, and be healthy? Perhaps, but I haven't met that fortunate person yet!

Supplement Sense

Google the word *vitamins* and you'll get millions of hits, most with the wildest claims you've ever heard. Supplements are hyped to increase energy, reverse cancer, prolong life, stimulate sex drive, and more. There are so many hucksters hawking stuff that you don't know what to believe or what to take. It's confusing, to say the least. In this chapter, I'll help you navigate these rough waters of information and show you what to take, based on credible scientific research and your personal health concerns.

If you took only a few supplements, they should be a group of key products, including a multivitamin/mineral that I call *core-level healing.* These form the basic, foundational supplements you need as nutritional health insurance.

Multivitamins and Multiminerals

The recently published work on multivitamins and multiminerals is encouraging. For example, a study reported in the *Journal of Nutrition* showed that individuals taking a daily multivitamin supplement experienced fewer heart attacks than those who did not. The study found that men taking supplements had 22 percent fewer heart attacks, and women taking supplements had 33 percent fewer heart attacks than those people who didn't take supplements. Why such positive findings? We know for a fact that several vitamins and minerals help protect against clogging of the arteries and heart disease.

Vitamins and minerals have also been shown to help suppress the growth of various forms of cancer and help prevent cancer from returning. The reason for this has to do with the ability of these nutrients to prevent free radicals from attacking cells.

Let me elaborate. Most of us have heard the terms *free radicals* and *antioxidants.* Free radicals are unstable chemicals that are missing electrons. So they go around and steal electrons by attacking cells, tissue, and DNA in an attempt to gain stability. Antioxidant nutrients step in and prevent this damage, often by donating electrons to free radicals and thus neutralizing them.

Antioxidants are very important in protecting the body against free-radical abuse—and in doing so, protect against free-radical diseases such as heart disease, cancer, and other chronic disease. Also, antioxidants are thought to slow down the aging process. Common antioxidants are beta-carotene, vitamin C, vitamin E, and selenium.

Based on the overwhelming evidence in their favor, taking multivitamins and multiminerals—especially those containing antioxidant nutrients—may be one of the best self-healing habits you can adopt. They're good insurance for times when your diet falls short.

Vitamin D

Another core-level healer is vitamin D. Until recently, vitamin D deficiency was thought to be almost as rare as the bubonic plague, eradicated by D-fortified foods such as milk. Normally, our bodies can manufacture vitamin D from the action of sunlight on our skin, but experts believe that many of us (especially the elderly and those who routinely use sunscreen) may not be exposed to enough sun.

Case in point: breast-cancer rates were about nine times higher in women who lived in areas with the least amount of sunshine, according to a 2008 study published in *Breast Journal,* in which researchers analyzed the correlation among sunlight, vitamin D, and breast cancer in 107 countries.

There are other health casualties when vitamin D is in short supply, either because of sunlight or diet: colds, flu, weak bones, heart disease, colon cancer, diabetes (types 1 and 2), depression, high blood pressure, arthritis, immune problems, and obesity. So many of us are now deficient in vitamin D (about 60 percent of all adults, say the Centers for Disease Control and Prevention) that physicians are now advising that patients be tested for shortfall. The test is the 25-hydroxyvitamin D test, a simple blood test as part of your annual routine blood work. Your level for optimal health should be above 60 to 80.

Vitamin D comes in two forms: D2 (ergocalriferol) or D3 (cholecalciferol). D3 is what your body makes after you get adequate sun exposure. This is the most usable form, so you want to look for the D3 form on labels of multivitamins and other supplement products.

Plant-Based Extracts

You and I both know we need to eat more fruits and vegetables to stay healthy, but we're only human and we don't always listen to good advice. For this reason, I advise supplementing with fruit and vegetable extracts, available in capsules or powders you can mix with water or juice, as another core healer. These supplements offer a well-absorbed source of phytonutrients. Phytonutrients, or phyto-chemicals, are disease-fighters in plant foods.

Studies into these supplements have been encouraging. One of the most recent studies I read was published in 2011 and examined whether an extract could prevent the common cold. Nurses and other health-care professionals from a university hospital took four capsules of fruit and vegetable dietary supplement or a matching pla-cebo daily. At the end of a six-month experimental period, researchers found that supplementation decreased cold symptoms by 20 percent.

Researchers are also having luck using fruit and vegetable extracts against heart problems. In a study done at Logan Chiropractic College in 2009, researchers tested the effects of a fruit and vegetable powder extract on blood pressure. Twenty people took the extract; twenty people served as controls. The extract contained a number of healthy substances, including algae, barley grass, milk thistle, and concen-trated extracts of many fruits and vegetables. The daily dosage was two scoops a day, taken for 90 days. The results were rather amazing. The supplement takers experienced significant drops in both systolic and diastolic blood pressure. On average, blood pressure normalized to 128/83. And that happened without blood-pressure medication!

How can you capitalize on this knowledge? For starters, pump up your fruit and vegetable intake daily. If you need the added assur-ance that you're getting enough phytonutrients to keep you healthy, I would definitely add a powdered fruit and vegetable extract to your diet; it's part of my own supplement program. The evidence in favor of this type of supplement is too powerful to ignore.

Immune Repair

Beyond core healing, I recommend "immune repair" supple-ments, especially if you come down with a lot of infections or viruses. Everyone, really, can benefit from immune protectors.

Omega-3 Fatty Acids

What do conditions as different as breast cancer, arthritis, and diabetes have in common? All are connected, in some way, to the workings of the immune system. Evidence has been piling up for years that the immune system may be helped by omega-3 fatty acids—special fats found mostly in fish.

Why would fish be advantageous for the immune system? The immune system is controlled partially by hormone-like substances called prostaglandins and leukotrienes. When you consume fish oil, either through fish or supplements, these substances are altered. And, most of the diseases I just listed are thought to involve prostaglandins or leukotrienes.

So exactly how might omega-3 fatty acids help fend off disease?

In cancer, for example, researchers suspect that omega-3 fats may hinder tumor development by blocking the formation of the types of prostaglandins that cause tumors to grow.

A link between arthritis and omega-3 fats is suspected, as well, because of evidence that leukotrienes and thromboxane (a type of prostaglandin) are involved in causing the painful symptoms of arthritis.

Investigators have long been interested in how omega-3 fats might protect against diabetes—a chronic disease that leaves the body deficient in insulin or incapable of using insulin correctly. Indeed, diabetes is rare among the Eskimos, who eat a fish-rich diet, and some experts believe that their diet provides a natural state of immunity that prevents the development of diabetes.

If you already have diabetes, omega-3 fats may also be a benefit because people with this ailment are particularly prone to cardiovascular disease. Omega-3 fatty acids are being used more and more to help treat diabetes, because of research showing they may decrease the rate of heart disease, reduce inflammation, and lower triglyceride levels.

Clearly, anyone can benefit from supplementing with omega-3 fats and eating more fish (two to three fish meals a week). I can't promise you that this good habit will cure you or guarantee a life free of cancer, arthritis, and the like. But along with everything else you can do to maximize your self-healing potential, omega-3 supplementation can certainly help. I don't think anyone can afford not to supplement with this nutritional self-healer.

GLA (Gamma-Linolenic Acid)

Omega-3 fats are not the only beneficial fats. Another is gamma-linolenic acid (GLA), a part of the omega-6 family of polyunsaturated dietary fats. It comes from the seeds of an Eastern flower known as borage. Although experts consider omega-6 fats and their by-products to be inflammatory, GLA is different. Mounds of studies show that GLA can fight a host of diseases and conditions. Among them: chronic inflammation, skin problems, asthma, rheumatoid arthritis, narrowing of the arteries, diabetes, obesity and overweight, and even cancer.

In the body, GLA converts into an anti-inflammatory substance that prevents blood clots and makes blood vessels more flexible. If you combine GLA with omega-3 fish oils, which have their own anti-inflammatory properties, you've got a double whammy of protection.

Curcumin (from the Herb Turmeric)

One of the most healing plants in the world is the herb turmeric. It contains an active compound called curcumin, which appears to have healing powers for a wide range of conditions:

— *Arthritis.* Taking curcumin may improve joint stiffness, swelling, and pain.

— *Respiratory problems.* Curcumin relieves coughing, excessive sputum, and stuffy noses.

— *Digestive disease.* Curcumin exerts anti-inflammatory power on gastrointestinal problems, including gastric ulcers, irritable bowel syndrome, inflammatory bowel disease, and pancreatitis.

— *Brain health.* Because there is less incidence of Alzheimer's disease in India compared to the U.S., medical researchers believe at least one common denominator may be the fact that Indians eat a lot of turmeric in their foods, and thus take in a lot of curcumin. Curcumin acts as an anti-inflammatory and may protect brain cells from damage.

— *Cancer.* Increasingly, researchers are looking into whether curcumin's healing powers may extend to cancer. So far, animal studies have found that curcumin can inhibit the growth of ovarian cancer cells. The jury is still out, but curcumin may be promising against cancer.

Reishi Mushroom Extract

Some of us are prone to getting colds in the winter or even the spring. If so, consider taking reishi mushroom extract daily if you're among the susceptible. This extract strengthens the immune system.

Called the "mushroom of immortality" in China, reishi mushrooms contain the compounds polysaccharides. These are large, complex sugar molecules that bolster the immune system by increasing the activity of macrophages (big white blood cells) that, in Pac-Man fashion, engulf harmful microorganisms and damaged cells.

Certain polysaccharides in mushrooms are getting a lot of attention because they seem to fight tumors and enhance the immune system. For example, the polysaccharide called beta-glucan (found in reishis and other medicinal mushrooms) has been shown to bolster the activity of the immune system and call into action certain cells that can attack cancer.

In lab dishes, reishi stopped cell growth and even killed off prostate cancer cells, according to a study published in May 2004 in the *International Journal of Oncology.* That same year, another study found that a reishi extract fought tumors by cutting off their blood supply. That study was published in *Acta Pharmacological Sinica.*

Reishi is also a powerful antioxidant. When 14 healthy adults took a reishi-based powder, scientists measured an "acute increase" in their antioxidant activity. Reishi mushrooms can also reduce blood pressure. Based on these findings, I'd say this mushroom is an all-around self-healer.

Whey Protein

One of my favorite supplements is whey protein powder, which is a waste product of cheese production. In the past 15 to 20 years whey has been recognized for its enormous immune-boosting potential.

Whey protein may help fight infections and perhaps even battle cancer. One reason is that it enhances the production of glutathione (which I mentioned in Skip's story at the beginning of the chapter), arguably the most important antioxidant in the body. Glutathione deactivates and gets rid of a wide variety of toxins, drugs, hormones, and chemicals from the body.

Whey protein is bursting with other immune-enhancing particles, which, once digested in the gut, can be taken up by infection-fighting cells, increasing their number. Clearly, one of the best ways to bolster glutathione stores and other immune boosters is to supplement with whey protein powder. It mixes well with water, juices, and other beverages. Use it to fortify smoothies.

Licorice (Glycyrrhiza glabra)

For many of us, the word *licorice* brings to mind thoughts of candy that comes in red or black. Licorice is actually made from a healing herb, *Glycyrrhiza glabra,* which has been used to treat many conditions, including viral diseases, asthma, coughs, bronchitis, ulcers, heartburn, arthritis, and gastritis.

One reason *Glycyrrhiza glabra* is an immune-repair substance is because it exerts an anti-inflammatory effect on liver cells and protects them from viruses. A few studies show that this herb might be a potent cancer fighter.

You can obtain the herb in various forms, including capsules, tablets, tinctures, and extracts. It is also available whole, sliced, and as the cut-and-sifted root.

Avoid licorice if you have heart disease, liver disease, or hypertension; if you are pregnant; and if you are taking diuretics or heart medications.

Blood-Sugar Regulators

As I mentioned in Chapter 2, it's vital to self-healing that we stop eating so much immune-suppressing sugar. Certain supplements can help.

Alpha Lipoic Acid

This nutrient is a highly researched antioxidant that has several vital duties in the body. Like a traffic cop at the cellular level, alpha lipoic acid directs calories from fats and sugars into energy production. It is also involved in breaking down fats and carbs into fatty acids and blood sugar so they can be converted into fuel for energy—actions that help normalize blood-sugar levels. In one study, lean and obese individuals with type 2 diabetes were given 600 milligrams of alpha lipoic acid twice a day for four weeks. Supplementation improved blood sugar and helped cells use insulin more effectively.

As an antioxidant, alpha lipoic acid also protects the body against disease and works with other antioxidants such as vitamin C, vitamin E, and beta-carotene to terminate free radicals. In the process, antioxidants become crippled. Alpha lipoic acid has the capacity to step in and restore them to their original form and strength.

This supplement has also been used as an "oral chelator" to remove heavy metal deposits from the body. Further, it helps support healthy liver function.

L-Glutamine

L-glutamine is the most abundant amino acid in the body. It has an impressive résumé of benefits, and one has to do with blood sugar. If you've ever developed cravings for sweets and starchy food, one reason is that your blood-sugar levels might have dropped. This means your brain isn't getting the fuel it needs. Take some L-glutamine, and you'll stabilize your blood sugar and put an end to your cravings.

Evidence also suggests that L-glutamine might help you lose weight by causing your muscles to burn up more glycogen (stored carbohydrate) rather than store it as fat. Plus, glutamine is the number one amino acid used as energy by the cells of your intestinal tract, so it's vital to good digestive health.

L-glutamine has been used clinically to treat gastrointestinal disease, wound healing, infection, HIV/AIDS, and bone marrow transplantation.

Anti-Stress Support

Who doesn't get stressed out every now and then? Of course, there are prescription drugs you can take to calm down, but my remedy to relieve tension always circles back to lifestyle solutions: regular workouts, a balanced diet, some form of regular meditation, and the following supplements:

L-Theanine

Getting relief from stress may be as simple as sipping a cup of green tea. Green tea contains an amino acid called L-theanine, which studies have shown can help you relax within about 30 to 40 minutes of taking it. It works in two ways: First, it directly stimulates the production of alpha brain waves, which create a meditative-like state. Second, L-theanine helps form a brain chemical called gamma-aminobutyric acid (GABA). It increases levels of two other major neurotransmitters, dopamine and serotonin, which together produce relaxation.

Good Fats

The brain is made up of mostly fat, and thus requires fat from nutrition throughout every state of life. The brain's favorite fats? The omega-3 oils EPA and DHA—which you can get in adequate supply by taking three grams daily of a good quality fish oil. Both fats have been found to help alleviate depression and anxiety. One caution, however: if you suffer from chronic depression or anxiety, or panic attacks, then please seek help from your doctor or a psychiatrist.

Digestive Repair

If we could look inside our bodies, we'd see that our guts are a mess, thanks to all the junk food and toxins we eat and ingest. The result? Gastric reflux, constipation, stomach aches, and more. And many people are lactose and gluten intolerant, which further upsets the digestive system.

Remedies such as laxatives, antacids, and other drugs are not the answer. The answer is to give our guts some tender loving care with better nutrition, and certain supplements are a good start.

Probiotic Supplements

Inside our guts, some bacteria are "good guys" and some are "bad guys." The good guys, or "probiotics," are obtained from fermented foods and beverages such as yogurt and kefir, as well as in supplements. Probiotics establish a barrier in the digestive system that kills off the bad guys—harmful bacteria, like salmonella—that would otherwise penetrate the gut and wreak havoc throughout the body.

Probiotics do so much good for your body. For example, they replenish good microflora after taking antibiotics (which tend to kill off these helpful bacteria), help us digest food, boost nutrient absorption, support immune function, promote healthy teeth and gums, help reduce cholesterol, protect against eczema . . . and on and on.

Probiotics really are super self-healers that just about everyone should take. The reason is that we lapse into poor diets, we take a lot of antibiotics, we're overly stressed, and we deal with so many other lifestyle issues. By taking probiotics, we take one more step toward protecting our guts, and indeed our entire bodies.

Digestive Enzymes

I always used to remind my patients that they can't expect to heal adequately if they can't digest their food. To ensure digestion, I'd recommend digestive enzymes.

These supplements help the body break down proteins, carbohydrates (and sugars), and fats, and are used to treat food allergies such as lactose intolerance and malabsorption (a condition in which your body doesn't properly absorb nutrients).

But they're also immune boosters. When a germ invades the body, the immune system sends out a virtual army, including antibodies, to attack it. Some of these antibodies actually attach to the germ and form clusters. These clusters of interlocking germs and antibodies are called immune complexes (ICs). Normally, immune complexes are rapidly ushered out of the bloodstream by specialized immune cells. In someone with an autoimmune disease, however, the ICs continue to circulate. Eventually, they get trapped in tissues and organs of the body, where they trigger inflammation and tissue damage. Enzymes come along and can dismantle the immune complexes so that they can be eliminated by the body.

If you suffer from poor digestion or inflammation, look into taking digestive enzymes.

Specific enzymes that are best to use include:

— *Betaine hydrochloride.* This enzyme stimulates stomach acidity and activates pepsin, a naturally occurring enzyme in the stomach. Pepsin breaks down protein into amino acids.

— *Bromelain.* Found in pineapples, bromelain is classified as a "proteolytic enzyme," which means it helps break down proteins, but it does much more than simply help you digest a steak. Bromelain has many other health benefits: it helps accelerate healing of injuries, heals inflammation, and may help improve the side effects of some cancer treatments.

— *Papain.* This is a papaya enzyme that breaks down protein and works much like bromelain, primarily as an anti-inflammatory. The two are often used together.

— *Pancreatin.* Extracted from pork or bovine sources, this enzyme helps treat lactose intolerance.

— *Lipase.* Lipase is synthesized from microbes and helps breaks down fats, particularly in meats and dairy products.

To improve your digestion, take enzyme supplements just before meals. That way, the enzymes will not compete with food and more of the enzymes can be absorbed into your bloodstream. To reduce and treat inflammation, take enzymes 20 minutes before meals on an empty stomach. Generally speaking, after taking enzymes to treat inflammation or pain, you should feel better in three to seven days. More chronic conditions, such as rheumatoid arthritis, may take one to three (or more) months before you notice a change in your symptoms. Discuss the use of these supplements with your health-care practitioner, and be sure to follow the manufacturer's label directions for exact dosage recommendations.

Joint Health

Joint health can deteriorate for many reasons: aging, overtraining from exercise and sports, and degenerative diseases such as arthritis. The usual treatment is to take prescription drugs, but we know from clinical studies that certain natural treatments may be just as effective. Some examples:

Hyaluronic Acid (HA)

To work optimally, joints must stay lubricated, and HA, a component in joint fluid, can help. As a prescription treatment for arthritis, it's sometimes injected directly into the joint cavity. Taken in supplement form, it can reduce inflammation and ease swollen joints.

Supplement manufacturers make HA from chicken cartilage. Vegetarians, vegans, or anyone allergic to poultry should not take this supplement.

Glucosamine and Chondroitin Sulfate

This duo is the most familiar of all joint-repair supplements. Glucosamine is a building block of joint cartilage, and chondroitin sulfate is a substance found in cartilage that helps keep it elastic. Some argue that neither is very effective; however, there is a significant body of research to the contrary.

Glucosamine is made from shellfish, and chondroitin from animal products. Vegetarians, vegans, and anyone with an allergy to shellfish should avoid these supplements.

Methylsulfonylmethane (MSM)

If you suffer from osteoarthritis (the most common form of arthritis), get acquainted with MSM. You'll find it in just about every joint-repair formula on the market.

MSM supplies the body with sulfur, which helps form the collagen that makes up our connective tissues. Research into MSM is encouraging. In the first randomized controlled trial on the use of MSM for joint pain, published in the November 2005 issue of *Osteoarthritis and Cartilage*, researchers found that people who took six grams of MSM daily for three months had less arthritis pain and improved their mobility, all without any side effects.

Cardiovascular Support

Heart disease still reigns, sadly, as the number one killer in the U.S. among both men and women. As such, it has been intensively researched, which has revealed key steps you can take to protect yourself. Among them: lose weight, especially around your waist; eat good fats such as olive oil and omega-3 fats; take baby aspirin under your doctor's guidance; supplement with fish oil; eat more fruits and vegetables; exercise; don't smoke; and get stress under control. For extra protection, you can add in supplements. Here are two to consider.

Coenzyme Q10

Produced in the body, coenzyme Q10 (CoQ10) helps turn food into energy. It exists in every cell, but is most concentrated in the heart, where it protects heart cells from free-radical damage. Many studies have shown that supplemental CoQ10 lowers blood pressure and lessens the risk of heart disease. You can boost your body's natural production of CoQ10 by amplifying your diet with B vitamins, especially B6. To keep up your B levels, make sure you get plenty of whole-wheat products and avoid heavily processed carbs (which are generally low in nutrients).

Red Yeast Rice Extract

Is your total cholesterol mildly elevated—say 200 to 220? If so, don't be surprised if your doctor recommends the natural remedy red yeast rice extract. Red yeast rice is produced by fermenting a type of red yeast called *Monascus purpureus* over rice. This process boosts the concentration of mevinolin, a natural ingredient that's similar to the active ingredient in two cholesterol-lowering statins: Zocor and Lipitor.

A study published in the February 1999 issue of *The American Journal of Clinical Nutrition* found that those who supplemented with red yeast rice for 12 weeks had impressive reductions in their total cholesterol, LDL ("bad" cholesterol), and triglycerides compared to those who received a placebo. Levels of HDL ("good" cholesterol) weren't altered in either group during the study. Many health-care practitioners recommend that you take CoQ10 and red yeast rice extract together to get the best heart-protective results.

Brain Support

No one wants to think of losing memory or brain power, but it is bound to happen. There's evidence that between ages 25 and 45, our ability to learn, remember, and recall can decline by as much as a third—unless we take some steps to stop it. Those steps include mental stimulation, a healthy diet, physical exercise, and stress reduction. Supplements are also part of the brain's self-healing prescription.

Minerals

Minerals are vital to mental function, performance, and thinking. Two honorable mentions are magnesium, which enhances memory, especially in middle age and older, and controls the ability to learn and then form memories; and zinc, which can sharpen your attention span and increase memory. Both are available in a good multimineral supplement.

Good Fats

I can't say enough about good fats. Fats, especially omega-3 fatty acids, regulate memory, learning, and intelligence. One of the most miraculous stories regarding good fats—namely fish oil—was circulated widely in the media in 2006. It was used to treat the sole surviving miner in the 2006 Sago Mine disaster in West Virginia. He suffered a massive heart attack from more than 40 hours of carbon monoxide exposure. He was in kidney failure and liver failure, he was dehydrated and hypothermic, and he was in a deep coma. His doctors didn't know how to save him. Although he was given three hypobaric oxygen treatments, there was nothing that could help repair his damaged brain.

As a last-ditch effort, they decided to treat him with fish oil, administered in extremely high doses, up to 19 grams a day, and delivered via a feeding tube inserted in his stomach. The treatment worked. After three months of rehabilitation and fish-oil treatment, he recovered normal brain functions—an amazing story of self-healing when the body is given what it needs to get better.

Choline

Choline is a B vitamin that helps form a "memory brain chemical" called acetylcholine. The more acetylcholine your brain produces, the better your memory. Choline may reduce the risk of Alzheimer's disease. In fact, many of the drugs used to treat Alzheimer's disease work by blocking the brain's breakdown of choline.

GlyceroPhosphoCholine (GPC)

GlyceroPhosphoCholine (pronounced "gli-sero-fos-fo-ko-lean"), or GPC, is a tiny molecule derived from choline that is naturally present in all the body's cells. GPC is a brain booster that heals at many levels.

To date, only 23 clinical trials have been done with GPC, but each one produced positive findings. GPC improves attention span, mental focus, memory, and thinking skills. What sparked my interest in GPC is its ability to help the brain heal following stroke or traumatic brain injury. Researchers at the University of Palermo in Italy tested GPC for its effect on 2,044 stroke victims—with impressive results. The supplement improved the patients' mental performance by 27 percent compared with patients not given the treatment. This research was published in the *Annals of the New York Academy of Sciences.*

In Europe, GPC is regulated as a prescription drug used to treat Alzheimer's disease. In the United States, GPC is available as a dietary supplement. The usual recommended dosage is 1,200 milligrams daily.

Vinpocetine

We might call it a "senior moment," or joke that we feel "brain dead," but all of us have had small lapses of memory at one time or another. As we age, though, these bouts of memory loss can become more frequent and may get more serious.

Vinpocetine, a derivative of the periwinkle plant, is considered an excellent supplement for improving concentration, attention span, alertness, and cognition. It enhances blood and oxygen circulation to the brain; delivers more fuel to brain cells; and prevents the sticking together, or "aggregation," of platelets, which can block blood flow.

The supplement works on mild dementia caused by lack of blood flow to the brain, but is not effective against Alzheimer's disease.

A caution: Vinpocetine is a blood thinner, so it should not be used if you're taking other blood-thinning substances or drugs such as aspirin, vitamin E, ginkgo, or blood-thinning medication (such as Coumadin, heparin, or Trental), except on the advice of your doctor.

Vinpocetine has been sold as a drug in Europe for over 25 years and has been found to be safe and effective. It is sold as a dietary supplement in vitamin, food, and drug stores in the U.S.

Acetyl-L-Carnitine (ALC)

This supplement is a close relative of l-carnitine, an amino-acid-like substance found in proteins. ALC is found throughout the body, but primarily in the central nervous system. It is involved in providing precursors (building blocks) to make acetylcholine (the memory neurotransmitter).

ALC can move freely across the blood-brain barrier, which means it can "get into the brain." ALC also goes to work in the mitochondria of cells, where it helps to produce cellular energy so that cells can do their jobs.

Clinical trials show that in patients with Alzheimer's, ALC improved the effectiveness of medications that patients had not responded to earlier.

Ginkgo Biloba

Perhaps the best-known brain support supplement is ginkgo biloba, an extract of the leaves of the ginkgo tree. The herb contains two beneficial chemicals: flavonoids and terpenoids. Flavonoids are powerful antioxidants that reduce the damage caused by free radicals. Terpenoids improve circulation by widening blood vessels and reducing blood clotting. This improves blood flow to the brain, which boosts short- and long-term memory, and leads to clearer thinking.

In October 1997, the *Journal of the American Medical Association* (*JAMA*) published a study noting that ginkgo biloba was "capable of stabilizing and, in a substantial number of cases, improving the cognitive performance and the social functioning of demented patients for six months to one year." That was a pretty impressive finding because medical researchers stated that a natural remedy was indeed an effective one.

Researchers have since found that ginkgo has many self-healing attributes: it helps heal tissue damage in spinal-cord injuries; protects against inner-ear damage; and improves learning, test taking, and thinking.

This herb thins the blood, so don't use it with blood-thinning agents such as aspirin, steroidal anti-inflammatory drugs (NSAIDs, like ibuprofen), or with anticoagulants such as Coumadin (warfarin) or heparin.

Purchasing Quality Supplements

It used to be that nutritional supplements were not well regulated. You didn't know what you were buying, or if the active ingredient in the supplement even existed in the product in therapeutic doses. Thankfully, these regulatory issues have been mostly resolved, and consumers are much better protected. As of June 2010, all nutritional-supplement manufacturers have to abide by GMPs, or Good Manufacturing Practices. They are regulations, enforceable by law, which are designed to protect consumers and give us more confidence in the supplements we use.

Also, I advise people to use professional-brand supplements. There are sold only through a health-care professional and with his or her guidance. Generally, these supplements are formulated on what is considered critical for a therapeutic effect, based on research. They are superior to what you find over the counter in grocery stores and other retail outlets.

In Chapter 12, I'll show you how to design a supplement program that meets your needs, along with recommended dosages for each supplement you decide to take.

Although I believe wholeheartedly in taking nutritional supplements, I will be the first to emphasize that this important practice should not replace eating a healthy, nutritious diet. In other words, food first, supplements second.

Keep in mind, too, that while a supplement program can help maximize your self-healing potential, it's not meant to cure any condition. It's your total lifestyle, not an individual dietary supplement, that establishes self-healing.

I have always tried to live a self-healing lifestyle myself. Early on, I discovered that if I ate well, took supplements, exercised, and focused on positive beliefs, then I would set an example and be better able to motivate my patients to do the same. And that is where real self-healing occurs—when people are empowered to change for the better, rather than look to someone to "fix" them.

Part of the self-healing equation includes regular exercise. We all know that physical activity makes us look great on the outside, but what most people don't realize is that exercise ignites the healer within and restores balance to our entire body. Keep turning the pages to find out how.

CHAPTER FOUR

ACTIVE HEALING

Johnny is an 11-year-old charmer, an active boy, the blond wisps of his hair swinging across his forehead as he goes. In the carpeted den of his house, he moves intently from fussing with a video game, which doesn't seem to be working, to examining a set of toy trains. Then he returns to the video game, which still isn't working. Finally, he stands up and stomps down to the kitchen.

Johnny rummages through the pantry, locates a box of macaroni and cheese, and wordlessly bangs it down on the counter. His mother heats up a bowl of it on the stove and sets a place for him at the kitchen table, but the food sits untouched, for Johnny has trudged back up the stairs, a frown of concern on his small face. There, he will flit from one toy or object to another in a compulsive fashion.

Johnny has autism, a mysterious brain disorder that interrupts language and social skills. The term *autism* actually covers a range of disorders with common behaviors: an obsession with repetitive patterns, and difficulty communicating or behaving in a socially ap-propriate manner. Autism appears to stem from problems in brain development, most often in the womb. Some autistic children occupy a misty world we can't seem to reach or understand, and it can be tough to teach the severely autistic to talk and express basic emotions of sadness or happiness. Often, the autistic child—four out of five are boys—just can't relate well to other people. Johnny's story was brought to my attention by Lisa Speaks, who works for Parker University as Clinic Director of Projects and Strategic Planning.

A neurologist once told Johnny's parents that he would never be "normal," but the neurologist didn't know Johnny's mother and father. If you show me a successful child with autism, I'll show you determined parents. It's the parents who will fight for their children and get them the services they need. Johnny's parents were determined to bring their son out of his shell.

One way to do that was to help Johnny achieve what he wanted most: to ride a bike, especially since most of the kids were already doing it. But his poor coordination prevented him from attaining his goal.

Johnny's medical doctor advised that in addition to his other therapies for autism his parents enroll him in "active therapy," which is basically a program of exercise to build strength, coordination, and balance. Open and willing, his parents enthusiastically agreed.

Science backs up their decision. Studies show that exercise reduces impulsivity in autistic children, increases their attention span, and helps them have more productive lives. Some of the best activities include jogging, dancing, horseback riding, swimming, and ball playing. Because little is known about this perplexing epidemic—and because what helps one autistic child may not help another—no one can predict how much progress an autistic kid will make with exercise. Exercise doesn't "cure" autism, but it helps improve behavior.

In the first active therapy session, the therapist produced a very large ball—about the size of a beach ball—and handed it to Johnny. His poor motor skills prevented him from holding on to it.

Each time Johnny came to his sessions, he worked with the ball. It was frustrating at first because it kept slipping out of his grasp.

Then Johnny had a breakthrough. One day he grabbed the ball and held on to it for dear life. The therapist next introduced a thick red elastic band into his treatment. She wanted him to stretch it. Imagine everyone's delight when, by the third week, he was exercising with the elastic band and pulling it all by himself.

The therapist also stretched Johnny's muscles, and the results were amazing. She then started rolling the ball to him along the floor, and it wasn't long before he could actually catch it. After more work and games of toss-the-ball, his nervous system began to function as it should and his coordination kicked in.

That's when Johnny's healing really took off. His parents said that even his attitude was noticeably different. The sessions calmed him now and fostered an "I can do it" attitude that he carried into other activities.

In therapy, Johnny move from tossing the ball and stretching the band to working on foot coordination. The therapist placed him on a stationary bike and helped him pedal by moving his legs for him. Naturally, this took a lot of time—and even more patience. Johnny's obvious excitement, however, made the patience easy. Clearly, he was making slow but sure progress.

Johnny's enthusiasm for the whole process lit up the entire active-therapy facility. His parents loved watching his progress. Beaming with smiles, he'd clap his hands after every successful effort. By the end of each therapy session, he was proud and happy, not to mention quite tired.

By this point, Johnny was well on his way to the hoped-for outcome. Two special days arrived soon enough: You can only imagine the emotional thrill when he first pedaled the stationary bike without assistance and later when he was able to ride his very own bike. Everyone marveled over his progress. Some even called it miraculous. Suddenly, a life that neither he nor his parents dared ever dream became a reality.

Exercise—the Ideal Self-Healer

I love this story, because it shows how close exercise comes to being the ideal self-healer. If we could invent a pill that does everything exercise does (reduce the risks of heart disease, osteoporosis, and certain cancers such as breast, colon, and bladder; improve anxiety and depression; and strengthen the immune system, to name a few), we'd all be popping that pill on a daily basis!

But unlike a pill or an injection, exercise has nothing but beneficial "side effects." There's no nausea, drowsiness, drug interactions, discharges, blurred vision, depression, or suicidal thoughts as is possible with medication. Instead, exercise gives you energy, mental clarity, healthy blood pressure and cholesterol levels, better circulation, and countless other wonderful side effects. It puts you in a great mood. Who wouldn't want all that!

And exercise doesn't have to cost a cent. You can go for a walk, or do many forms of exercise in the comfort and privacy of your own home with little or no equipment. Sure, gym memberships can be costly; however, a family membership usually costs far less than medical bills for a family per year.

So I ask you: If your doctor prescribed physical activity that suited your abilities, would you be willing to regularly comply?

The bottom line is that exercise is medicine—medicine you can take to live a longer and healthier life. But how does exercise accomplish all this? Why is there so much healing power in physical activity? What I have to share may surprise you.

How Exercise Heals

Before I talk about how exercise heals the body, let's talk about what happens when we don't exercise. Inactivity is tied to all sorts of health problems: depression, osteoporosis (thinning and weakening of the bones), dementia (loss of mental abilities), heart disease, obesity, some cancers, and type 2 diabetes. In fact, so many people are inactive these days that some experts have coined a new term for the epidemic: *sedentary death syndrome.* The condition helps cut short an estimated 250,000 lives in the United States annually, according to research from the University of Missouri.

All the diseases I just mentioned have one thing in common: chronic inflammation. Inflammation is a swelling and redness in the body's tissues that is usually brought about by an injury or an infection, and it usually doesn't last long. It's one of the body's natural protective mechanisms, but when it becomes chronic, it can turn destructive.

During inflammation, certain immune cells called cytokines flood the body. One of them is interleukin 6 (IL-6). I know that sounds like a made-up galaxy in a sci-fi movie, but it is a protein produced by muscles, fat, and other tissues. When you're under stress, injured, or infected by a germ, lots of IL-6 gets churned out. When you're at rest, levels of IL-6 are low. Then when you exercise and work your muscles, your body starts cranking out more IL-6.

At first, IL-6 puzzled scientists. They observed something odd: When IL-6 is produced by immune cells, it causes inflammation. When muscles make IL-6, it reduces inflammation. Why might that be? It turned out that exercise holds in check other chemicals that normally work hand in hand with IL-6 to cause inflammation. Put another way, exercise guards your body against chronic, harmful inflammation.

But the insights into IL-6 were just the beginning. Further studies found that working muscles produce many different proteins—as many as 600 cytokines, all very different from each other, and playing different roles throughout the body. For example: IL-8 instructs the body to form new capillaries, the body's tiniest blood vessels. IL-15 encourages muscle growth and helps prevent the buildup of belly fat. (Abdominal fat is more harmful to overall health than fat elsewhere in the body.) Some cytokines might even send an anticancer message.

The main idea here is that exercise heals by triggering the release of healing chemicals. Clearly, the human body is designed to self-regulate and self-heal under the right conditions, and exercising is among the most important of those conditions.

Exercise and Immune Balance

Every second of every day, your body is under siege by armies of microscopic invaders. What keeps your body from succumbing to the infections and diseases that these bacteria, viruses, parasites, and fungi are trying to inflict? Thank your body's defense force, otherwise known as the immune system.

Your immune system is made up of many different types of immune cells. Among them are T-helper-1 (Th1) cells and T-helper-2 (Th2). Th2 cells attack bugs when they first enter the bloodstream; if the bugs get established, Th1 cells go to work. If the Th1 part of your immune system is weak, it can take a long time to shake off colds, flus, and other infections (and there is an increased risk of more serious diseases). What's more, the immune-system balance of Th1 and Th2 cells is often at the root of many conditions, including autoimmune issues and allergies.

Exercise helps regulate this balance by enhancing the activity of Th1 cells. For example, low-intensity exercise, such as walking, yoga, or tai chi, has been shown in research to boost the Th1 side of the immunity equation. Case in point: Out of China is a study that tested the effects of tai chi on the immune system. In the study, 30 healthy tai chi devotees had their T-cell count compared to 30 who did not practice tai chi. Before exercising, a blood sample was drawn. Already, those trained in tai chi had a higher number of T cells than the untrained. Then after a 20-minute bout of tai chi, the exercise group gave another sample. There was a 13 percent average increase in active T cells over their original level! The practical applications of this research are obvious. I'd say that if you find yourself often coming down with colds, the flu, or other infections, try 30 to 60 minutes of walking, yoga, or tai chi five to seven days per week.

Exercise may also slow the decline in immune function that comes with aging. When you compare the immune systems of old and young people, the most striking finding is the decline in T cells. A study conducted by researchers at Appalachian State University in Boone, North Carolina, looked at 13 highly conditioned elderly women whose T-cell activity was nearly equal to that of a control group of college-age women and 60 percent greater than another control group of elderly, sedentary women.

These women, whose average age was 73, had been exercising moderately for around an hour a day for about 11 years. They had the heart and lungs of women in their 40s and weighed 23 pounds less on average than the sedentary group. They were neither depressed nor stressed out, and their dietary intake of nutrients was better. I'd say this study elucidates the immune-boosting power of exercise!

Exercise on the Brain

Everyone gets the blues from time to time, yet some people stay depressed. Left unresolved, depression can sap your energy, suppress your sex drive, keep you from concentrating, lead to insomnia, and generally take all the joy out of living. One effective remedy is to sweat it out through exercising.

In your brain, exercise activates key neurotransmitters that elevate your mood, namely serotonin and norepinephrine, the very same chemicals used in most antidepressant medications. While these medications can provide much-needed relief to some patients, clinical trials have shown that 40 to 50 percent of depressed patients don't even respond to them the first time around. Plus, there are some nasty side effects from these medications. Exercise, on the other hand, lifts depression by altering these same neurotransmitters more quickly and without side effects—and thus should be considered as a first-line intervention for depression. Exercise is a drug, a natural one!

Self-Healing Secret: Sleep

Just as activity is healing, so is sleep. During sleep, your body repairs damage caused by stress or environmental toxins, and sorts out memories from the day. When you get less than six or seven hours of sleep each night, your risk for developing diseases begins to increase, blood pressure increases, and excess stress hormones are pumped out. Less melatonin—which suppresses the growth of tumors—is produced. (Be sure that your bedroom is dark; darkness helps your body produce melatonin.) You get caught in a bad cycle. On the other hand, adequate sleep:

- Energizes you. It makes all your internal systems (such as your immune system) more alert and alive.

- Helps you remember and process things better.

- Helps you lose weight. People who get fewer than seven hours of sleep a night are more likely to put on weight. Lack of sleep wreaks havoc on the balance of hormones in the body that affect appetite.

- Lifts your mood by allowing your body to produce enough serotonin, a feel-good brain chemical.

Here's how I suggest you improve your sleep habits:

1. Eat at least three to four hours before going to bed, allowing your food time to digest.

2. Cut back on caffeine or nicotine on a daily basis, especially after 3:00 P.M.

3. Create a soothing sleeping environment—no messy bedroom or television blaring with violent shows.

4. Meditate or read for a few minutes at bedtime (although I don't recommend reading murder mysteries or thrillers).

5. Discuss sleep issues with your health-care provider, and ask for advice.

6. Do deep breathing, and think relaxing thoughts while lying in bed.

7. Nap during the day. I give you permission to do this! Napping can protect your health and make you more productive. A study of 24,000 adults in Greece showed that people who napped several times a week had a lower risk of dying from heart disease. Napping also improves memory, cognitive function, and mood.

8. Talk to your health-care provider if you have sleep problems that remain chronic.

Healing Empowerment

Exercise bestows what I call *healing empowerment.* Dealing with a serious disease can make you feel out of control and helpless in the face of medical procedures. But then you begin to get active, and all of a sudden you feel more in control, energetic, and stronger. Exercise can give you a wonderful sense that you're participating in your own recovery.

Take cancer, for example. For people dealing with cancer, exercise can be a stress reliever, a mood booster, and a strength builder. It also helps people deal with cancer-treatment-related fatigue by decreasing resting heart rate and yielding more energy. A study in the *Journal of Clinical Oncology* found that breast-cancer patients who exercised lived longer.

A caveat: Choose an activity that fits your energy level and is less taxing such as walking, doing yoga or tai chi, or any kind of gentle stretching. All these forms of activities will increase relaxation and well-being, and even help relieve pain.

Start Moving, Start Mending

Although all exercise is self-healing, I want to focus on the following activities. Each has been studied rigorously for its benefits in the prevention and treatment of diseases that so commonly plague us.

Moderate Aerobic Exercise

Just two-and-a-half hours (150 minutes) of moderate aerobic exercise a week will provide "substantial health benefits," according to 2009 guidelines published by the U.S. Department of Health and Human Services. The guidelines are designed so that people can fit enjoyable physical activities into their daily schedules.

Moderate aerobic activity includes brisk walking, jogging, dancing, swimming or water aerobics, gardening (digging, lifting, carrying), tennis and other recreational sports, and bicycling, to name just a few. If you're so inclined, try more vigorous activities such as race walking, jogging, running, swimming laps, and hiking. For more extensive benefits, gradually increase your aerobic activity to five hours a week.

If you want to do something different, I'd suggest Zumba, a Latin-inspired program that infuses international music and dance into a typically hour-long workout that will leave you happy, energized, and healthy. You don't need to know how to dance; it's a workout anyone can do, while burning up to 700 calories an hour. And, there can be self-healing benefits to this fun form of exercise.

Healing Dance

Dawn's story begins with these words: "Zumba was instrumental in helping me rebound from a debilitating health condition. At 48 years old, I am healthier and stronger than I have ever been."

In 1973, Dawn was diagnosed with scoliosis, at age 13, and wore a body brace for three years to stabilize her spine and prevent increased curvature. She was released from her orthopedic surgeon's care in 1978 and did not give her scoliosis a second thought. "As far as I was concerned, I was cured!"

But in 2004, Dawn began to struggle with chronic back pain. She had difficulty standing for periods longer than 45 minutes, and her back would stiffen up. Incapacitating pain throbbed through her lower back and hips. The pain became her constant companion, interfering with her daily activities, both at work and at home.

"Simple things like cooking, cleaning, and grocery shopping were tasks I found nearly impossible to complete," she said. "At night, I was often unable to sleep due to excruciating back and hip pain. My chronic pain left me feeling very discouraged. I couldn't help but wonder if I was in this much pain at age 44, what did my future hold?"

Dawn researched her condition and connected with a physiatrist, a physician who specializes in rehabilitation, whose clinic was 150 miles from her home. Extensive diagnostic testing revealed a 30-degree curve in her lumbar spine and a leg length discrepancy of 1.3 cm.

Her scoliosis was much worse than it was when diagnosed in high school. The physician prescribed a course of physical therapy that concentrated on core strengthening exercises.

In 2006, a friend introduced Dawn to Zumba. "She told me about the core strengthening benefits and wondered if it might help me build my core strength. As I watched her demonstrate, I wanted to join in, but was hesitant that the movement might stress my back muscles."

A month later, Dawn decided to participate. After only eight classes, she was amazed at how much stronger she had become. "My back and hip pain had decreased significantly; I was sleeping well, and my lower body started feeling better. Zumba has had such a positive impact on my physical health and well-being. It's really amazing."*

There are many healing benefits to be gained from regular, consistent aerobic activity. Among the benefits attributed to following these guidelines are improvements in:

---

*This story is used with permission from Zumba Fitness.

- Body composition (reduction in body fat)
- Bone health
- Reduction of breast-cancer risk
- Circulation
- Reduction of colon-cancer risk
- Depression
- Reduction of diabetes risk
- Endurance
- Heart function
- Hypertension
- Respiratory function
- Weight control

Qigong

You may not have heard of *qigong* (pronounced "chee gung"), but it is China's ancient system of self-healing. It focuses on breathing, postures, and mental concentration to balance body, mind, and spirit.

The word *qi* literally means "energy cultivation" and is based on the traditional Chinese concept that qi is a vital life force that flows through the body. When qi becomes blocked (through emotional pain or physical illness, for example), you may heal yourself by doing qigong.

In China, people practice qigong to treat diabetes, asthma, cancer, poor circulation, internal-organ problems, arthritis, nerve pain, low-back pain, high blood pressure, autoimmune disorders, and other physical diseases. In 2002, researchers at the Robert Wood Johnson Medical School in New Jersey reviewed over 50 studies on qigong therapy for cancer. Their findings were encouraging: cancer patients who integrated qigong into their treatments had a better survival rate than patients using strictly conventional methods.

Qigong may be helpful if you are concerned about:

- Anxiety
- Cancer, and treatment-related side effects
- Chronic inflammation
- Depression
- Fall prevention
- Hypertension

Pilates

Pilates is a series of yoga-like flexibility and muscle exercises developed by the German fitness guru Joseph Pilates, a gymnast and boxer. It was originally practiced by dancers and athletes trying to minimize injuries. Eventually, Pilates migrated from dance studios to health clubs. There's a large book and video industry that has also sprung up if you'd like to try Pilates at home.

With Pilates, you control all your movements from the "core"—the muscles in the center of your body that connect your abdomen to your lower back and buttocks. The idea is that if the center is not working well, the body doesn't function as well either.

Pilates has been scientifically studied for its benefits in improving the following conditions:

- Aging
- Body composition (reduction of fat and increase in lean muscle tissue)
- Fibromyalgia
- Flexibility
- Mood
- Muscular endurance
- Pain management
- Scoliosis
- Sleep quality

Strength Training

My main form of exercise is strength training—and I'm thankful I do it. The National Centers for Disease Control says that lifting weights a few days a week helps fight against heart disease and diabetes, plus helps you keep your weight under control. It also helps improve emotional well-being.

Put as simply as possible, strength training means giving muscles some kind of resistance, causing them to contract, and therefore to strengthen. You can use a variety of tools to build strength and muscle tone: hand weights (plastic bottles filled with sand or water work just fine), stretchy resistance bands, or even gravity and your own weight. Everything has value.

You can strength train at home or in a gym or health club. For most beginners, it takes just two or three sessions per week of 20 to 30 minutes each to make great improvements in muscle tone and strength.

If you've never attempted a strength-training program before, first consult a professional fitness instructor who can do everything from evaluating your fitness level and designing a training program to showing you how to properly use strength-training equipment.

Researchers have found that strength training offers many health benefits and can be used to prevent, improve, or treat the following conditions:

- Aging
- Arthritis
- Back pain
- Body image
- Depression
- Diabetes
- Fatigue
- Heart disease
- Immunity

- Joint strength

- Muscular endurance and stamina

- Osteoporosis

- Sleep quality

- Strength

- Weight control and obesity

Tai Chi

Tai chi, one of the world's most widely practiced forms of exercise, has become very popular. You can do it almost anywhere, and no equipment is required. The philosophy behind tai chi is similar to that of qigong: to restore the free flow of vital energy.

Tai chi is technically a martial art, although no belts or ranks are awarded. Classes begin with a series of slow and precise body movements or "forms" that may take up to 20 minutes to complete.

Tai chi incorporates breathing exercises designed to improve circulatory and respiratory function. Practitioners try to achieve a fluid, whole-body movement from start to finish, while enhancing strength and coordination.

Tai chi has spurred a lot of research—with promising results. It provides relief from stress, hypertension, arthritis, rheumatism, and back pain. Studies at the Johns Hopkins Medical Institution showed that tai chi reduced blood pressure in mature adults as much as regular aerobic exercise without speeding up their heart rates.

I'd consider tai chi if you're concerned about any of the following:

- Arthritis

- Back pain

- Balance and mobility in Parkinson's disease

- Bone health

- Fall prevention

- Fibromyalgia

- Flexibility

- Knee osteoarthritis

- Heart disease

- Hypertension

- Immunity

- Mood

- Muscular strength

- Respiratory function

- Rheumatoid arthritis

- Sleep quality

- Stress

Yoga

Personally, I love yoga. It's not a religion or a doctrine, but a comprehensive system for conditioning the body: increasing flexibility, building strength, developing balance, and releasing tension created by stress. It strengthens specific muscle groups, and its stretches relax deep muscle layers from within.

Yoga has been well studied for its power to improve digestion, boost respiratory and circulatory systems, confer an anti-aging effect, and help balance you emotionally and mentally. Certain yoga poses stimulate the endocrine system or other glands in the body. Other poses keep your blood vessels elastic for healthy blood flow. Yoga breathing techniques help prevent arrhythmias of the heart. Standing poses strengthen your heart, and forward bends improve the function of your nervous system. Yoga can even help you heal after a major illness. It really is an amazing form of self-healing exercise.

Consider yoga if you are concerned about any of the following:

- Aging

- Anxiety

- Arthritis
- Asthma
- Back pain
- Carpal tunnel syndrome
- Cholesterol issues
- Depression
- Diabetes
- Hypertension
- Osteoporosis
- Scoliosis
- Sleep quality

If you're serious about starting and staying with an exercise program—and I hope you are—first ask the question, "What is my goal?" Do you want to lose weight, relieve stress, normalize cholesterol or blood pressure, regulate blood sugar, rehabilitate from an injury, lift depression, or just feel better overall? Exercise does all of this and more. Once you decide what you want to achieve, select an activity that is right for you—one that you enjoy and can easily fit into your lifestyle. Then start moving and mending!

At times, our "number" will come up, and we'll have to come to grips with some sort of health crisis. We might get sick, have an accident, get injured, or be diagnosed with a life-threatening disease. Whatever the case may be, we'll need to be treated. There are so many treatments available to us now—ones that can restore, balance, and alter the quality of health. I call these the "healing arts," and they go a long way toward enhancing the self-healing powers of the body. That's the subject of the next chapter.

CHAPTER FIVE

THE NEW
HEALING ARTS

After suffering from multiple sclerosis for nearly 20 years, Joanne, 55, turned to complementary medicine to help relieve the physical and mental deterioration that conventional medicine could not get rid of. The disease that destroys the protective covering around nerve fibers in the brain and spinal cord shut down her body. She had lost nearly all her mobility, relying on assistive devices to walk. Joanne had no bladder control, and her thinking was foggy and disoriented. If you said something to her, she would take several minutes to respond, if she did at all. Joanne's husband, William, could no longer care for her and keep a job at the same time. He was faced with putting his wife of 30 years into a long-term care facility.

As a last-ditch effort, William suggested that they visit a chiropractor. With Dr. Jeff Spencer, Joanne underwent chiropractic care, along with nutritional counseling to create an anti-inflammatory diet of healthy fats, plant foods, and other natural foods. Dr. Spencer treated Joanne for three months, and she followed his instructions religiously. The effects were what many might consider miraculous. Within the first month, Joanne regained her mobility and did not need help walking. By the end of three months, she had near-normal cognitive capacity and turned into a chatter box. Not only could she take care of herself, but she could also tend to her husband's needs. William's eyes glazed over with tears when he told Dr. Spencer about his wife's transformation.

I've always believed that our society depends too much on drugs and surgery, and not enough on complementary care. Twenty years ago, acupuncture in America, for example, was considered outright quackery. Not so today. The Chinese use it, and 1.3 billion people must know what they're doing! Nowadays, in clinics and hospitals around the country, acupuncture and other nontraditional therapies are gaining a much wider acceptance.

In 25 years of healing, I have used a variety of treatments, products, and techniques to help people get better. When I was in private practice, I'd evaluate a person and determine what made him or her unique. I'd provide chiropractic care and perhaps recommend nutrients, herbs, exercise, medical therapies, or whatever else I believed was clinically required. I'd do everything in my power to turn my patient's own healing power back on. I would not be treating illnesses or disease processes, only giving what I felt would help the body try to heal itself. I'd then step back and let the process unfold. The body is much wiser than we are. My main job was to determine what the body was missing—and then provide it as quickly as possible.

The concept of self-healing has broadened over the years. In 2010, I surveyed more than 500 health-care professionals, including medical doctors, and asked them what they believed to be the top "self-healing" treatments and techniques—those that genuinely work and are held to the same standard as conventional Western medicine. I've brought that information together for you here. I call these approaches the *new healing arts*—innovative therapies that are offering real help.

The New Chiropractic

In the mid-1980s, I was studying premed at the University of Dallas, with the goal of becoming a neurosurgeon. At the time I was rear-ended in a car accident and developed severe whiplash. At the hospital, where I was volunteering as part of my training, an orthopedic doctor in charge of my work gave me the card of his chiropractor. I had no idea what a chiropractor was or even how to pronounce the word *chiropractic*, but I trusted the doctor's advice and decided to make an appointment.

The doctor of chiropractic was confident, caring, and enthusiastic. He seemed to enjoy his practice. His clinic had an uplifting, positive atmosphere; I'd never experienced anything like it in any other doctor's office. I asked him that question we have all asked: "What do chiropractors do?" The answer I received remains the most concise and elegant description I have ever heard. He told me that chiropractic is rooted in this simple principle: *The power that made the body heals the body.*

I was astounded and knew deep inside that this statement resonated with me. That visit changed the course of my life, because I realized that chiropractic was the ultimate form of health care. I wanted to learn more about it. I was so intrigued by the idea of a health-care system that respects the inherent self-healing powers of the body that in time, I decided to become a chiropractor myself. I chose my profession from my heart, and for more than 20 years, I like to think that I've brought healing and relief to thousands of people. I helped teach them how to make better choices every day for better health. Watching the self-healing miracles take place over the past 20 years has inspired me to devote my life to helping men and women discover what they can do to live a healthy, natural lifestyle so that they can live fully and age gracefully.

Most people think chiropractors treat back or neck pain, or maybe headaches. Yes, we do treat those. But rather than try to relieve the symptoms, chiropractic tries to correct the cause—and encourage the body to self-heal. What I've learned over the years is that the body has a far greater capacity to heal itself than most doctors give it credit for.

The best application of chiropractic in our lives is preventive maintenance—just like we'd take care of our cars. We know it's easier to keep a car in good running order if we regularly maintain it. Well, our bodies are the same way, and chiropractic is one way to keep the body in good running order. And one of the ways we do this is by keeping the spine well adjusted. Adjustments remove nerve interferences from the body; this keeps communication lines open between the brain and the rest of the body. In addition, we also encourage a fully functioning nervous system, good nutrition, water, proper rest, inspired thoughts, and movement.

Chiropractic allows for the body to be as stress-free as possible. In other words, while many people live on the stress roller coaster, people who stay well adjusted find that they experience a steady road to better health through better living. That's why a chiropractor analyzes your body for nerve interference that occurs as a result of our stressful lifestyles.

The daily stress of our lifestyles and the accidents we may experience can cause subluxations, or pressure on nerves. Subluxations cause misalignments of spinal bones (vertebrae). These misalignments unduly stress the spinal nerves and spinal cord, which are considered in chiropractic to be the body's main communication line. When the stress from subluxations goes unchecked long enough, the results can be devastating. It can cause the millions of chemical reactions inside our bodies to become diluted, triggering respiratory problems, allergies, digestive problems, reproductive problems, skin conditions, pain, and more.

Chiropractic doesn't cure any of these conditions, but by getting adjustments, your nervous system functions better, you can boost your immune system, and you can restore motion and provide your body a means with which to take care of unwanted conditions faster.

Stroke of Healing

Twenty-four years ago, while trying to fall asleep, Christopher turned his head to one side, when all of sudden, the right side of his body went numb and the room started swirling. He felt like he was underwater and trying to swim to the surface.

Something's wrong, he thought. Christopher called out for help, and a friend dialed 911, while he tried to makes sense of something that was senseless.

Within minutes, two paramedics appeared, asking questions: "Are you dizzy?" "Do you have any pain?" An oxygen mask appeared, then an IV. "We're taking you to the hospital," said one of the paramedics.

Someone mentioned that he might have had a stroke. To Christopher, this was preposterous! A perfectly healthy guy doesn't wake up feeling fine and then have a stroke. (The official diagnosis would be a brain stem lesion.)

Twenty minutes later, he was wheeled into the emergency room. A nurse taped a heart monitor to his chest. He underwent a battery of tests, including a CT scan of his brain.

Christopher was transferred to the intensive care unit and put on a mechanical ventilator so he could breathe. Meanwhile, the attending neurologist informed his family that Christopher would probably not make it through the next few days.

Christopher was not about to let this prognosis become true for him. Life became a training camp—a race to restore severed connections. Two chiropractors visited him and gave him adjustments. There were small victories: Shortly after the first adjustment, he could wiggle the fingers on his right hand. Soon he was off the ventilator and able to use a wheelchair. With the unofficial consent of the attending physician, he continued to receive chiropractic adjustments while undergoing an intensive regimen of rehabilitation. A little over a month after being carried in, he walked out under his own power with the aid of a cane.

Since then, Christopher has taught at a chiropractic college, become an attorney, and co-founded a successful business. He is again able to drive a car and pilot a light airplane. He has some residual health issues, and while he may never be completely normal, he knows how lucky he is.

"I realize that while medicine prevented me from dying, it was chiropractic care that made the expression of life possible," Christopher says. "My message to practitioners and patients alike is to focus on your intent to allow the body to express its healing potential. It will positively and significantly affect what happens to you."

A Life Saved

As a chiropractor, I know that we routinely incorporate the art and science of the profession into our practice. No chiropractor is a great healer all the time—that would be impossible. But all of us have great moments, and in these moments we combine research-based practices with our own experiences of working with patients and their families. This is when the magic occurs. I would like to tell you about a time when magic occurred for me and for a patient with whom I was working.

In 1995, the plate-glass door to my office swung open and in walked a very large lady—she must have weighed at least 350 pounds. Her name was Rosie, and she was accompanied by a somewhat smaller man, obviously her husband, who did his best to assist his wife as she inched to the front desk.

When I entered the consultation room, I found a lady in her mid-30s whose beautiful face was contorted in pain and anguish. Her medical history was ravaging. Rosie had been diagnosed with a variety of conditions since early childhood. For more than 20 years, she had been subjected to an increasingly complex and ever-more powerful array of pharmaceuticals—none of which provided more than temporary relief.

To make matters worse, she had been diagnosed with fibromyalgia, plus possible reflex sympathetic dystrophy (RSD), a chronic pain condition caused by a malfunction of the nervous system. Rosie described her condition as excruciating pain, which lasted 24 hours a day. Her medical doctors had also given her a poor prognosis: "Learn to live with it, and take your meds. There is no cure."

With the onset of these conditions, Rosie rapidly put on weight. She had no energy and couldn't sleep at night. She eventually had to quit her job. These days, she spent most of her time in bed, praying for the blessing of sleep.

I administered a variety of chiropractic adjustments to remove neural interferences so that her body could start to heal naturally. For the first couple of weeks, I saw her daily. As her function improved, I adjusted her three times a week. Rosie continued to improve to the point where she required only once-a-week adjustments. After six months, she tearfully told me that her husband's company was transferring him to a different state. I was more than happy to help her locate a chiropractor near her new home.

About a year after I became president of Parker University, I got a call from Rosie.

"Rosie," I said. "How are you?"

"Oh, Dr. Mancini, I've been losing weight—more than 175 pounds so far. I feel like I have my life back. I was able to go back to work and have a great job, too. Everything is wonderful!"

Then she proceeded to tell me something that forever changed me.

"When I first came to your office, I was deeply depressed. My husband was about to divorce me. He said that every time he tried to get close to me, I would push him away. Every time he needed something, I wasn't there for him—or for my kids. My whole family turned against me, and I'd lost my job. Right before I saw you the first time, I realized I was losing everything I cared about. I had nothing to live for!

"When you said that our bodies are designed to heal themselves, and that the power that made the body can heal the body, a concept I'd never heard from any other doctor or physician, I felt hope. When you told me that the main objective of chiropractic is to remove the interferences preventing the body from healing itself, this all made sense to me."

Then she told me something for which I was totally unprepared.

"Dr. Mancini, what I didn't tell you is that just two days before I first saw you, I bought a gun. I had already made up my mind that I would kill myself if I didn't feel that chiropractic could help me. I just want to thank you for saving my life."

I was speechless. It was at that moment I recognized that the power of the human body and of chiropractic to intercede when necessary are so much more than what is recognized by most. I knew in my heart that if I never saw another patient, then maybe I became a chiropractor just for this one person.

Yes, we know that people often recover from their pain over time. We also know that they get back to their regular activities: work, sports, travel, whatever they love. Yet our spine and nervous system impacts our lives on so many levels—physically, mentally, and spiritually. That is the reason why, every single day, I do what I do: help people maximize their health potential so they can maximize their life potential.

If you haven't had your spine and nervous system checked by a chiropractor recently (or ever), no matter your age (from newborn to elderly), it's time you do so, whether you are suffering from any condition or feeling great. Subluxations are often referred to as "the silent killer," because they can be present for years before symptoms ever appear, all the time causing dysfunction, which will create serious issues in the future. Although chiropractic is not condition specific, people with a variety of conditions have responded favorably to chiropractic care, when subluxations were corrected. (For more information on the wide range of conditions treated by chiropractic, turn to Chapter 13.)

Myths and Facts about Chiropractic Care

Despite its success over the years, there are a lot of myths circulating about the practice of chiropractic. Let's take a closer look at some of the more common ones.

Myth #1: Chiropractors are not real doctors.

Fact: The road to becoming a doctor of chiropractic is a challenging one. A chiropractic institution grants a Doctor of Chiropractic (D.C.) degree. Before being eligible to enter chiropractic school, a student must have had completed a minimum of 90 hours of prechiropractic or premed courses with a strong science foundation. Most students come in with a bachelor's degree. Chiropractic is a three-and-a-half to four-year program. As part of their education, chiropractic students also complete an internship working with patients in a clinical setting, supervised by licensed doctors of chiropractic. By the time chiropractic students graduate, they have to pass four sets of national board exams, as well as state board exams in the states where they want to practice.

The biggest difference between chiropractors and medical doctors has little to do with education, but more in how they treat patients. Generally, medical doctors are trained to use medicines and do surgery. Thus, if you have a biochemical problem, such as diabetes, hypothyroidism, or an infection, medical doctors can help by giving you medicine to treat it. Because science recognizes that the nervous system is the master system controlling all other systems, chiropractors feel it makes sense to always make sure your nervous system is functioning optimally before using other treatments.

To elaborate: If you have a misaligned spine interfering with normal nervous system transmission or you have soft-tissue damage causing pain, there is no chemical that can fix it. You need a physical solution to correct a physical problem, a neurological solution to correct a neurological issue. That is where chiropractic can really help. Chiropractors provide neurological and physical solutions—adjustments to correct subluxations, exercise and diet recommendations, stretches and muscle therapy—to help the body heal from conditions that are physical in origin, such as back pain, muscle spasms, headaches, poor posture, and others.

Myth #2: Medical doctors don't like chiropractors.

Fact: Many medical doctors today regularly refer patients for chiropractic care. Many hospitals across the country now have chiropractors on staff, and just as many chiropractic offices have medical doctors on staff. Chiropractors and medical doctors are much more comfortable working together in cases where the two forms of treatment mesh. I believe in using both traditional medicine and chiropractic to complement each other. I don't want people to leave their primary doctor, but they should have chiropractic care, too. What medicine does not address, chiropractic can, and vice versa.

Myth #3: Chiropractors only treat back pain.

Fact: Chiropractic care has successfully treated people with a variety of conditions, such as dysmenorrhea (painful menses), ulcers, migraine headaches, and ear infections in children. While we don't claim to cure these conditions, we believe that many of these problems are aggravated and oftentimes caused by disruptions in the nervous system as a result of spinal dysfunction (subluxations). By correcting these subluxations, we help people self-heal and regain control of their lives.

Myth #4: Once you start going to a chiropractor, you have to keep going for the rest of your life.

Fact: I hear this myth more than any other! Sure, if you're being treated for a specific problem, the treatment plan normally ends when your problem is resolved. If your problem is chronic or recurrent, or you wish to avoid it in the future, periodic care can help you stay healed. It's a personal decision as to whether you want to continue chiropractic care. If your goal is to maintain health and a properly functioning nervous system at all times, you'll definitely want to make chiropractic part of your health-maintenance plan.

Myth #5: Chiropractic care is expensive.

Fact: When I hear that comment, I always ask, "Compared to what?" How much is your health worth to you? At a chiropractor, you pay for services rendered, and in most cases, your health insurance covers your treatment. You may want to consult your health-insurance carrier to see if your chiropractor is in their network and covers your treatment. Investing in correcting the cause of your health concern and in keeping yourself healthy is the very best investment you can make. The fact is that getting sick is expensive and has become the number one cause of personal bankruptcy in America. The cost of investing in products and services that promote your better health and well-being has consistently shown to be a far better investment because of the wide-ranging positive side effects, including feeling better, performing better, being able to better take care of your family, and being happier overall. What price can you put on your better health?

Yes, it's true that most people expect their health insurance to cover the cost of being healthy, but the reality is that health insurance is designed to pay for expenses when you are sick. My advice to you is to invest in yourself and use insurance only when you have a health condition that requires medical attention.

The Healing Power of Cold Laser Therapy

A handheld, flashlight-like device directs a barely tangible beam of intense (but not hot) light at injured tissue beneath the skin. A quick flash heals soft-tissue injuries, cervical neck pain, carpal tunnel syndrome, repetitive stress injuries, tendinitis, hamstring injuries, arthritis, and wounds, among others. Sounds like a scene from *Star Wars*? No, just healing business as usual. This medical procedure—called *cold laser therapy*—is an impressive way to help the body heal. In fact, cold lasers speed the healing process. Take a hamstring injury, for example. What normally would take at least seven days to heal, cold laser therapy cuts healing time down to two or three days.

During treatment, a health-care practitioner passes a high-wavelength light through the area of pain or injury. The light activates an increase in cell metabolism in the area. The immune system rallies as a result, and healing accelerates.

Unlike surgery, treatments involving cold laser therapy are noninvasive and require no downtime. There are no gels or ointments applied prior to the treatment. You might feel the pressure of the head of the laser on your skin, although some patients report only a small tingling.

Over the last four decades, more than 2,000 clinical studies have been published worldwide on cold lasers, which are FDA approved. Most of the studies demonstrate that this healing technique is effective for a variety of clinical uses. But I think the most compelling evidence comes straight from real-life patients. Take a look:

Sports Wellness

Jessica was a star first baseman for her prep-school team. In three playoff games, she batted .750 (9-for-12) with five RBIs. Her coach, Larry Harvey, would shudder to think about what it would be like not to have Jessica batting third in his lineup. His fear came to roost when Jessica severely sprained her wrist and tore some ligaments, when, going after a fly ball, she collided with a teammate.

"It just got so swollen, I couldn't move it," she said. "I had a hard time putting my clothes on in the morning."

Coach Harvey had heard about a soccer player who had undergone a relatively new medical treatment called "cold laser therapy." He brought it to Jessica's attention.

At first, Jessica was skeptical. "Wow, this is such a hoax," she said. "It isn't going to work." But she was willing to try anything.

If not for this treatment, Jessica's role on her team might have been limited to singing the national anthem before the home games. To fix her injured wrist, she underwent the therapy.

Jessica said she didn't feel anything during the procedure, and after the second treatment, she began to see improvement. She developed increased movement in her wrist and, after some initial soreness, her pain vanished.

No More Neck Pain

Life was interrupted for Deanna on May 30, 2003, when, out of nowhere, a midsized car came barreling straight toward her truck. *Bam! Screech!* The impact caused her truck to spin around completely before coming to a total standstill, dangerously in the opposite lane. By the grace of God, none of Deanna's four children, all passengers, were hurt.

Right after the crash, Deanna felt fine, but that evening her body started aching so severely that she had to go to the ER. Doctors said she had dislocated her shoulder and sent her home with pain medications, anti-inflammatory drugs, and muscle relaxants.

None of this worked, however. For the next several months, Deanna suffered in constant pain, despite taking all the prescribed medicine. She was referred to an orthopedic doctor who injected her shoulder with steroids—but to no avail. The pain only intensified. Deanna couldn't push a grocery cart, shut the door to her truck, or even get up from sitting on the floor.

She found herself taking more and more medication. She quadrupled her muscle-relaxant dosage, and took increasing doses of Tylenol, ibuprofen, and naproxen. She began taking sleeping pills, too. The pain would not go away, regardless of what she took.

There is a particularly horrible aspect of chronic pain: the psychological damage it causes. Deanna became so emotionally distraught that she told her husband that she'd rather be dead than go on living with the debilitating pain.

Fortunately, a good friend suggested that Deanna see the chiropractor Dr. Dave Shiflet. Deanna was willing to try anything and made an appointment right away.

Under Dr. Shiflet's care, Deanna received a series of adjustments, plus cold laser therapy. With the blessing of her family doctor, she stopped taking all the medications and began taking natural supplements instead. After the very first treatment, Deanna had no neck pain and could turn her neck from side to side for the first time in nine months. She was shocked by how much better she felt. She continued the treatments and credits them with giving her life back. As she told Dr. Shiflet: "I don't think I will ever completely understand how the laser therapy and the adjustments worked, but I know without a doubt that my quality of life has increased more than I thought possible. It is a miracle to me and always will be."

Healing a Stubborn Infection

Cold laser therapy has other applications. Take the case of Michelle: In just one day, a mysterious and very aggressive infection materialized in Michelle's upper-right armpit. The infection was painful and inflamed. At the infection site, the skin began turning ashen. Technically, this can mean necrosis—or tissue death.

A surgeon removed excessive amounts of the dead tissue. In a matter of days, the infection returned, and the surgeon repeated the procedure. Just as quickly as he took out the dead tissue, the infection came back with a vengeance.

The medical team treating Michelle was baffled, but not deterred. They decided to use cold laser therapy at the site of the infection. Michelle received this treatment daily for one week. By the end of the week, the infection was gone and it never reappeared, ever. There was complete healing.

Energy Healing

Energy healing is based on the Eastern medical paradigm that we all have a life-force energy. If it's out of balance, we become ill; if it's in balance, we become healthy. There are many different techniques used by energy healers to restore this balance. I've listed several in the following table.

You wouldn't want to replace traditional medicine with energy healing, however. If I have an irregular heartbeat, for instance, I want a cardiologist to fix it. But as traditional medicine kicks in, I may then turn to an energy healer to help accelerate the healing process.

Forms of Energy Medicine

Treatment	How It Works	When to Consider It
Acupuncture	Super-thin needles are inserted at specific points (gateways or acupoints) along a network of energy channels (meridians) in the body. Meridians correspond to specific organs or organ systems.	• Addictions • Allergies • Arthritis • Asthma • Dental pain • Fibromyalgia • Gastrointestinal disorders • Irritable bowel syndrome • Migraines and other headaches • Nausea from chemotherapy • Pain control • Respiratory ailments • TMJ
Aromatherapy	Uses the scent of essential oils from flowers, herbs, and trees to promote health and well-being. The oils can be sprayed into the air and inhaled, or absorbed through the skin via massage, hot baths, or hot or cold compresses.	• Allergies • Arthritis • Asthma • Back pain • Depression • Insomnia • Muscular aches • Stress

Forms of Energy Medicine		
Treatment	How It Works	When to Consider It
Homeopathy	A healing discipline founded on the belief that just as large amounts of certain natural substances can produce symptoms, smaller doses of these same substances can relieve those symptoms. The remedy is thought to promote the body's own defenses against whatever is causing the illness. Homeopaths believe that the more diluted (weaker) an agent is, the greater its healing power.	• Allergies • Delayed muscle soreness • Influenza • Migraines • Tension headaches
Magnetic field therapy	Magnets are placed on or near the body to reduce pain and swelling and speed healing. Supposedly, the magnetic field increases circulation, improves oxygen supply, and removes waste from cells in the area. Additionally, the magnetic field is supposed to block nerve signals carrying pain messages to the brain.	• Arthritis • Headaches • Joint pain • Low back pain • Strains • Toothaches
Reiki	Reiki is based on the idea that there is a universal (or source) energy that supports the body's innate healing abilities. Reiki practitioners place their hands lightly on or just above the person receiving treatment; this technique is supposed to enhance your own healing response.	• Anxiety • Depression • Pain reduction

Forms of Energy Medicine		
Treatment	How It Works	When to Consider It
Therapeutic touch	This technique is a variation of the ancient healing method known as "laying on of hands." It involves lightly touching or holding the hands above the body in order to manipulate the energy field.	• Headaches • Nausea • Pain • Premenstrual syndrome • Thyroid problems

Tapping Into an Inner Power

One of the easiest-to-learn healing methods I have ever encountered is called Emotional Freedom Technique (EFT). EFT is a form of energy healing; it is designed to resolve many physical and emotional problems by simply working with the body at certain energy points. Before I explain EFT in detail, let me share with you a rather amazing testimony to its power.

It was 2008. Michael was almost 50 years old. He had a long family history of heart disease, and whenever that's the case, there is also a risk factor for others in the family to develop heart disease. After being diagnosed with high cholesterol at age 28, he was put on cholesterol-lowering drugs and remained on them.

At 3:30 A.M. one day, Michael awoke with searing chest pain. He prayed that it wasn't his heart and tried to calm himself by thinking it was probably something more benign such as indigestion. He popped a tablet of an over-the-counter acid reducer and hoped the pain would subside, as it had in the past.

Nothing happened. Michael took five more acid reducers, and still nothing. The pain got so severe that he took a nitroglycerin tablet. The pain was gone within minutes, which was good, but it scared him, because the resolution of pain through nitroglycerin was a clear indication of a heart problem, not indigestion.

Convinced that he was having a heart attack, Michael headed for the emergency room where the cardiologist suggested a series of tests.

The cardiologist eventually marched into the room and informed Michael that he definitely had blockages and would require an angioplasty right away. It was then 9:30 P.M., and his doctor wanted to schedule the procedure for 7:30 the next morning.

Michael pleaded with him to wait until next week, and the doctor informed him that he might not be alive if it was postponed. So he agreed to go ahead and do it.

Michael's good friend and chiropractor, Dr. Rick Wren, called to check on him after the cardiologist left. He made Michael promise to do something called the Emotional Freedom Technique as many times as he could before the next morning. EFT is a type of psychological acupuncture that employs tapping rather than needles. You simply tap with your fingertips on certain areas on the body known as meridians in order to stimulate them. Yes, I know this might sound a little woo-woo right now, but stay with me here.

Michael went through the tapping process no less than 50 times before the next morning.

The angioplasty team came to retrieve Michael around 7:00 A.M. He lay on the operating-room table feeling overwhelmed and ashamed to have allowed himself to get into this situation.

An hour later, the procedure was over, and the cardiologist was walking alongside the people pushing Michael's gurney and showing him pictures of his arteries. One of the blockages had completely disappeared. The cardiologist was puzzled and astonished. Of course, so was Michael!

"I can't figure it out," said the cardiologist. "You can't leave the hospital until you tell me exactly what you did to make this happen." Michael explained that he did EFT.

"It makes no sense to me," the cardiologist replied, "but I can't argue with the results."

EFT appeared to unblock one of Michael's arteries overnight. If that wasn't a miraculous example of self-healing, then I don't know what is!

So how does EFT work exactly? Developed in the 1990s, EFT evolved from meridian-based therapies, such as acupuncture and acupressure. Both attribute disease and emotional dysfunction to disturbances in the energetic field. Energy is believed to flow through our bodies along meridians or pathways that connect to each other, and to our organs, much like an electrical circuit.

If we're under stress of any sort—either emotional (anxiety, for example) or physical (a food intolerance)—then the energy meridian most affected will shut down or get blocked. The other connected meridians try to compensate in order to keep the energy flowing. But eventually, they get overloaded and blocked. The result is pain or other symptoms.

These problems often stem from negative emotions stored within the body. EFT utilizes gentle tapping on the body, as tapping is believed to open energetic centers to release these emotions. According to proponents, EFT can help heal many conditions, including eating disorders, phobias, post-traumatic stress syndrome, chronic pain, anxiety disorders, and many serious physical illnesses.

If EFT interests you, it's best to locate a qualified practitioner to lead you through the process. You'll learn where and how to tap, and how to employ breathing and affirmations as part of the therapy.

Massage Therapy

Massage therapy isn't exactly new. In fact, it's the oldest and most natural of the healing arts. Yet it was not scientifically studied as a healing art until about ten years ago. So I include it here because so much "new" research has recently brought its healing power to light. For example:

Reduce Lower-Back Pain

Unfortunately, there have been no blockbuster cures for low-back pain, although it is a popular topic of discussion. Just recently, I read that one of the best ways to help reduce pain is through massage.

In one study, 24 people were assigned to a massage therapy or a progressive muscle-relaxation group. Sessions were 30 minutes long, twice a week for five weeks. On the first and last day of the five-week study, participants completed questionnaires, provided a urine sample, and were assessed for range of motion.

By the end of the study, the massage therapy group, as compared to the relaxation group, reported less pain, depression, and anxiety and improved sleep. They also showed more flexibility in their back (this was amazing, as function is not always an easy thing to regain if you have chronic back pain), and levels of the "feel-good" hormones serotonin and dopamine were higher. I love reading about these outcomes—all achieved without pain medication!

Heal Faster

If you've ever been hospitalized, therapies such as massage can help your overall healing. Recovery from cardiac surgery is a good example. Anyone who undergoes long procedures or surgery for heart problems is prone to having back and shoulder pain, anxiety, and muscle tension following treatment. In one study, heart patients who had undergone bypass surgery received either a massage or participated in quiet relaxation (the control group). Those who received massage therapy felt significantly less pain, anxiety, and tension.

Improve Pregnancy

There are few gifts so precious as the healthy birth of a healthy child, which is why I want to bring your attention to this study. Often, for reasons unknown, pregnant women suffer with depression, but research has found that massage therapy can be helpful. The reason hinges on the fact that massage lowers cortisol, a stress hormone implicated with depression. Further, mothers-to-be who undergo massage therapy tend to give birth to healthier babies, according to research. I find these happy endings to be nothing short of miraculous.

Now for a real-life miracle:

Healing Touch

Jeff Kirstein is a licensed massage therapist in Plano, Texas, and a friend of mine. He shared with me the story of "Mr. B," who sought Jeff's help with some serious digestive-tract problems. Several years ago, Mr. B's appendix exploded—literally. This caused blockages in his digestive system that required hospitalization to remove them—a painful, uncomfortable treatment.

Jeff began treating Mr. B with deep myofascial work in his abdomen, as well as providing full-body-massage treatments. As therapy progressed, Jeff learned that Mr. B also suffered from bipolar disorder. ("This is where the story gets interesting," Jeff told me.)

Mr. B was taking many medications, and they left him fatigued and in a continual fog. Meanwhile, with regular massage, his digestive issues began clearing up. As his digestion started working again, he needed less medication, probably because massage increases the body's own feel-good chemicals (which is what drugs for mental health do). Under his doctor's supervision, Mr. B cut his medication doses in half; with this, his fog, tiredness, and inability to think clearly all vanished. Mr. B is feeling whole again, all because of getting just one massage a week. Jeff sums it up like this: "I believe that our bodies are designed to heal if we just give them the things they need. Mr. B receiving his weekly massage is a great example of this."

How exactly does massage perform these self-healing miracles? For one thing, the hypnotic rhythm of the strokes creates relaxation. As a result, you feel calmer and more relaxed. Massage promotes circulation of the blood and lymph, and restores the health of muscles, tendons, and ligaments. Then, as I mentioned, massage naturally elevates positive brain chemicals like serotonin that make you feel less stressed and more at peace. There is a definite brain-calming factor to massage.

Forms of Massage

There are many different types of massage. You'll want to choose the one that helps you with your particular issue.

Massage	How It Works
Deep tissue	This form of massage is effective for general relaxation. It utilizes slow strokes, direct pressure, or friction applied across the grain of the muscles.
Myofascial release	The focus is on the fascia enveloping the muscles. If you suffer from an injury, inflammation, or physical trauma, the fascia tighten, causing pain and restricting range of motion. MFR helps relax the fascia by applying gentle pressure to the problem areas.
Reflexology	This method massages the feet to bring relaxation, balance, and healing to the body. It works on the theory that there are 70,000 nerve endings in the feet that connect via the spinal cord to all parts of the body. Putting pressure on those nerves helps heal the corresponding organ or region of the body.

Forms of Massage	
Massage	How It Works
Shiatsu	This Japanese "finger pressure" therapy works by stimulating the body's energy flow to promote health. The Shiatsu practitioner uses thumbs, fingers, elbows, and even knees and feet to apply pressure along the body's energy lines, or meridians. The goal is to stimulate circulation and the flow of lymphatic fluid and to help release toxins and deep-seated tension from the muscles.
Sports massage	Preventative and therapeutic, this form of massage can help improve flexibility, range of motion, and sport performance.
Swedish massage	This is most common form of massage. It involves a combination of basic strokes, and concentrates on the muscles and connective tissues for improved circulation, relaxation, pain relief, and overall well-being.

In these first five chapters, I've offered guidance and tools on physical self-healing. I hope it has empowered you to take some necessary action steps. Remember that your body has the power to deal with injuries and disease. Just as you can assist your body to heal physically with good nutrition, proper rest, and exercise, you can also learn to access your natural emotional healing power. In the next part of the book, I'll show you how to reclaim this aspect of your innate healing potential.

Part II

EMOTIONAL SELF-HEALING

When you connect with your inner self and explore your inner landscape, you'll be able to remove blockages that stand in your way of self-healing. Unblocking your emotional self is easier than you might think. I'll show you some simple ways to achieve this and, in the process, take your health to a whole new, much more vibrant level.

CHAPTER SIX

YOU THINK, THEREFORE, YOU HEAL (OR NOT)

Try this simple experiment with me: Get a small drinking glass and fill it with water. Next, drink or pour out about half the water. Sit down and look at the glass.

Think for a moment about the old saying: the pessimist sees the glass as half empty, and the optimist sees it as half full. Then think about yourself, imagining that you are like that glass, and the water represents your level of health. Are you half full of health? Or half empty?

I'm a half-full person—an optimist, if the term is properly defined. True optimism is not synonymous with Pollyannaism. Nor is it blind foolishness, like the partygoer who insists that he's "sober enough" to drive home. If you're a true optimist, you believe that you can control your destiny, turn a negative into a positive, and find meaning in a bad situation. Optimists rarely give up, and because they hang in there, they usually succeed.

By contrast, pessimists feel out of control. There are many common phrases that capture the essence of pessimism: "seeing the glass half empty" or "the sky is falling." Both phrases express the belief that problems will persist, and no amount of problem-solving will help.

Optimism and Self-Healing

I'm sure you know where I'm going with this: Optimistic thinking makes you healthier. If you're an optimist, you feel you can take charge of and influence your health for the better. Suppose a doctor told you that you need to lose weight and start working out. The optimist in you would say: "The doctor's right. I've been eating too much junk food. I need to eat more fruits and vegetables, and cut back on calories. I'm going to start going to the gym at least three times a week."

The same words from a doctor might lead your pessimistic best friend to say, "Oh, forget it. It's too hard—I can't stick to it!" Pessimists feel helpless, so they never get motivated to make healthy choices. The messages they tell themselves become negative self-fulfilling prophecies.

Even science tells us that optimism is self-healing. A number of years ago, psychologists at Carnegie Mellon University in Pittsburgh followed a large group of heart-bypass patients and rated them on an optimism scale. They found that the most optimistic patients were less likely to suffer a heart attack in the course of the surgery (which can happen), suffered fewer complications, and recovered faster.

Then consider the famous nun study: Researchers read the auto-biographical essays of 180 nuns living in the U.S. that were written in the 1930s when the women were young (average age was 22). They found that the nuns who wrote optimistically of their lives went on to live longer—an average of ten years longer than other nuns.

And the results of a Dutch study on the health effects of optimism and pessimism on the elderly were published several years ago in the *Archives of General Psychiatry:* optimists had a 55 percent lower risk of death by all causes. A Mayo Clinic study, conducted over a 40-year period, also concluded that optimists live longer than pessimists. And in a 2008 Duke University study, cardiac patients who were pessimistic about their outcome were twice as likely to die early as those who were optimistic. Pessimism, to speak frankly, just isn't healthy. An attitude rooted in sickness can lead to sickness. You can either think of yourself as healthy or sick. The choice is up to you!

The Power of an Optimistic Outlook

Be an optimist! According to the Mayo Clinic, you'll enjoy a wide range of health benefits such as:

- Lower rates of heart and cardiovascular diseases

- Greater resistance to colds and other infections

- A positive outlook for the future

- Better interpersonal skills

- More friends and longer-lasting relationships

- Lower stress levels

Meet Three Self-Healing Optimists

Curing the Incurable

Scott's junior year in high school was the busiest year of his life. He was taking advanced classes, holding down a coaching job, playing sports, and participating in theater productions. He worried about not being able to afford to go to college and put a lot of pressure on himself to earn money. All of the stress and worry eventually took its toll.

One day Scott was doubled over by severe abdominal cramps. They were unrelenting, day after day. He started losing weight rapidly and missed a lot of school. His stomach cramps became unbearable.

Scott's family doctor referred him to a gastroenterologist who diagnosed him with ulcerative colitis (UC), an autoimmune disease of the colon that causes severe abdominal pain, hard-to-control voiding, and bleeding. When diagnosed with UC, you supposedly have it for life, with only one inevitable treatment option: have your colon taken out.

Over the course of the next six months, Scott's symptoms worsened. He did not respond well to the three or four traditional medicines he was on. He kept getting sicker, spending months at home, unable to eat solid food or attend school. He couldn't go out very much because he was afraid to be away from the bathroom.

At this point, Scott had exhausted the traditional medicines, and the only ones that seemed to hold out hope were steroids. His doctor started Scott on a round of steroids to quell the symptoms, and it worked. The symptoms abated over the next several months. But Scott soon developed other problems: a weight gain of 20 pounds, and angry, out-of-control emotions. Both are common side effects of steroids. He was miserable and he was making everyone around him miserable. But his doctor kept insisting that this was the only way to treat him.

Scott's life fell into a tiresome, depressing pattern, as he was never quite sick and never quite well. This is when he became completely fed up with his treatment. Nothing had really worked over a year's time, or it had only made things worse, causing side effects that were actually worse than the disease.

No one really knows what causes ulcerative colitis, and his doctor delivered the assurance that nothing he had done had caused it, but over time, Scott found out otherwise. In deciding to get rid of this "menace" in his life, he discovered that the menace was him.

Scott intensely researched UC and discovered that his stress, poor diet, and negative attitude were blocking his road back to health—all issues he felt were under his control. "I had overextended myself," he confessed, "creating more stress in my life than the body is meant to bear. That lifestyle lends itself to eating quick, unbalanced meals, which reflects within."

To relieve his stress, Scott studied meditation, relaxation and breathing techniques, and energy healing. He changed his diet, made time to rest and relax, and created a more balanced schedule. He also emerged from the negativity that had been holding him back. During the course of his illness, he had come to believe that his condition was unchangeable—a thought that limited his ability to heal. So Scott began to change his thoughts; he stopped thinking of UC as "unchangeable." He decided that there was no condition he couldn't modify into something better.

Over the next six months, he worked on releasing his limiting thoughts, weaned himself off the steroids, implemented daily meditation and relaxation techniques, and altered his diet.

What happened was powerful and miraculous in its outcome. Scott became disease-free—something that rarely happens with ulcerative colitis.

"I Believe I Will Heal"

As a young man in his early 20s, Juan was told by a doctor that he had a malignant tumor growing in his esophagus. If left untreated, it would kill him. Grueling treatments would be required, but without any promise of success. However, Juan believed in his body's ability to self-heal and valiantly decided to pursue holistic treatment options.

Luckily, the doctor he consulted shared Juan's beliefs—and supported his decision to begin a self-healing journey.

To Juan, that journey was mostly about changing his frame of mind, which is exactly what he did. If he held any persistent thoughts of negativity or limitation, he would gently sweep them aside and replace them with encouragement. He accepted responsibility for his own healing—or more accurately, he adopted an optimistic belief system that said, *I believe I can heal.*

Not only did he change his mind-set, but he also changed his lifestyle and eating habits. This was all part of taking responsible action for his health.

Juan followed his own "protocol" aggressively for a year. There was no conventional medical treatment, simply a change in thinking, beliefs, and lifestyle. Never once did he doubt the outcome of his efforts, and after one year, the malignancy was gone. Today, Juan is a healthy, vibrant 53-year-old. He would tell you, as he told me: "The healing process is the one thing that can get our bodies back to perfect health. In many cases, mine included, it's a better state than the one we were in before our health was affected."

Juan is living proof of his own words.

She Discovered True Wellness

As far back as Brandi could remember, her health was always precarious. As a child, she was anemic and given an awful-tasting, iron-fortified black syrup to treat it. She was always underweight. At age nine, her tonsils were removed, and she hemorrhaged profusely because her anemic blood refused to clot. As Brandi emerged from general anesthesia, her heart rate escalated to an alarming level before returning to normal. Her mother was summoned to the recovery room at once, because the hospital staff thought she might not survive.

Throughout Brandi's high-school years, her sicknesses continued. She came down with every illness you can imagine, including colds, flu, impetigo, and chronic fatigue syndrome (CFS). She failed every fitness test she took, and couldn't execute a single sit-up.

When she was 16, Brandi started to notice large lumps on her lower back. She couldn't get up in the morning without intense pain and stiffness. Her mother took her to a physician who x-rayed her spine and discovered she was missing one of the lower vertebra. He said nothing could be done to remedy the problem except to take medication.

From a very young age, Brandi believed that "sickness" was a natural state for her. As she grew older, she solidified that victim mentality. Every physician she consulted asked about her genetic predisposition to disease, and every time that question was posed, Brandi shrank a little more into her sickness belief system.

As if life couldn't get any worse, at age 19, Brandi was diagnosed with cancer of the cervix. In due course, she was treated with the standard protocol of surgery, radiation, and chemotherapy. That completed, Brandi was pronounced "in remission."

When Brandi was 21, her bladder and kidneys started to fail. Even after painful, invasive, diagnostic procedures were conducted, no cause could be determined. Her physicians said they were unable to find anything "wrong." Brandi was advised to continue taking anti-inflammatory drugs, autoimmune suppressants, and antibiotics. Emotionally, she was exhausted and withdrawn, unable to fully engage in life.

Brandi found herself in a dark valley of illness, doubt, and despair. She could only look upward . . . to the mountaintop, the place that encourages us, and that's what she did. She climbed her way, slowly, out of the hellish valley, seeking health and healing.

Rather than listen to those who dwelled only on her disease, Brandi turned to a chiropractor and listened to his message. She learned something profound, something she had never, ever heard before: that the body is a self-healing creation, with an inborn ability to become well. This knowledge flipped a switch in her mind. In her own words: "I began to reject my previous acceptance of sickness as a normal state. No longer would my body be the storehouse of disease. I made a conscious decision to reject the three chemical stressors that were keeping me in a constant state of sickness: antibiotics, painkillers, and digestive medication."

With a hunger to learn, Brandi started attending health lectures. She discovered the vital roles that an optimistic attitude and a properly functioning nervous system play in regulating health and wellness. And over time, her health began to improve, although gradually. "After I changed my attitude, everything else improved in perfect harmony," she said. "I began to see the possibility of a healthy future."

After Brandi turned 28, she started running as a form of exercise. Not long afterward, she competed in an ultra-marathon in the mountains. To date, she has run in four half-marathons! She no longer takes any medications and has been drug-free for more than seven years. These days, she travels around the world and teaches others about their potential to heal. She says, "Each morning, I wake up and ask myself, *What can I do today to sustain and feed my soul?* Every day, I expect more of myself and more of my health. I no longer think of sickness as my constant companion. In fact, sickness and I have gone our separate ways—permanently!"

Don't let anyone ever tell you there's no such thing as a miracle!

Your belief system is critical because either you believe you were designed to be healthy or you believe that you were designed to be sick. I've had patients for many years who believed that having a headache every day and taking a handful of aspirin for it was normal. More than 80 percent of Americans experience lower-back pain—is that "normal," too? Just because everybody's going through it, does that make it acceptable? Whenever there's a virus going around at a school, many of the children get sent home because they quickly become infected. Yet why are there still some kids sitting in the same class, exposed to the same viruses, and their immune systems are working well enough to keep them healthy?

It's not so much a matter of what's going on in the external environment; rather, it's more about your internal environment. Belief in sickness can promote sickness, but belief in health can promote health.

Think Well, Be Well

No one is born an optimist or a pessimist. Both are ways of thinking that can be learned or unlearned. It's possible to change your mind-set just like you change the kind of clothing you wear. You *can* learn to replace pessimistic thinking with optimistic thinking.

Try these few steps, and more often, you'll indeed see that the glass is half full.

Think with Clear Intention

When I reread the three previous stories, one thing pops out at me: Scott, Juan, and Brandi were very clear in their intention that they wanted to be disease-free. They let nothing block the path of that clarity. So first, be clear on what you want. A more active life? More energy? Healing from a disease? Better eating habits? Weight loss?

Your subconscious mind is responsible for 95 percent of your habitual behavior and responses, so it pays to be clear about your intention—and set that intention in your mind like concrete. Start believing that your body can self-heal, and you'll start attracting health and healing.

Having a clear intention also means being doubt-free. Expect good health. Believe it's already yours, and act like you already have it. Act like an optimist. Expect good things and dream big!

Advising you to pretend that you're an optimist might sound like I'm telling you to act like a fake. I'm not! Every time you take "act as if" to heart, an amazing thing happens. The fakeness you feel gradually fades away, and the new role and accompanying attitude begin to fit as comfortably as an old pair of slippers.

Focus Optimistically

See yourself healthy, active, and vibrant. Feel the emotions connected with a healthy, pain-free body. Give this all your positive energy, and feel good about it! There is energy and vibrations in all your emotions and feelings. Any thought you have, when combined with emotion, becomes a vibration and will attract back what you are focusing on.

Catch any negative thoughts about yourself, others, places, or situations, and banish them from your mind. Immediately replace them with positive thoughts. For instance, if you find yourself saying, "This is the worst day of my life; I'll never get out of this mess," you need to pause and say, "Wait a minute! Is this really the worst day of my life? I've had better days, but this isn't the worst. I'll find a way to resolve this situation."

Sure, you may experience times of disappointment, but the optimistic person springs back swiftly and is able to go about the business of productive living.

Optimistic people know, too, that they have no control over what is happening outside of themselves—the external environment. The only thing that we can control is how we respond to the external environment. I'll give you an example of something that happened to my wife, Alicia, and me.

When Alicia was pregnant with our first child, we went through a procedure to determine whether the baby had Down syndrome. While we waited for the results, we were shown a videotape to help us understand that if the test came back positive for Down's, we would be given an opportunity to end the pregnancy. My wife and I, for the first time, had to discuss an issue we'd never had to address before. We sat there and said to ourselves, *If this baby happens to be challenged in some way, if this baby happens to have special needs, will we love him or her any less? Would we want another baby? Will we try conceiving again?* I don't know if you've ever been in that position, but it was a defining moment for us. We recognized that the baby was part of us, and we knew a child with special needs would be a blessing. That is how we chose to respond.

While we were sitting there, the doctor came back and said, "Everything is fine. Congratulations on the new baby."

One secret of a self-healing life is to decide to choose the positive. Regardless of the situation—good or bad—we must find something joyful and drop every thought of negativity. Trust in the expression that "this may be a blessing in disguise"—because to optimists, this is true!

Turn Thoughts into Action

Our actions allow our thoughts to become our behavior. You can have the greatest thoughts in the world, but if you don't put some action steps behind those thoughts, you limit yourself from ever becoming anything or achieving anything.

Here's one way to turn your thoughts into action:

Take a sheet of paper and draw a line down the middle. In the left column, write down your top three thoughts, the ideal things you want to attract—it could be related to your career, relationships, health, whatever you want.

In the right column, make a separate list of everything you do in a 24-hour period. Compare the two lists. Do your actions support your thoughts and desires? If not, then you need to change your actions.

The first time I did this exercise I found that I wasn't putting enough of a priority on my number one desire: better health. For one thing, I wasn't working out as much as I knew I needed to. So I looked at my day. I had such a full agenda that the only way I could fit in a workout on a consistent basis was to get up earlier in the morning. Now I prioritize physical fitness as part of my morning routine, every single day. While examining my list, I also realized that I wasn't paying enough attention to my nutritional intake. I was skipping breakfast, eating a fairly healthy lunch, but having a not-so-nutritious dinner, often eaten too late at night.

Time for a change. I prioritized breakfast, with an emphasis on having a protein shake made with all the essential nutrients I needed. Next, I made sure to have dinner before 6 P.M. and not eat anything afterward. These actions completely changed my way of being and feeling when it came to my physical health.

The lesson here is not to get stuck in a rut and bemoan life's ups and downs. Make some changes! Life will take on a new meaning when you're living with positive expectations.

Our attitudes are formed, little by little, by our thoughts. If we for any reason feel that we can't be healthy, happy, and prosperous, then this is an attitude that needs changing. It *can* be changed, just as it was formed, by changing our thinking.

Dare to change your thinking. Align yourself with the good by thinking positive new thoughts. Your attitude will change, and your life will change, too.

❖ ❖ ❖

CHAPTER SEVEN

EMOTIONS THAT HEAL, EMOTIONS THAT HARM

Now and then, someone asks me whose healing story I most remember, and I flash through a mental Rolodex of the thousands of people who have crossed my path over the years.

One recent story comes to mind: Kara, a petite, bubbly redhead, who at age 47 was diagnosed with a malignant brain tumor. Her doctors held out little hope.

"In just about every instance, you make a choice to laugh or cry," she said. "I was dealing with serious stuff, but I didn't want any doom and gloom. I've never been one to sit and cry, so I laughed my way through it."

Kara went through surgery to remove the tumor. Afterward, she endured countless radiation treatments over a ten-week period. Throughout it all, she still managed to keep her sense of humor.

What happened next was a genuine medical surprise—a miracle. Her doctors changed their original prognosis. They now believed that she would live. And of course, she did! Laughter turned out to be the best healing medicine.

Laughter, joy, hope, and any number of positive emotions are healing. By contrast, negative emotions such as sadness, worry, or anger do just the opposite: they block the healing energies of the body. Emotions have such a powerful effect on our health; let's now take a closer look at why.

Our Emotions Turn into Chemistry

The relationship between emotions and healing is not just a mind game or a matter of semantics. There is a true physical relationship between your emotions and nervous system, endocrine system, and immune system. What you feel turns into the chemistry, biology, and the immunity of your body.

So much of what goes on in your body is under the control of *peptides* and *receptors*. When you feel happy, your brain produces happy peptides; when you're sad, your brain produces sad peptides. Peptides travel to cells and enter them through doorway-like receptors. Once inside, they influence many of the cell's actions. For example, they might cause your face to turn "white as a sheet" when you're scared or "beet red" when you're enraged or embarrassed. They do so by regulating blood flow and signaling receptors on blood-vessel walls to constrict or dilate.

Every hour of every day, millions of cell divisions occur in your body to replace the old cells that die. If I feel sad for just one hour, I've produced billions of new cells that are more sensitive to depression-type peptides. Those new cells are creating a body that is more apt to feel depression than joy.

Since your body is remaking itself like this, doesn't it make sense that you'd want to produce more happy peptides than sad ones? Of course you do! And you can do so by creating the best possible emotional health you can. That might be as simple as just smiling or laughing more. Those positive thoughts transform positive emotions, producing happier peptides, which will visit your cells and keep your body in a state of emotional equilibrium.

Much has been written and taught about the impact of emotions on the body. It's not difficult, for example, to feel the effects of emotions such as frustration, jealousy, vengefulness, or fear on your physical well-being. You can probably recall a time in your own life when anger or stress made you physically ill. Your state of mind and emotions significantly influence how often you get sick, how fast you heal, and in extreme cases, whether you live or die.

Here's what happens when your emotions, as they say, "get the best of you."

Arguing with Others

Let's say you get into an argument with someone—and you're really mad. There's a lot going on under the surface than you might think. For one thing, your endocrine system churns out stress hormones, such as epinedrine, norepinephrine, and cortisol. Your blood pressure keeps zooming up. None of these physical responses bodes well for your body. And if you remember the argument even a week later—and relive it in your mind—your blood pressure will zoom up again, according to a study published in the *International Journal of Psychophysiology.* That's exactly why you need to learn to let arguments and disagreements go!

Lovers' quarrels are anti-healing, too. In fact, if you and your spouse or partner go at it habitually, your bodies might take twice as long to heal. Researchers at Ohio State University proved this in an intriguing experiment with married couples. The researchers created blisters on the couples' arms using a suction device. They then asked the couples to relive arguments that were particularly emotional in nature. This situation caused the wounds to heal 40 percent more slowly than when the couples were calm and in control of their emotions. Why was this? The researchers were measuring molecules called cytokines in the blood. Cytokines trigger inflammation—a process that can delay healing. Cytokines were higher in the couples' blood when they were reliving an argument. Clearly, when you're in a constant negative emotional state, your health can truly suffer.

Suppressing Anger

Often, we're advised to "let it out" or vent our anger. Other times, we're told to "keep a lid on it," or hold it in. Which advice is right? Really, both situations can interfere with self-healing. Researchers in Michigan looked into the long-term health effects of suppressing or venting anger. They assembled a group of women who were yelled at without cause by authority figures, and then studied the women's physiological reactions. The women who held their anger in, habitually, were more apt to die from heart disease, stroke, or cancer. Other research has observed that venting anger, even for a few minutes, can increase the risk of heart attack or stroke by up to five times in those over 50.

You don't have to be over 50, though, to harm your heart. In a 1998 study published in the journal *Psychosomatic Medicine,* University of Pittsburgh researchers found that women who are hostile, hold in their anger, or feel anxious in public have thicker carotid arteries (two large arteries in the neck that supply the brain with blood). Thickened carotid arteries are an early sign atherosclerosis, the buildup of plaque in artery walls.

Everyone is going to get angry once in a while; it's a natural reaction to a situation, and it doesn't always harm your body. It is destructive, however, when you get angry habitually or don't deal with it constructively. If someone slashed the tires on my car, it's natural that I'd get mad. But if I held on to that anger for weeks, constantly thinking about the incident and feeling hostile toward the slasher, I'd ultimately be harming *my* health.

If you harbor unresolved anger, learn to recognize that behavior and try to change it through techniques such as relaxation, meditation, or even anger-management classes. Be extra attentive if you have risk factors for heart disease, such as physical inactivity and high cholesterol.

Feeling Blue

When I was a premed student in the early 1980s, there weren't many illnesses that medicine tied to depression, and we weren't taught a thing about how treating depression might help people heal. These days we know that not only can depression aggravate an existing illness, but it can also increase one's odds of developing several serious health problems, from heart attacks to autoimmune diseases, such as lupus and rheumatoid arthritis.

I'm not just talking about the occasional blues brought on by the occasional disappointment. I'm talking about depression that lasts longer than two weeks—the kind you can't shake, disrupts your sleep, drives you to binge on food or alcohol, or makes you feel chronically sad. That kind of depression can make illness worse. Case in point: In a three-year University of Washington study of 4,154 patients with type 2 diabetes, investigators found that those with diabetes who were also depressed had significantly higher death rates than those who had diabetes alone. That's a scary finding. It tells me that chronic depression can certainly interfere with self-healing. That's why depression must be treated and addressed, through counseling, nutrition, perhaps medication, or holistic techniques, in order for self-healing to take place.

Do You Suffer from Depression?

Depression blocks self-healing. If you're depressed, ask your doctor what treatment options are available. Chances are that appropriate treatment can improve you, physically and mentally. Of course, everyone experiences brief bouts of the blues from time to time, especially during stressful events. But you should consider seeking professional help for your depression if it lasts more than two weeks and is accompanied by any of these symptoms:

- Insomnia, early morning wakefulness, or excessive sleeping

- Persistent feelings of sadness, emptiness, hopelessness, guilt, or worthlessness

- Feelings of hopelessness and pessimism

- Loss of interest in or pleasure from activities that were once enjoyed, including sex

- Fatigue and decreased energy

- Overeating or appetite loss

- Aches and pains, headaches, cramps, or digestive problems that do not let up even with treatment

- Difficulty concentrating, remembering, or making decisions

- Thoughts of death or suicide

- Restlessness or irritability

Source: National Institute of Mental Health: **www.nimh.nih.gov.**

Stressed Out

Sorry to use the *S*-word again, but stress and anxiety also depress the immune system. Stress hormones go into overdrive, causing insomnia, exhaustion, increased stomach acid, and irritability. Repair processes slow down or halt altogether, and the immune system gets lazy. You don't remember things as well. Your blood pressure climbs, your heart rate goes up, and your body dumps cholesterol into blood vessels. A cascade of events occur that lead to illness and depression.

When stressed, we're more likely to catch a cold or the flu. A Carnegie Mellon study published in the *Journal of Health Psychology* showed that people who had been chronically lonely, upset, sad, or agitated, or who were jobless or had family problems, were more likely to catch a cold than those who had secure jobs and solid family relationships.

Here's the irony, though: A little bit of stress can actually bolster your immunity. Your body senses the stress, and fortifies its defense system to compensate—at least temporarily. But chronic stress weakens your resistance to infection.

You'll respond differently to stress than I might. What feels like a catastrophe to me might be small potatoes to you. If you're frequently feeling stress or anxiety, you have to take steps to manage any situation in your life that is provoking this, from a bad job to a bad relationship, so that your body's self-healing powers can operate at full capacity.

When Stress Gets Under Your Skin

Soon after a heartbreaking split with his fiancée of six years and losing his home, Rocky developed raised, itchy, tormenting red spots all over his body. He was diagnosed with hives and took antihistamines in hopes of quick relief. Rocky, a former golf pro, was a student at Parker University at the time.

An attack of hives is usually the body's response to a food or drug allergen; soy, shellfish, aspirin, and penicillin are frequent offenders. The allergen triggers cells beneath the skin to churn out a chemical called histamine, which brings on the hives. Stress hormones play a part, too. They dilate blood vessels, which increases blood flow to the skin. Sometimes, stress can trigger hives within minutes of exposure to the allergen.

The antihistamines worked only partially. The hives would disappear for a day and then return. Life went on like this for Rocky for nearly a year. One day, he forgot to bring his antihistamine tablets with him to school; and by lunchtime his lips were swollen two inches thick, top and bottom. His breathing was also labored. Alarmed, Rocky sped to the staff doctor, who treated him and sent him home.

As a chiropractic student, Rocky acknowledged that he wasn't treating the fundamental problem, only masking it by trying to alleviate the symptoms. Stubborn skin problems often have emotional causes. When hives are chronic like this—lingering for weeks, months, even years—there is usually chronic stress as well. He knew he couldn't keep taking antihistamines without also working on the stress in his life.

Skin problems have a definite psychological component. Researchers at the University of Pennsylvania School of Medicine found that a protein called "substance P" is secreted by nerve fibers in our organs during heightened anxiety. This reaction appears to clog the skin's tiny blood vessels with white blood cells. The result is inflammation.

Rocky felt that his own condition was rooted in some sort of psychological problem. He consulted a health-care practitioner who was trained in a procedure called Neuro Emotional Technique (NET), which is used to heal physical or behavioral problems caused by unresolved emotional issues. The therapy identifies emotional blocks through muscle testing and a patient interview. Once the emotional block is located in the body (usually linked to a specific organ), the NET practitioner asks the patient to concentrate on the emotional issue and place one hand on the organ area and the other on the forehead. Next, the practitioner will tap on specific acupuncture points on the spine, using the edge of the hand or a special device. Muscles are tested again to see if the issue was cleared or whether more work is required.

Rocky was skeptical at first, but he stayed with it. The redness, itching, and bumps slowly disappeared. Learning how to relax more effectively also helped him.

Rocky didn't believe that NET had cured him. He kept waiting for another skin breakout, but it never happened. Fast-forward a few years: he has not had a hive or even the remotest sensation that hives would appear.

"NET helped remove the physiological reaction that my body was having to stress," he says. "I'm not saying that this technique can cure the world, but it changed my life!" Rocky found the courage to step out and do what was right: solve the underlying problem of his affliction. Healing depends a great deal upon your willingness to dig down deep and unearth the emotional pain that's keeping you ill. But let me encourage you—emotional stability can be built up just as physical strength can.

How to Manage Your Emotions

Emotional health is a powerful healer. The bottom line is this: Emotionally healthy people tend to get sick less often and heal faster than those who let their negative emotions get the best of them.

Maybe you think you can't be a member of that group, that you can't help getting upset easily, or that it's not possible to control your emotions. You're wrong. You're not at the mercy of your moods. You have the power to control your emotions and set the emotional standards by which you live. Here are several mind-body techniques that will help you.

Control Your Anger

Rarely does anyone win in an emotional argument, and more often than not, arguments bruise relationships. If you catch yourself in a heated, escalating argument, retreat and find a quiet spot. Take up to 20 slow, deep breaths. At the same time, assure yourself that you are in control of your emotions, and that you will get through this. These actions can lower your heart rate and blood pressure almost immediately. Walk back into the room for a discussion. If that isn't possible, retreat again.

Stop Negative Emotions in Their Tracks

The longer you let negative emotions overtake your life, the longer you'll suffer, psychologically and physically. You may feel consumed by these feelings, and while what you feel is anger toward others, who you really end up hurting is yourself. You get so wrapped up in the painful past that you can't enjoy your present. Learn to let go. You are not defined by your past; you are prepared by your past.

Reduce Stress

I know this might sound like "duh" advice, but you've got to reduce the stress in your life. If you're up against tight deadlines, cross items off your to-do list. Practice deep breathing to help you relax and let go of worries. Or employ relaxation skills: tense and relax every muscle in your body, one by one. This helps you achieve calm and peace.

More than anything, change the way you look at things in order to reduce stress. You can't control what's going on around you, but you can control how you react to it. Take charge of your thoughts, your emotions, and the way you deal with problems. Maybe you have to learn how to say no more often, or avoid the people who stress you out. Perhaps you have to look at things in a different light. Instead of fuming over a flat tire, ask yourself if this is really worth getting upset over. Is there a better way to focus your energy?

In life there will be many circumstances over which you will not have control, but you can always control how you react. Viewing stressful situations from a more positive, productive position is one of the main differences between people who heal effectively and those who do not.

Live Truthfully

Do you have any past emotional wounds that have not healed? If you're mired in some sort of psychological pain from the past, seek counseling to help you break free. You may need to clear away psychological clutter, get freedom from fear, and gain a kind of clarity that leads to a stronger sense of well-being. It's about making peace with the past.

When you can do that, you have the freedom to wake up each day with a fresh start, no matter what happened to you yesterday. You'll regain your ability to trust and love. And you'll take more time to count your blessings and less time to complain about what went wrong in your life.

"Internally Jog"

Laughter and humor have been called "internal jogging." I feel that this is what happens when I laugh. My entire being reacts to laughter with healing. It's as if the trillions of cells in my body are having a great workout.

And indeed, they are: Laughing burns calories, since it's possible to move as many as 400 muscles when you laugh. Some researchers estimate that laughing 100 times offers a workout equivalent to 15 minutes on a stationary bicycle. Your heart rate goes up, and you increase blood flow to the brain. Likewise, you help trigger the release of endorphins, feel-good chemicals that create a natural, euphoric high.

In his book *Anatomy of an Illness,* Norman Cousins credited laughter and humor as tools he used to fight a serious collagen-vascular disease. He found that one ten-minute bout of laughter gave him two hours of painless sleep.

We know from numerous studies that laughter:

- Relaxes tense muscles

- Reduces production of stress-causing hormones

- Lowers blood pressure

- Helps the blood stay oxygenized

- Wards off depression and helps people heal emotionally
- Provides an outlet to manage unwanted stress

Tap into the healing power of laughter! Watch comedies or TV shows or read the comics or cartoon books. Hang around with people who crack you up. All of these actions will lighten your life and promote self-healing.

Cry If You Want To

To cry is to heal. When you cry, you release negative emotions through your tears, and there is scientific proof of this. One rather fascinating study looked at two different types of tears: true emotional tears (the kind released when you're sad, depressed, or otherwise emotionally distraught); and tears released when you peel onions. When emotional tears were analyzed chemically, researchers found that they were loaded with stress chemicals. So when you cry emotionally, you're literally getting rid of stress! Tears related to peeling onions have none of these stress chemicals; the tears are simply a physical reaction to irritants in onions. The take-home message of this study is that tears serve a healing function by cleansing the body of harmful stress chemicals—so don't try to fight back your tears!

Relax!

When you're feeling relaxed, you'll heal faster. Some proof of this comes from a study conducted at the University of Massachusetts Medical School and published in the journal *Psychosomatic Medicine*. In the study, patients with psoriasis (a chronic skin disease) were taught how to relax. They listened to relaxation tapes while undergoing ultraviolet light treatments, the standard treatment for the disease. The rate of skin healing for those who listened to the tapes was nearly four times faster than for those who used the UV treatment alone!

Look into relaxation techniques. Try taking a class in yoga, meditation, guided imagery, or deep breathing. These activities release worries and quiet your nerves. The more you practice them, the less anxious you become.

Whenever you're tense, work to identify what thoughts and emotions might be causing the tension. For example, you might be worried about something, or focused on all the bad things that are happening or could happen in a particular situation. Correct your thinking and drop any thought or feeling that creates tension. Let go of every doubt and question in your mind. Disassociate yourself from them. Picture them contained in a balloon that is floating into the sky, out of your sight. Do this exercise on a regular basis, and you'll go a long way toward freeing yourself from stress and strain.

Dr. Albert Schweitzer, the great philosopher and physician, was right when he said, "Each person carries his own doctor inside him. . . . We are at our best when we give the doctor who resides within each patient a chance to go to work." And one of the many ways we can do so is by nurturing what I call "the trust factor," a powerful healing concept that works in the face of the toughest odds. That's the next stop on our self-healing journey.

CHAPTER EIGHT

THE TRUST FACTOR

When he was seven years old, my son Gianni fell off his bike one day while out riding on the sidewalk in front of our house. There was no visible sign of injury, but he was crying, complaining that his knee hurt. I applied a Band-Aid—one with a superhero on it—and kissed it. He felt instantly better—no more pain—just by the soothing effect of putting the tiny bandage on his knee, although there is no medical reason it should have made him feel better.

Gianni's expectation that the Band-Aid would fix him was a powerful thing. And it is the type of expectation that we see operating at all levels of healing. The more you believe you are going to benefit from something, and you trust in it, the more likely it is that you will experience a benefit. It is the power of your belief and expectation that produces the improvement in your health.

No one yet understands why. This "trust factor" may activate the body's self-healing capacities or interact in some way with drugs or other interventions. Some scientists say a person's trust in a therapy causes the body to churn endorphins, which act as natural painkillers.

These ease pain and reduce discomfort. In other words, believing in the healing can literally make it happen.

There are three levels to trust: trust in your treatment, trust in your healer, and trust in your body's ability to self-heal. Each is extremely powerful in outcome.

Trust in Your Treatment

If you believe that a treatment will work, your positive expectations make that treatment more effective.

Here's a story to illustrate my point: For her part, Mrs. Mitchell decided that she had little to lose in seeking care from a colleague of mine, Gil Ramirez, D.C. With a large afghan covering her legs down to her feet, Mrs. Mitchell steered her wheelchair into his office and announced: "I want you to fix this." At which point, she pulled up the afghan to reveal swollen, inflamed feet with pus oozing from her toenails and her feet blackened all the way up and over her ankles.

As he looked at the poor woman's condition, Gil said, "I think you're in the wrong place. You should be in the hospital."

She stared at Gil and replied, "No, I've been to the hospital already, and they can't help me. They want to amputate."

Then she took Gil's hand and said in a somewhat softer tone, "I know you can help me. I trust you."

Gil was stunned. He thought to himself, *This woman, a complete stranger with gangrene up to her knees, tells me she has faith in me to help her! Well, she has more faith than I do!* But then he realized that she had faith in the treatment, not him.

Gil and Mrs. Mitchell talked more, and he tried to dissuade her, but before he knew it, she had talked him into trying to do something . . . and not just try to help, but to heal!

After a short but futile attempt at explaining chiropractic philosophy, Gil wrote up a disclaimer saying that she insisted treatment despite his protests, and that she didn't hold him responsible. Gil really believed she did not have a hope in the world, but Mrs. Mitchell signed the form and they started treatment.

Gil took a three-view set of x-rays of her neck and got her onto the adjusting table for their first session. He advised her to come back in a couple of days for another adjustment. This went on for about a month.

Mrs. Mitchell kept encouraging Gil as they continued treatment, and one day, some pink skin emerged where once there was only black. As time passed, she steadily improved. After five months of care, Mrs. Mitchell walked into Gil's office and said she was okay and didn't need any more adjustments.

Her experience was, in Gil's words, the most beautiful of human encounters. Gil had given her his accumulation of wisdom and compassion. From her, he received absolute trust.

If a person trusts that a treatment is going to help, whether it's chemotherapy or a pill, then most likely it will—and Mrs. Mitchell's case is a strong testament to this.

The message a healer gives with a treatment can also affect how rapidly it begins to work. This premise was tested in one study of 30 people who underwent relaxation training to help lower their blood pressure. Half of the group was told their pressure would begin to go down immediately following the first session, and the other half was told that their blood pressure response would be delayed until at least after the third session. The patients who expected an immediate response showed a seven times greater reduction in blood pressure when compared with those led to expect a delayed response.

There is incredible healing power at work when you believe in the treatment. How can you acquire this mind-set? Well, you can start by researching various treatments and costs, finding a good specialist, and insisting on receiving the best options for your diagnosis. Here are some questions you can ask that will help you acquire trust in your treatment:

- What is the goal of my treatment?
- What are my treatment options?
- How effective are they?
- Should I think about complementary treatments?

- What is your experience in using this treatment?

- May I talk to other patients who have had this treatment?

Satisfying answers to these questions will build your trust in the treatment you're seeking.

Trust in Your Healer

A colleague of mine, Richard J. Parenti, D.C., was troubled because his receptionist, Cindy, told him she couldn't have children. She and her husband had been trying for four years and had seen many doctors, including fertility specialists. They all said that while they didn't know what was wrong, the couple would never have children.

"As long as I can remember, all I've ever wanted was to become a mother and have lots of babies," Cindy said, sadly. "I see parents with babies, and I wonder if we will ever know the joy of having a child of our own."

Dr. Parenti suspected that her problem stemmed partly from believing in what the doctors told her—and if she didn't believe in their ability to conceive, then they probably wouldn't be successful.

A few months later, Cindy's husband came by to pick her up from work one night. Dr. Parenti persuaded them both to let him check their spines. He found nerve interference in Cindy's lower spine, the area where the nerves that supply her ovaries exit. And in her husband, he found interference in the first spinal nerve in the neck.

"I felt confident that this interference, along with Cindy's belief that she couldn't have children, were the sources of the problem," Dr. Parenti confided to me. "I didn't share this with them because I didn't think they'd believe me, especially since I was a new doctor just out of school. So I just asked them to let me correct the nerve interferences I found."

Cindy and her husband agreed. Three times a week, Dr. Parenti took them into a treatment room and adjusted their spines. By removing restrictions (subluxations), he felt he could free the wellness force, allow it to flow, and provide their bodies with the fullest expression of health.

Then one day, Cindy called in sick. She said she had the flu. The next day, she called in again, saying that she didn't quite know what was wrong with her. She had started feeling better the day before but became sick again in the morning. Dr. Parenti told her to get a home pregnancy test and then shared with her why he thought she hadn't been able to get pregnant before.

When Cindy called back later that day, she was crying. "All the doctors told me that I would never have a family," she said.

"All but one," Dr. Parenti replied. "I always knew you would."

"It's a miracle!" she cried.

Nine months later, Cindy gave birth to a healthy eight-pound boy, who, today, is six years old.

One of the essential elements of the healing process is the relationship you have with the healer. It must be based on trust—a firm belief that your healer is honest and will not cause you harm. When you have this conviction, you feel more comfortable confiding in your healer and seeking advice. And a relationship implies an ongoing interaction between two parties who respect each other. In the presence of this bond, healing is more likely to take place.

By contrast, if you go to healers whom you don't trust, you are less likely to take their opinions about what you ought to do, and you're also less likely to believe that you're going to heal.

You must come to the point of trust, and it begins with finding the right doctor or healer, knowing the technology is the best that's out there, and just feeling a sense of "this is right for me." Yet finding a practitioner you trust can be a challenge in today's baffling world of medicine.

Choosing a Healer

Each of us wants the right to choose our own doctors, but choice is largely dictated by our health plans or insurance providers. I want to feel that the doctors whom I've developed a relationship with care about me.

If your insurance changes, should you switch your doctor? Perhaps stay with the insurance carrier but opt for a more expensive policy that allows more choices? It's not just a financial decision, though. It's an emotional one because you trust the doctor who coached you through a high-risk pregnancy, who diagnosed your puzzling symptoms, or who offered moral support throughout your open-heart surgery.

Imagine being in one of these situations and being forced to switch doctors in the middle of your care!

Some families can afford to stick with their doctors, but many others don't have that luxury. They don't have the money for a higher co-pay and can't pay out-of-network fees. When you're sick, the last thing you want to worry about is the bill.

When you're not well and going to a new doctor, you're also feeling vulnerable, weak, and even powerless to some extent. Something is happening to you that you can't control. Oftentimes, you have to explain your whole life story, when you'd rather be going to somebody you've seen for the last ten years and who already knows your entire health history. You'd rather go in and say, "Doctor, I'm here and I hurt." And then, the doctor prescribes an effective treatment because he or she knows your medical history. When you lose a doctor who really knows you, you lose important memories of your case.

With the cataclysmic changes going on in the health-care industry, it's likely at some point you may need to find new providers. So how can you make the best of the situation and find healers you trust?

Most of us find our doctors by chance, get lucky, and end up with a healer we trust. If not, we might fault ourselves for failing to research like we do when shopping for a new TV or car. We also ask our family members and friends for recommendations, but that's not always the most reliable method, as we often judge doctors by their bedside manner, rather than on their diagnostic skills.

We must also be slightly skeptical of referrals from other physicians. There's some bias attached because they may favor their friends, people with the same hospital affiliations, or doctors who send them patients, too.

I feel the best source of referrals is from an insider. Try to find a nurse, a medical assistant, or a doctor friend you trust who will talk honestly about who's competent and who isn't. These people are often more trustworthy, because they feel less loyalty and have worked with, or observed, many professionals in action.

Once you have a solid recommendation, how do you follow up? First, check credentials. Board certification is the minimum requirement these days. Where a doctor went to medical school is often less important than where he or she served a residency. This information can often be verified by state medical boards or medical societies.

Meeting with a Healer for the First Time

Once you've tentatively decided on a doctor, make an appointment for an interview. Ask doctors about their practice philosophy. Do they believe in minimal intervention? Preventive care? What is their attitude toward complementary medicine? How much do they rely on high-tech procedures? Can you get in readily—on an emergency or walk-in basis? Is the doctor available by phone when you have a question or concern?

My own choice is for a doctor who keeps up with the latest treatments, who pays attention to me when I speak, who understands my needs, and who, if the cause of the problem is not obvious, will tenaciously pursue the diagnosis. I want no doctor who is quick to treat my symptoms before having sufficient knowledge of what's wrong with me.

Training and experience are also important. If I had a heart attack, I'd want the best cardiologist to get me through it. Then I'd want to get to an N.D. (a doctor of naturopathy), a D.C. (doctor of chiropractic), or a primary-care M.D. who is open to other forms of healing. The real work of healing and keeping patients healthy is in prevention, and that is a weak spot in conventional medicine. Our current medical system is a great lover of "Band-Aid measures," but that doesn't work so well anymore. We want medical professionals to show us what to do to prevent disease and how to create our own self-healing measures.

How supportive will the doctor be? Healing is harder without a supportive doctor. A supportive doctor will encourage second opinions and want you to be well-informed and satisfied. You want to feel that they care.

Notice, too, the subtle clues around the office. Is the office staff caring and helpful? Is the initial exam comprehensive? Does the doctor explain what he or she is doing during the examination? Does he or she ask about facts that could bear on your medical history, such as your job, relationships, family life, or sexual orientation?

Find out how the doctor feels about pursuing second opinions. Good doctors won't feel threatened if you want to get one, nor do they become touchy when you want to know more about your condition. And they listen to you when you're describing what's wrong or asking questions about your illness. Indeed, my dream doctor is someone who listens to me, explains my condition clearly, and validates any symptoms, such as pain, that I'm experiencing.

Once you trust your healers, you usually believe what they tell you. So if they explain that something will make you better—and you trust them—this positively affects your outcome. There were times in my own practice when patients were perfectly fine, but didn't feel that way. I might recommend a vitamin tablet for what they imagine is the problem. It's all in the mind. My patients take it and because of their trust in me, it might act as a placebo. They go home feeling positive and the next day, they wake up feeling fine. A trusting healer-patient relationship is also believed to have a positive placebo effect in itself and may definitely improve health outcomes.

But I advise against blind trust in your doctor or any other healer. Is this person choosing the right treatments for your condition? Does he or she consider complementary therapies that might be more effective? Many people trust their health-care providers, but their effectiveness is only as good as the knowledge they possess. Doctors, like other trusted advisers, aren't always right. All of my recommendations, by the way, apply to any healer: naturopath, chiropractor, psychologist, rehabilitation therapist, and so on.

In the end, choosing a doctor is like picking a friend or spouse. You can't expect perfection. I believe in empowering yourself by learning as much about your medical condition as you can—its causes, treatment options, and rates of disability. The more educated you are about your care, the better care you will receive.

How to Ask for a Second (or Third) Opinion

I strongly recommend that if you lack confidence in one doctor, or just feel unsure about your diagnosis or treatment options, get a second opinion and even a third. Here are some suggestions on doing so:

— *Ask for a referral.* Ask your doctor to recommend another physician or specialist so that you can seek another opinion. This is about you and your life, so don't worry about hurting a doctor's feelings! Most doctors welcome a second opinion, especially when surgery or long-term treatment is being considered.

— *Find a different doctor.* If you don't feel comfortable asking your doctor for a recommendation, contact another doctor you trust. Call university teaching hospitals and medical societies in your area for names of doctors. Some of this information is available online.

— *Talk to your insurance provider.* Always check with your health-insurance provider to make sure the cost of a second opinion is covered. Many carriers do cover this.

— *Gather together your medical records.* The doctor you're seeing for a second opinion needs as much information as possible about your case, so arrange to have your medical records sent. This can help you avoid repeating any tests and can get the new doctor up to speed quickly. Also make sure you get a copy for your own files.

— *Visit the second-opinion doctor.* For a competent second opinion, you need to be seen by the doctor for a physical examination and a thorough review of your medical records. Ask the doctor to send a written report to your primary doctor and get a copy for your records.

Trust in Your Body's Ability to Self-Heal

Clearly, it is the treatment and the healer's ability that seem to mobilize powerful self-healing mechanisms within the body, but there is more: you really want to believe that it's possible to heal yourself.

I want to share with you two stories that illustrate how powerful this belief is.

From Wheelchair to Walking

Eighteen-year-old Joshua was an avid snowboarder who was a bit of a daredevil. One afternoon he attempted a jump at Buller Ski Resort, a few hours' drive northeast of Melbourne, Australia. Joshua hit the icy launch ramp and was airborne. Moments later, he was upside down. In midair he realized he wasn't going to make it to the other ramp and just before he hit the ground, he tucked his head in and attempted an army-style forward roll to avoid a concussion—and crushing his skull.

On impact, his chin got buried in his chest. When he bounced off the ground, his head whiplashed back and his helmet hit between his shoulder blades. He heard a massive *bang*—like the discharge of a shotgun at close range. He knew his neck was broken.

Joshua was airlifted to a prominent spinal-care facility in Melbourne. His parents were told that if he survived, he would be a quadriplegic. The prognosis was grim.

One day shortly after Joshua entered the hospital, a surgeon at his bedside explained very carefully, and with condescending certainty, that Joshua needed a reality check: "You are a quadriplegic; you will never snowboard again. You're going to spend the rest of your life in a wheelchair."

Joshua's mom overhead him and became enraged. She shouted, "Doctor, we are positive people. If you don't have anything positive to say, then say absolutely nothing! Do I make myself clear?"

Relentlessly searching for any positive input, Joshua's mother sent his MRIs to close family friends in California. They forwarded them to a renowned spinal surgeon at Cedars-Sinai Medical Center in Los

Angeles, but his prognosis was the same: that Joshua would never walk again.

Undeterred, his mother played hours and hours of video showing Josh riding his motorbike and snowboarding. She brought in his motorbike helmet and snowboard gear, and stuck it all under his nose, so he could smell the leather, the dirt, the sweat. She surrounded his bed with extreme-sports photos of Joshua in action. She did everything possible to prevent her son from mentally adjusting to life as a quadriplegic. Her objective—and Joshua's—was to visualize a return to everything that had previously been meaningful in his life.

Encouraged by his mother's belief in the body's ability to heal itself, Joshua kept visualizing movement in his limbs. After about a week of intense concentration, his hard work in combination with other therapies started to work. Before long, he was able to wiggle the big toe on his left foot. It was an exciting achievement.

From the hospital, Joshua was transferred to a rehabilitation center where he encountered still more medical-establishment negativity. The way the physiotherapists saw it, their job was to help him adjust to life in a wheelchair, but Joshua kept telling himself that he would walk out of that place under his own power. And days before his 19th birthday, he was finally ready to be discharged. He rolled his wheelchair about four feet, then locked its brakes. He stood up unassisted, accepted the crutches his girlfriend gave him, and walked ten feet into the Melbourne sunshine.

These events occurred ten years ago. Today, although Joshua walks with a limp—and with the aid of an ankle brace on his right foot and a walking stick—he also rides a Harley, drives a car, and does some occasional snowboarding. To the bafflement of the medical establishment, Joshua's MRIs continue to show that 90 percent of his spinal cord is nonfunctional. Technically, he is still a quadriplegic. Joshua asserts that it is his belief in his body's innate healing intelligence that helped him so miraculously.

A Healer's Total Belief in Self-Healing

Dr. Arno Burnier, D.C., is a friend and colleague of mine. On a warm summer day, in 1983, Arno and his wife, Jane, were about to go on a motorcycle ride when he decided to pull into a state park in Flemington, New Jersey, and teach Jane how to drive. Since he used to race bikes, he was well versed in operating them. It was hot and muggy, so they decided to take off their leather jackets and helmets. After all, what could possibly go wrong in a nearly empty parking lot?

Jane straddled the Kawasaki, and Arno sat behind her. He showed her the throttle, clutch, front brake, and rear brake operation. He told her to slowly turn on the throttle, but the next thing he knew, they were up in a perfect wheelie with her frozen grip on the handle bar and Arno unable to reach the brakes. They blasted across the parking lot and missed hitting a car by a few inches—a collision that would have taken both of their right legs off. The bike kept flying over the asphalt until it reached the embankment of the sidewalk. The rear wheel hit and they were airborne. Jane was thrown in front of the bike in the grass, and Arno landed on the back of the motorcycle.

Arno set the bike upright and assessed the damage. Once the bike's motor was turned off, he quickly turned to Jane to see if she was okay. She appeared unharmed. As he collected himself and started back toward the bike, Jane screamed: "Oh my God, look at your arm!"

Arno felt a rush of searing pain in that instant. His arm was ripped open from the shoulder to the elbow. The wound was wide and loaded with sand, gravel, and pieces of rubber. His arm had acted as a brake to the rear wheel. The spinning tire had laid a track on his arm, taking the skin, subcutaneous tissues, and fatty layer with it. Arno stared in disbelief at his arm, which was open down to the muscles.

His first thought was to clean the wound immediately. He walked down a small hill to the park's little bathroom with the intention of pouring water on the gash. The closer he came to the faucet, however, the more his entire nerve system and insides hissed. Arno could not see himself putting water on it. Instead, he listened to his gut feeling, turned around, and began to walk back up the hill.

You'd think that Arno would have called 911 or at least driven himself to the nearest emergency room. But he is someone who believes so strongly that the body is self-healing and self-correcting that he decided to allow his body's innate intelligence to do its own doctoring.

And Arno saw immediate proof of this. He took another look at the wound and noticed that the entire gash was flooded with a thick layer of serous fluid, which meant that immune cells had rushed to the area and were sealing the wound from edge to edge.

Jane and Arno got back on the bike and rode the final 30 miles home. While attempting to dismount, they both realized how much they had been injured. Both of their pelvises were seriously strained, which likely was caused when the bike came up between their legs as they were ejected on impact. Jane's neck was also stiff, and Arno guessed she had sustained a lateral whiplash. Arno was also certain that his lower jaw was broken. They both went to bed fatigued and shaken up by the crash.

As soon as Arno dozed off, the pain got so intense that he moved his arm a bit. The motion somehow gave him some relief, so he spent the night moving his arm back and forth in slow repeated motions. The constant motion kept the fluid covering the gash elastic and supple as it dried overnight. By morning the wound had sealed.

Arno began to wonder, *What would have happened if I had had the wound washed, cleaned, and bandaged; then taken a sleeping pill, painkiller, and antibiotics? I would have slept soundly. But I'm sure that the next morning, when it was time to get up again, the first movement of my arm would have pulled the edge of the wound, causing it to bleed.*

Since Arno felt that he had to keep his arm in motion, he went to his office to conduct business as usual. He cut the left sleeve of his shirt, keeping the wound exposed. He could hardly walk, yet moving eased his pelvic pain. When patients saw his arm, they were shocked. Most were frightened and told him flat out that he was insane and needed to go to the hospital to have a tetanus shot, get the wound cleaned, and have a skin graft.

Arno told me: "In my mind, I was at peace and really wanted to see what my body was capable of. I thought that, if my body built my arm from scratch in the first place, maybe it could repair the damage. Faith and trust were my allies."

But by then, Arno could hardly speak; his jaw was nearly shut tight. All day at work, he muttered through his mouth.

Two days later, Arno delivered a seminar scheduled in his office, but was still struggling to speak. Among the 30 some people attending the talk, one was the chairman of the board of Hamilton Hospital in New Jersey. He walked up to Arno at the end of the talk and said, "I couldn't understand a word of what you said, yet seeing you up there with your arm hanging out, your frozen jaw, and your apparent distress, I believe you have something I want." The man ended up receiving Arno's care for years thereafter.

The wound kept drying up and soon formed a thick scab. Over a period of months, the scab became thinner. It started to detach itself from the top of Arno's shoulder downward. Some people suggested he pull it, but he refused.

Then the top of the scab began to coil grotesquely on itself. Again some people suggested that he at least ought to cut the coil, yet Arno let it be. Eventually, the entire scab disintegrated and fell off. It took with it the sand, gravel, and rubber. At first the layer below the fallen scab was thin, pink, and ugly, but soon began to improve. Today, Arno doesn't even have a scar or any skin discoloration. His pelvis also healed over time with no residual discomfort.

From the time of the crash, Arno developed frequent headaches due to his broken jaw. Then, many months after the accident, he was sitting outside, reading a book while sunbathing. As the warmth of the sun hit the side of his face, he felt a sudden "clunk." His jaw shifted on its own, realigning itself. The headaches vanished and have never returned. His body had healed itself fully and in an amazing way.

Behind these wonderful accounts of self-healing lies one great truth: Genuine belief is the most powerful asset you can possess. Look around you, read about, and listen to people who have stories of their miraculous cures, or who, like Joshua or Arno, had worked out their own healing life plan.

When you believe in your healer, in your treatment, and in your own self-healing ability, nothing is impossible.

The final piece of the self-healing paradigm is spiritual. History shows us that the most inspiring people of our times believed in a spiritual base that gave them the strength, comfort, peace, joy, and confidence for great accomplishments. Finding your spiritual source is a powerful way to gain self-healing, and that is what we'll talk about next.

Part III

SPIRITUAL SELF-HEALING

A strong spiritual belief system is a major advantage in self-healing. Regardless of preference, faith in a higher power or spiritual practices and rituals seem to strengthen our healing forces. Daily prayer and meditation improve conscious contact with this spiritual power . . . as does creativity and the healing spiritual triad of forgiveness, gratitude, and love.

CHAPTER NINE

CREATIVE FORCES

Stacy, a 37-year-old flight attendant, had been everywhere—that is, everywhere that consultations, diagnosis, and treatment can take a patient. Stacy suffered from severe migraine headaches and relied heavily on pain medication. She had been to migraine and headache specialty clinics, two or three university medical clinics, and herbalists. Her migraines were so bad that sometimes she was confined to bed for 24 hours to sleep off a nasty one.

Stacy had come to my office primarily because of neck stiffness, but in the course of my examination, she timidly asked if I could do anything for her migraine pain. Since she had never had chiropractic care before, and because my exam indicated that her head pain got worse when I pressed on her neck, I knew it was likely she'd respond positively to my care.

Living with migraines can make life almost unbearable. There's usually a painful throbbing on one or both sides of the head or even around the eyes. The sufferer may experience other effects such as nausea, vomiting, and an increased sensitivity to noise and/or bright light. Nearly 30 million Americans—and three times more women than men—suffer from these painful attacks, according to the National Headache Foundation. An episode typically lasts four hours but could continue for three days.

While migraines tend to run in families, no one really knows what causes them. There are some theories, though. One is inflammation in the brain caused by overactive nerve cells that overstimulate blood vessels. Another theory is that migraines are triggered by low levels of serotonin, a brain chemical that regulates pain perception. Low magnesium levels in the brain may also cause migraines, which is why these headaches often respond to supplemental magnesium. Also, in women, fluctuations in estrogen and progesterone levels seem to bring on migraines.

I spent an hour asking Stacy about her migraines: what seemed to trigger them, how often she got them, how long they lasted, where they started, how they progressed, and if there were possible environmental causes. We also discussed her life: the joys and the stresses, as both can set off head pain.

When I'd sit down with patients who were in pain, I'd ask them what they were hoping for. Most wanted the right treatment to make the pain go away—which is what Stacy wanted. Others said they wanted the pain to be less intense. They wanted to be able to do everyday activities, like taking care of their kids, being able to work, going for walks, or making plans for the weekend.

I'd usually explain to patients that if a particular painkiller worked, it probably wouldn't make the pain go away altogether, but it might help improve their quality of life. If a doctor prescribes pain medication for you, it will usually reduce your pain intensity by about a third or more, and that's helpful to most people. You might get even more relief, but it's unusual for the pain to go away entirely.

I suspected that one of Stacy's problems might be too much medication. In a lot of cases, pain medication just makes people feel worse. Ironically, if you use painkillers frequently (even the over-the-counter variety), you'll experience even more chronic pain. And the longer you use painkillers, the longer your chronic pain will persist, as the likelihood of chronic pain increases with the length of time you use analgesics daily. In studies, people who took daily painkillers for six months or longer were more than 20 times more likely to have chronic migraines, almost ten times more likely to experience other types of chronic headaches, and three-and-a-half times more likely to have neck and/or lower-back pain. Still, pain continues to be treated mostly with pills. It's crazy!

I feel that pain—including migraine pain—is best managed through multiple approaches, which means trying different treatments in conjunction with each other: nutritional supplements, relaxation techniques, chiropractic adjustments, massage, and more. Healing is about more than what pill you take.

I suggested to Stacy that we work with her physician to wean her off the pain medications, we continue her chiropractic treatments, and that she try some nondrug pain-management techniques such as relaxation and visualization.

A serendipitous event occurred during this time, in the form of a chance invitation from a friend. It was the first in a chain of remarkable shifts in Stacy's health. Her friend invited Stacy to a paint-your-own pottery store, where people could create their own ceramic pieces, make fused glass pieces, or learn to use a pottery wheel. Stacy was attracted to the process; she found it very satisfying to make something from the nothingness of ceramics or clay. Enamored, she made all of her Christmas presents at the store. It was when pieces she donated to charity auctions started fetching as much as $500 that Stacy realized she might be producing pieces of actual value to people.

"Pottery restored my sanity," she told me later. "It took my focus away from the pain and put it on my pottery. When you get in touch with your creativity like that, it can be a rewarding and healing experience."

It is always exciting for me to hear about the things that medical science is making possible. Blockbuster pharmaceuticals, high-tech medical devices, and miracle cancer treatments grab headlines—and the optimism is justified, at least somewhat. But pottery-making? Stacy had stumbled upon an unlikely cure: the healing power of creativity.

Creativity and Self-Healing

The notion that pottery helped Stacy deal with her physical pain is not as far-fetched as it might seem. The relationship between art and healing has been around forever, even documented in the Bible and other venerable texts. In most cultures throughout history, music, dance, rhythmic drumming, and chanting have been essential parts of healing rituals. In a more modern context, art and music therapies are used in hospitals and clinics because health-care providers now realize that creativity is healing and life-enhancing.

One of the most intriguing studies done in this area was the 2006 federally funded Creativity and Aging Study. It hinted that participating in an arts program may confer rather amazing health benefits, especially with age. The study was led by researchers at George Washington University's Center on Aging, Health & Humanities. In 2002, they recruited 300 people, ages 65 to 103. Half participated in arts programs, which included singing, creative writing, poetry, painting, or jewelry making; and the other half was not involved in arts of any kind.

After two years, those in the arts group reported better overall physical health and fewer doctor visits than the others. They also experienced fewer falls and felt less depressed or lonely. Medication usage increased with age in both groups, but the arts group went from using an average 6.1 drugs to only 7, while the control group jumped up from using 5.7 drugs to 8.3. The arts programs also made the participants feel more independent and less in risk of needing long-term care. Pretty remarkable, I'd say.

Obviously, creativity makes us healthier—but how?

Neuroscientists unaffiliated with this study assert that artistic expression stimulates the growth of new brain cells—an amazing process called *neurogenesis*. Now, when I was a premed student in the '80s, the dogma was that if a brain cell dies, it's gone forever. But we know that's not true. Your brain continues to make new brain cells with corresponding improvements in performance, as long as you're engaged in creative pursuits, you exercise, and you engage in mental "work" such as crossword puzzles. So don't worry: You may have killed some brain cells last weekend, but more will be created, as long as you use your head—literally.

Creativity on Stress

When your body is under stress, it evokes what is called the *fight-or-flight response,* and stress hormones are released. This reaction jacks up your blood pressure, breathing rate, metabolism, and muscle tension. If chronically elevated, these hormones can suppress your immune system, which can lead to health problems and pain.

Do something creative, and you'll break that stress cycle. Creativity quiets your mind. This is the opposite of the fight-or-flight response. Research illustrates that a quiet and focused state of mind alleviates pain and bolsters the immune system. Being creative also stimulates endorphins, your body's natural painkillers, in the same way exercise does. Once you get into the flow, you begin to desire that endorphin rush in the same way that you enjoy how exercising makes you feel. In Stacy's case, she knew she felt more relaxed and at peace when she made pottery. And being relaxed kept her distracted from the migraine pain.

The Power of Creative Expression

Down through the ages, every form of art—music, drama, art, dance—has been used as a way to communicate. Through art, you can learn to express your emotions in ways that don't employ words. If you give someone who is being treated for cancer, for example, a canvas and some paints, a painting will emerge—one that inevitably relates to his or her feelings.

The reason art therapy has become so important in medicine is that it allows us to express what we can't or don't want to talk about verbally, but that we can express through painting, sculpture, writing, or drama. It helps us release negative emotions and get to the core of healing.

I am moved by the often-told story of Holocaust survivor Alfred Kantor. He used art as a stress-relieving, emotion-releasing activity during his imprisonment in concentration camps, and in the process left one of the few visual records of that horrific period in history. To avoid detection, Kantor sketched and painted when no one was looking, mainly at night, and he would hide his sketchbook under the floor. His paintings depicted scenes of everyday life in the camps, including unspeakable atrocities committed by the Nazis: naked women being classified into those who would live and those to be killed, corpses being dumped into trucks from the gas chambers, the flames from the crematorium chimneys at night, and vicious SS guards.

This body of work was published in 1971 by McGraw-Hill as *The Book of Alfred Kantor.* He wrote that his art helped him survive and cope with the unimaginable horrors he experienced. I believe that creative expression kept his spirit alive.

And I believe that creativity can work in a similar way for all of us. A good example is depression. When we're depressed, we tend to withdraw and get lost in the sadness. But if we get involved in something artistic, it takes us away from the sadness and puts our focus on an activity with the potential to bring joy.

While researching this book, I read about a fascinating study called "Managing Depression Through Needlecraft Creative Activities." It involved middle-aged women who began embroidery or tapestry work in order to relieve stress and overcome grief. Dr. Frances Reynolds, the study's author, observed that women found that needlework relaxed them, distracted them from anxiety, and made them feel like they had accomplished something. The women also said it boosted their self-esteem and gave them a sense of control in often uncontrollable situations. Another benefit was the building of new relationships with other women who could act as a support system.

Art has enormous healing power and is effective in treating trauma. Art therapists have helped combat veterans with post-traumatic stress disorder (PTSD), as well as trauma victims of 9/11 and Hurricane Katrina.

There's even more. Researchers at Thomas Jefferson University in Philadelphia found that women with cancer who sculpted or sketched experienced less pain, insomnia, and overall stress during their treatment. And researchers at Chicago's Northwestern Memorial Hospital discovered that art therapy reduced fatigue and pain, and boosted appetite among a group of 50 cancer patients.

Music is also a powerful healing instrument, extensively reached for its benefits. Music therapy:

- Reduces pain intensity in various types of chronic pain, including fibromyalgia

- Controls lower-back pain

- Distracts patients from pain and other symptoms of illnesses

- Improves mood

- Relieves stress

One of the most powerful effects of music therapy has been found in the treatment of Alzheimer's patients. Researchers at Dartmouth College discovered that a part of the brain called the rostromedial prefrontal cortex responds to specific keys in a melody. This part of the brain also happens to help us retrieve memories and emotions connected to those memories. When a music therapist played a song recognizable to an Alzheimer's patient, an emotional connection was forged. The patient was able to retrieve memories, better organize thoughts, and connect to the present. Additional studies suggest that when Alzheimer's patients take part in music therapy, melatonin levels in their blood start to surge. Melatonin is a soothing chemical in the body. As this natural chemical increases, patients become less aggressive and agitated.

Another powerful way to promote self-healing is to dance your troubles away. Dance therapy helps kids who can't express their feelings verbally. And it's great for adults who need to come out of their shells; as well as elderly men and women who may be too lonely, depressed, or disoriented to talk. I've seen people strengthen weaknesses in their hands by learning to play a guitar, and someone born with one leg shorter than the other learn to walk more gracefully after taking dancing lessons. And there are many more healing miracles like these. Nursing homes, hospitals, clinics, and schools for children with special needs all incorporate dance therapy as a part of their standard care.

While enjoying making music or dancing, you're also building your self-esteem, a vital aspect in healing. Connect to your own creativity, and you'll create profound self-healing in your life.

Generate Great Ideas:
The Four-Stage Creative Process

In 1926, educational psychologist Graham Wallace studied well-known scientists and innovators and discovered that they typically followed four distinct steps in their creative processes:

1. *The preparation stage.* This consists of formulating the problem, studying previous work on it, and thinking intensely about it.

2. *The incubation stage.* A germination period follows where you step away from the problem and engage in some form of activity unrelated to the problem you're trying to solve. Have you ever observed that ideas often come to you when you're doing something else? Well, that's no accident. When you're highly pressured, it's very hard to do that creative thinking. In this stage, there is no active work on the problem; your subconscious is working on it.

3. *The illumination stage.* Important insights are gained in this stage. Often as a flash or "Aha!" as a brilliant idea shoots across your mind, frequently while you're doing something else.

4. *The verification stage.* You must test and evaluate your idea to determine its validity. The musical composition must be scored, for example, or the mathematical formula proven.

Anyone can apply these steps. For example, conduct research online or brainstorm with colleagues (preparation). Turn the problem or challenge over to your subconscious mind—"sleep on it," take a break, work on an unrelated task, or do something that stimulates your imagination and emotions (incubation). When you least expect it, the idea comes to you—the "Aha!" moment (illumination). Finally, subject it to criticism—evaluate it, test it, refine it, and implement it (verification). If it doesn't work, go through the process again.

Find Your Creative Outlet

With all the evidence I've presented that creativity heals, I want you to get more creative. I know what you may be thinking: *I'm not artistic . . . I don't know how to draw . . . sing . . . or dance. I'm not coordinated. And I'm not talented.* I understand where you're coming from, but you don't have to be artistic in the traditional sense. I remember looking at the art my sons produced in school. It was beautiful. They didn't do it for the critics but for themselves.

Kids express themselves with natural artistry from the time they first pick up a crayon. But most of us lose confidence in our ability to create art as we grow up. We're taught (wrongly) that we have to be highly gifted to participate in the arts, rather than simply focusing on the personal joy of expressing ourselves. I want you to restore the "kid" in you, creatively!

Everyone can be creative. Stacy loved to create pottery. You might try your hand at writing poetry, scrapbooking, painting, sewing, taking dance classes, acting in plays, doing photography—anything you enjoy. Maybe you like to work with your hands. Why not try gardening or flower arranging? Even everyday activities like cooking are forms of creativity. If you love to eat, take a cooking class!

I urge you to give this a try. A friend of mine, who had never picked up a paintbrush in her life, went to a class that catered to people who had never painted before. She was going through the process of grief after losing her husband to leukemia and needed an outlet to express herself and a way to get some relief from her depression. The painting class not only restored her mental health, but along the way, she also discovered that she was actually a very good painter! It made her feel alive and gave her a sense of purpose. So step out of the confines of your comfort zone; you just never know what might happen!

There's even creativity in problem-solving at work—and there are always plenty of problems to tackle on the job! Use the creative process to brainstorm new and better solutions, and approach this with a positive frame of mind. Trust me, you'll arrive at a viable solution quickly.

I believe the most important element in all this is to not judge yourself or worry about what others might think of your creative work. You're doing this because you want to, because you want to create a self-healing life, not to please other people.

Ignite Your Creativity

I've found that the key to feeling more creative is to rely less on your left brain, the center for logic, and activate your right brain, the center for feeling and creativity. Here are a few techniques that will help you:

— *Write.* If writing appeals to you, sit down each morning and write whatever comes to your mind. Don't edit a thing; just let the words flow. What should you write about? I suggest that if you're dealing with anxiety, trauma, or depression (or even joy), write about these emotions. You'll release pent-up feelings, including guilt, sadness, or anger—emotions that can block your body's ability to heal. Writing reduces levels of the stress hormone cortisol, too much of which can harm your immunity; and numerous studies have shown that writing lowers blood pressure.

It is important to put a positive spin on your writing, too. Bring out the benefits your situation may be making available to you, whether they are some new wisdom you acquired, an important lesson learned, or something that made you feel grateful.

— *Use your nondominant hand.* This technique feels a little awkward, but it is highly recommended by creativity experts. Close your eyes, take a pencil or pen, and draw on a piece of paper with your nondominant hand for several minutes. This process helps activate the right side of your brain.

— *Take a walk.* Einstein, one of the greatest creative thinkers of all time, took frequent walks to help him solve problems. And no wonder—walking is a gentle, meditative exercise that helps quiet your left brain. It also increases and promotes oxygen flow to the brain, energizing brain cells for sharper mental performance. Some scientists believe that exercise, in general, triggers the release of various brain chemicals that enhance creativity.

— *Daydream.* Henry Ford once employed an efficiency expert to evaluate the productivity of his company. The expert's report was favorable, although he expressed reservations about one employee. "It's that man down the corridor," announced the expert. "Every time I go by his office, he's just sitting there with his feet propped on his desk. He's wasting your money."

"That man," replied Ford, "once had an idea that saved us millions of dollars. At the time, I believe his feet were planted right where they are now."

Whether you're grappling with a way to solve a business problem or thinking up a new idea for that novel you want to write, just relax, close your eyes, and let your mind wander freely. Don't edit your thoughts. You'll be surprised by the creative ideas that come into your mind.

— *Believe in your creative power.* If I had to leave you with one piece of advice, it would be this: Believe that you can be creative! Psychologists have studied the characteristics of creative people—their conclusion? Attitude. Creative people simply believe they are creative. So, have faith in your creative abilities!

What do you truly love to do? What makes your spirit soar? Dancing, singing, or playing an instrument? What about drawing, painting, woodworking, or even a starting a new business venture or inventing a product? Creativity takes so many forms. Whatever the activity, add it to your daily or weekly routine. Creativity will lift your spirit, bring self-healing, and energize your life.

While I was studying to become a chiropractor, my instructors often told us that many of our patients would come to us not because they were sick or in pain, but because they were lonely and needed a place to go. I found this to be true. What was lacking in those patients' lives was something I have come to call the "healing triad"—a trio of spiritual sentiments that, when restored in your life, chart a course toward resilience, happiness, self-esteem, and a sense of hope. The healing triad is the topic of our next chapter.

CHAPTER TEN

THE HEALING TRIAD

I have gone through seasons of life that have been joyous and happy, and also endured times that were harsh and painful. Through whatever loss or hardship or even triumph I have faced, I try my best to practice *forgiveness,* show *gratitude,* and express *love.* Each of these actions forms what I call the "healing triad," a powerful path to self-healing. When these interconnected emotions are at work in your life, they will soften the edges of the problems you face, lift your anxiety, and honor your health. Let's start with forgiveness.

Forgiveness

Forgiveness is medicine, and unless you view it as such, you'll let feelings of anger, revenge, and hate fester in, and dominate, your life. Studies have shown that long-held resentment can have serious health effects, including high blood pressure and heart disease, and perhaps even cancer. Research from the University of Wisconsin–Madison found that people harboring a grudge had more heart problems than those who forgave.

People who cannot forgive may also take longer to heal from an illness or injury. This response was demonstrated in the study conducted by researchers at the Institute of HeartMath in Boulder Creek, California. They asked the study participants to dwell for five minutes on a situation that aroused hate, frustration, and resentment. In their bodies, levels of immunoglobulin A (an antibody that helps fight off infections such as colds and flu) dropped significantly as a result—and the effect lasted up to five hours. When the volunteers were asked to feel compassionate toward a person or situation for the same amount of time, their IgA levels rose.

Every one of us has been hurt by someone at some time. Perhaps you've had a friend who has stolen something from you or who has lied to you about something important. Understandably, you might get angry, hostile, or resentful. You might even feel like taking revenge. Certainly, those emotions will pass. You may either forgive that person, or simply part company.

Uniformly, people who forgive are less angry, less resentful, more hopeful, less anxious—and of course healthier. Letting your heart soften even a tiny bit can make all the difference in your health.

A Gift You Give to Yourself

Many people don't fully understand forgiveness. If you forgive someone, it doesn't mean that you have to resume a relationship with the person who hurt you. Some people are so mean-spirited that they may never change. If the act was criminal, you can forgive, but still press charges against that person and work to hold them accountable for their action. You can also forgive someone and choose to never see them again.

I look at forgiveness as a gift you give to yourself, not something you do for someone else. It helps you heal physically, emotionally, and spiritually by releasing any pain, anger, and resentment you have. And no one else even has to know about your decision to forgive.

Learn to forgive. It puts hurtful experiences behind you so that you can concentrate on positive things—an outlook that can lead to a much healthier, more fulfilling life. Forgiveness is like getting out of an emotional jail. It's freedom from harmful emotions. With forgiveness, you have peace of mind and healing in your life. Forgiveness is truly self-healing.

Gratitude

You'll find that gratitude is a fundamental teaching of most religions and spiritual disciplines. From a scientific standpoint, research hints that it has important health benefits, too, including better sleep, fewer illnesses, and greater resiliency to deal with stress.

Robert Emmons, a University of California psychology professor, has comprehensively studied the relationship between gratitude and mental and physical health. In 2003, he conducted a series of studies and found that people who kept a weekly gratitude journal slept better, exercised more regularly, and were generally happier compared with those who were asked to record only their complaints. Many similar studies have found that practicing gratitude gives us a greater sense of well-being in our lives, and the following stories bring such findings to life.

He Walked Again

It was a crisp, beautiful March morning. Morris went to his airplane hangar, pulled back the door, and prepared his Cessna 172 for a pleasure flight—a flight that would change his life forever.

After a careful preflight check, the wheels left the ground, and Morris was free from the earth below and soaring like an eagle. The scenery below was breathtaking—rivers and inlets, trees and fields, and the vast Atlantic Ocean hidden from the mainland by beautiful barrier islands.

After flying for an hour, Morris headed in the direction of home. As he prepared to land, he decreased his speed to the mandatory 75 mph because of the short runway. He was well above the power and electric lines that all airplanes avoid on descent.

Suddenly, without warning, his engine lost power. The Cessna started dropping. The plane struck some high tension wires and was whipped to the ground, crashing headfirst and upside down. The next thing Morris remembered was the mangled metal that was once his airplane, while paramedics worked on his mangled body.

The ambulance raced Morris to the hospital just in time to save his life. As the teams of doctors swarmed over him, his family was given the bleak news.

Morris's neck was broken at the first and second cervical vertebrae, and his spinal cord was crushed. His swallowing reflex was destroyed, and he did not have the ability to eat or drink. His diaphragm was gravely injured, so his breathing was lost. Almost every bone in his face and skull was broken. His bowel, bladder, and kidneys did not work. The nerves that controlled his heartbeat, respiration, and blood pressure were damaged. Almost every muscle in his body was injured, and he did not have voluntary control of a single muscle except for his eyelids. Morris could blink his eyes. For a long time that was the only way he communicated with the outside world: one blink for *yes* and two for *no.*

The most hope the doctors offered was that Morris might one day sit in a wheelchair and blink his eyes.

One day Morris woke up, and as his eyes met the morning sunlight, he remembered that no matter what he was going through, it was a blessing even to be alive and see the sun.

Each morning after that, Morris began his day by acknowledging a list of things he was grateful for. He gave thanks for the many blessings he had, even amidst his ordeal. This was a powerful and liberating ritual. It empowered him to deal with and eventually overcome the series of challenges he faced. With all this in mind, Morris began to formulate a plan for healing. Every day he prayed to God for the strength and courage he would need for the long hard battle. And in every prayer, he thanked God for saving his life.

Morris then tried to breathe on his own. He worked on taking hundreds of deep breaths with the respirator, even though each breath brought excruciating pain. He did not give up. One night, his prayers were answered. He took 300 deep breaths and rested. Suddenly, he breathed on his own three times. Over the next few months, Morris began breathing completely unassisted. The doctors discovered that he had built up his stomach muscles enough to replace the need for his diaphragm. This had never been done before!

His next goal was to talk. After hundreds of hours of speech therapy, Morris finally learned to say two words: *no* and *mama*. And then more words, and finally sentences.

His third major challenge was to eat on his own, without the use of a feeding machine. He reached that goal—with incredible joy, knowing that he was finally able to feed himself.

His final—and most ambitious—challenge was to walk. When Morris informed his doctors that he planned on walking out of the hospital on his own two feet, they just laughed. Undeterred, Morris attacked his therapy like a man possessed. He arranged for the orderlies to wake him up by 5:30 so he could be in therapy by 7:30, an hour and a half before everyone else arrived. They propped him up on the parallel bars, and Morris would struggle to stand up. Day after day, the fight moved him to action, and miraculously, Morris walked out of the hospital on his own five months later.

Medical research is beginning to show what Morris's story illustrates: a key factor in battling health issues is taking note of all that's good in your life.

She Found Meaning from Tragedy

I once had a patient—I'll call her Lauren—who was a very successful 31-year-old woman, an executive with a Fortune 500 company. She lived alone, and liked to jog. One day she went out for a jog, returned home, and decided to take a shower before going to work. All of a sudden, she heard a noise. A man had broken into her house and viciously raped her in the bathroom. "Don't scream or I'll kill you," he threatened. The sudden rage in his eyes convinced Lauren that he meant it. She begged for her life. "Please, please don't kill me," she heard herself saying. "I'll do anything." Lauren resolved to do whatever it took to survive. She separated her mind from her body. It was as if the rape were happening to someone else, somewhere else—not to Lauren.

Then he fled. When she was sure he was gone, Lauren wandered around the house in a daze, figuring out how her attacker got in and pondering what to do. Alone in the stillness, she picked up the phone and dialed 911.

Later that day, she came to my office. I could tell something was horribly wrong. She was disheveled, her hair uncombed; she was practically despondent. I immediately asked, "What happened?" She broke down.

"Oh, I'm just so embarrassed. I feel like I've been violated. I feel like I don't know what to do, and I just feel awful."

Even though she was sharing with me, I had no idea what to say. How could anyone, really, understand the tragedy she had endured?

Slowly, I said, "I know this has got to be one of the toughest things in your life. But I promise you that one day, you'll be able to view this experience from a different perspective. You will see that it enabled you to grow to a level that most people will never reach; your resilience is being stretched beyond any lengths that most people are tested. And if you surpass it, it will be one of the greatest things you could achieve in your life."

Lauren listened, and I felt she trusted my words.

Later on, the police apprehended the rapist. Lauren dreaded the thought of testifying at his trial, knowing she'd be grilled by the defense attorney and have to relive the entire experience. But she got through it, and the rapist was sentenced to prison. Lauren could breathe again.

She had survived the physical assault. Now came the hard part: coping with life as a rape victim. Lauren, however, made no attempt to hide what had happened to her. To heal, she went to group-therapy sessions made up of others who had also been raped. Eventually, she was asked to lead the group. Further, she became a national advocate and speaker on victims' rights. She reclaimed her sense of power by helping others. I saw her recently, and she brought me up to date on her life. She was married and pregnant, but the journey had been a tough one. For the longest time, she struggled to lift herself from the numbness caused by her assault. She couldn't go out on a date. She was terrified to have a man touch her. She found herself having horrible nightmares.

But slowly, she began to find meaning in the rape. "It forced me to reassess what value I bring to life. I remember the words you said to me, and those words kept inspiring me to recognize that even though it was very difficult, one day I'll be thankful. I just wanted to tell you that I am thankful. The rape let me find myself and attract what it is that I really wanted in life, which was a great relationship."

You know, we don't grow in comfort. We grow in discomfort. And though it's difficult, we often must accept, embrace, and be grateful for that discomfort.

The Gratitude Attitude

Life isn't always what we want it to be. But if you think about it, life is filled with so many blessings: freedom, positive relationships, opportunities, and so much more that we often just take for granted. The next time you're feeling overwhelmed, frustrated, anxious, or depressed, stop and evaluate the good in your life. Then give thanks—for nature, your friends and family, your gifts and talents, and hopefully your good health. Let these blessings guide your happiness; they are what give true meaning to your life.

Do this on a daily basis, especially when times are tough, and you'll rise above any negativity. Start counting your blessings daily. This simple practice can bring healing to your body and spirit.

Love

Ricardo Fujikawa, M.D., was leading a relatively ordinary life as a young doctor—practicing during the day, enjoying family life on the weekends—when he gave up the comforts of his life to serve as a volunteer physician for orphans in Kenya. Many babies in Kenya are infected with HIV and are abandoned by their parents because of it.

The AIDS pandemic continues to cut a deadly swath through Kenya and the rest of the continent. (Nearly 30 million Africans are HIV-positive, according to the World Health Organization.) Ricardo was very much aware he was about to experience something that would have a profound impact on his life.

A child was brought to Ricardo for care. Her family had been hiding in the bushes, and her mother was HIV positive. She had fed the child with only ashes and water for a couple of weeks. The baby teetered on a fragile precipice between life and death. She shook with pneumonia and lacked the strength to sit up straight. Her breathing was shallow and fast, showing how pneumonia had affected her lungs. Ironically, the name of this little child meant "mercy" in English.

The child's immediate need was treatment with antibiotics, but the drugs would not arrive for at least 24 hours. Ricardo was worried that she would not make it through the night. All he could do was hold the child in his arms and give her love. So that is what he did.

The next day, Ricardo purchased antibiotics in the nearest village and took them to the child. There had already been a miracle. The child sprang from her mother's arms and bounded toward Ricardo. An irrepressible smile had replaced much of the festering infection on her face.

Ricardo recalled, "That one experience taught me more than six years of medical school. I realized there was more to medicine than cutting up, and sewing up, people. No matter how ill, these kids are human beings, as all of us are, and they deserve love and compassion; they thrive on it. Often, when a life is broken, it can only be rebuilt by another caring, concerned human being."

The more love, connectedness, and social interaction we have in our lives, the healthier we can be. Why is this? One reason is that our immune system improves. All of us have cells in our bodies called natural killer cells. They're like super-soldiers in a powerful army, able to engulf invaders without being harmed themselves. Something amazing happens to those cells when love walks into our lives and loneliness walks out: those natural killer cells become more active.

This probably explains why having social-support networks makes us healthier. We know, for example, that certain diseases tend to be more common in people without many friends and family around: clinical depression, heart attack, high blood pressure, viruses, even cancer. Having deep bonds with other human beings is a certain route to self-healing.

As for love, what is it exactly? Love is the complete and unconditional acceptance of ourselves, so we may be able to have a complete and unconditional acceptance of others. That's how I define love in my life, and all love begins from within. If I can develop an unconditional acceptance of myself, that will give me the opportunity to have unconditional acceptance of others.

I know I have to extend love and friendship to others to receive it myself. When my son was in the first grade, he said to me, "Daddy, nobody wants to be my friend."

I asked him a simple question: "Well, honey, how many people are you being a friend to?"

He looked puzzled, "What?"

"How many kids in your class have you taken the time to get to know and find out what you have in common? How many kids have you gone up to and said, 'I want to be your friend.' How many?"

"Nobody."

"Well, what makes you think that they'll want to do the same for you when you haven't even offered to be their friend first?"

My son got what I was saying—that to have a friend, you have to be a friend. And before too long, he was one of the most popular and friendliest kids in his class.

I know that love can be different for many people. I also know that many only think of it as a physical means. But the love that I'm referring to, the unconditional kind, is the love that has no expectations. It is wanting to love, solely for the sake of loving.

This is the kind of love you find in strong, bonded families—like the following family.

True, Healing Love

Benny started working as a teenager laying track on the NY Ontario & Western Railroad, which was a very physically demanding job. He was quite a physical specimen, strong as an ox with huge arm muscles. He progressed to being a signal maintainer for the railroad, operating his own motor car and maintaining the wires, climbing telephone poles in all kinds of weather, and making sure all the signal gates were operational. He earned a meager wage.

Sadly, in the early 1940s, Benny was stricken with a rare, incurable disease, aplastic anemia, which sets in when the body stops producing enough new blood cells. Aplastic anemia leaves a person feeling fatigued and at higher risk of infections and uncontrolled bleeding. It can lead to rapid death.

Benny spent days in the hospital and was unable to work for nearly a year. No work meant no income, and there was no health insurance or welfare. Told he would die, Benny's wife, Frances, faithfully and lovingly visited him twice a day. They didn't own a car, so Frances walked to the hospital in the middle of day, returned home to make supper, and then walked back to the hospital in the evening, a total of nearly five miles each day. She was a critical part of his health care at the hospital.

While in the hospital, Benny required many blood transfusions, which he could not afford, but his Italian friends from the railroad came to his rescue numerous times by donating blood. Benny would often quip that he was now "half Italian."

At night Frances would take their five-year-old daughter with her. As they walked to the hospital, Frances would explain to her, "The doctors say daddy is going to die, but God decides when a person dies, so, we do not talk like that. The doctors are doing all they can do, and we will pray."

Many nights, the doctors told Frances that her husband would likely not live to see the morning. Night after night, however, he would somehow make it through. Then he sank into a coma and was near death. He remained in a special room set up for him next to the nurses' station. This was his room for 96 days. The doctor said, "We have tried everything and nothing works. He is going to die."

But Benny lived. He came out of his coma and once stable, the doctors released him to go home. Benny and Frances thanked the doctor, but the doctor admitted, "It was nothing we did." Frances didn't know for sure, but she suspected her husband was sent home to die. But she never, ever, believed he would die.

Benny's healing at home was long and arduous. Frances became his nurse, giving him painful liver shots, and slowly nursing him back to health with her love. It would take months. This bulk of a man had deteriorated to a shadow of himself, weighing only about 100 pounds. He needed a cane to stand and walk. Faith, friendship, love, and the prayers of many would be the answers to his struggle.

Eventually, Benny recovered from this "incurable" disease and he went on to lead a full life. He lived to be 85 years old.

His doctors pronounced it a miracle. And it truly was a miracle, since aplastic anemia remains an incurable disease today.

I believe that there was a deep, abiding, unconditional love between Benny and Frances, and it was a huge factor in Benny's healing. I've already discussed how negative emotions and chronic stress have devastating effects on our health, shutting down our immune systems and increasing our susceptibility to infection, cancers, tumors, and inflammatory disorders. *But love heals.* Not in a greeting-card kind of away, but at a cellular level that actually helps our bodies get well.

A big part of the reason is that love is largely a chemical event in the brain. When you love, and are loved, a stew of healing chemicals is released. Two of these chemicals, the so-called cuddle chemicals, vasopressin and oxytocin, encourage bonding; they entice you to become part of a committed pair. This reaction, in turn, pumps out DHEA, an anti-aging, anti-stress hormone that promotes cellular repair in the body. Oxytocin also reduces stress in the body by causing the nervous system to relax. It floods the tissues with oxygen, too, and when oxygenation increases, so does healing.

Pleasurable activities—including being in love—release more dopamine. Dopamine is a "reward chemical"; it induces the same sense of reward you get from food, alcohol, or drugs. The reward sensation explains why you want to repeat pleasurable activities again . . . and again . . . and again. Another chemical that may create intensely focused love is serotonin—a feel-good chemical secreted by the brain whenever you feel loved and connected. Love, in short, is a very healing emotion.

The Importance of a Hug

Every day my body gets a major boost of resistance to disease. Any ailment—either physical or mental—that might try to strike me has very little chance of success. Everything about my body and mind feels in a high state of regeneration.

What sparks this increase in my inner strength? A hug does it. In this world of highly evolved intelligence and mega-theories on what makes us all tick, I've found that for me, the most effective form of connection with another person dates back to the beginning of time. I'm often asked why I go around hugging people all the time, as if I'd known them forever. Well, I grew up with a Colombian mother and a father of Italian descent. I rest my case! We hugged all the time; we kissed all the time. I had grandparents who hugged me all the time, and uncles and aunts who hugged me all the time. To me, hugs are second nature.

When I was in college, my mom sent me a wallet-sized card that expressed all the benefits of a hug: trust in others, healing, love, openness, communication, and much more. She gave it to me as a reminder that we are a family of huggers, and though separated by states, I should continue the family tradition with my new friends.

Her gesture made me recognize that hugs are not just for me, because it made me feel good and it made me feel connected with others, but that it was actually for the purpose of making others feel connected.

These days, everybody is texting, e-mailing, and phoning each other. The hug seems to have gone the way of the VCR! So technology, along with our fast-paced schedules, has led us almost in the opposite direction from a good old-fashioned hug. Instead of finding a greater physical, emotional, and spiritual connection, we're becoming more and more withdrawn from the external world.

Benefits of Hugging

The simple act of hugging accomplishes many things that you may have never considered. For example, hugs:

- Feel good
- Dispel loneliness
- Overcome fear
- Open doors to feelings
- Build self-esteem
- Foster altruism
- Slow down aging (Huggers stay young longer.)
- Help curb appetite (We eat less when we're nourished by hugs and when our arms are busy wrapped around others.)
- Ease tension
- Fight insomnia
- Keep arms and shoulder muscles in condition
- Provide stretching exercise if you are short
- Provide stooping exercise if you are tall
- Offer a wholesome alternative to promiscuity
- Offer a healthy, safe alternative to alcohol and other drug abuse (Better hugs than drugs!)
- Affirm physical being
- Are democratic (Anyone is eligible!)

My "How to Hug" Instructions

When it comes to relationships, I usually express that the first exercise is a smile, because a smile opens up the opportunity for someone to feel that you're approachable; that they can engage you. Once you're comfortable with that, then it's time for a hug. It can be a half hug, it can be a full hug, it can be a handshake with both your hands. So start there: a smile, one handshake, two handshakes, a half hug, or a full hug.

A hug is a powerful instrument. It takes any relationship to a deeper level, because, you see, there's no way that you can give or receive a hug if there's not a feeling of "I want to be in this person's space." So once you cross over that space, you're automatically connected deeper to that individual. I'm the president of a university, and perhaps I'm bragging a little, but right now I get an average of 82 hugs a day. Of course, at the same time, I'm giving the same amount of affection out. I've been doing that for the last 15 years or so. And if I'm being that close with people, especially all kinds of people, whether or not they're influential or powerful (I believe everybody is important), then who is to say that maybe my willingness to hug is the most critical exercise that I do? Who can say that something that has allowed me to connect so strongly with others hasn't also allowed me to achieve the level of healing and success that I've realized?

I go to meetings mostly attended by very high-level educators, 50 years old and above, and I'm the only person in the room that they all hug, but they don't hug each other. That happens to me all the time. I'll go to a party or a meeting where everybody is just shaking hands, with a hard shake of a hand, including men and women, but I immediately lean myself into it, and 90 percent of the time people respond. A lot of times I may shake their hand initially, but when we say good-bye, I feel comfortable enough that I give a hug.

Hugs are productive. They demonstrate humanity and caring enough to make contact. That's the thing we all want to feel. It makes us realize that we're not alone in the world. We want to feel validated. We want to feel connected. We want to feel that there's a reason why we're here that other people value. It doesn't matter who it is.

The healing triad of forgiveness, gratitude, and love allows us to live in the present. Forgiveness frees us from deep and consuming past regrets that burden our health. And when we are grateful, we no longer focus on the things we wish we had, which opens us up to love.

Can you see how all three—forgiveness, gratitude, and love—naturally flow together? As the old saying goes, "Do not look back in anger, nor forward in fear, but around in awareness." When you bring the often chaotic process of your life to a healing stillness, you rest completely in each moment. You bring your best to life *now,* without regrets about the past or worries about the future. That is the power of the healing triad at work in your life.

For self-healing, it's absolutely vital to maintain a regular spiritual practice in your life, whether it's formal or informal, religious or non-religious. Spirituality is critical to the healing process, and in the next chapter, you'll see why.

CHAPTER ELEVEN

THE HEALING SPIRIT

If a new health treatment was discovered that extended the quality and length of our lives, prevented drug and alcohol abuse, improved treatment for depression, reduced recovery time from surgery, and enhanced our sense of well-being, wouldn't we all be scrambling to try it?

This hypothetical medical treatment really does exist, but it's not a new drug: it is spirituality. To my way of thinking, spirituality involves who we are in relation to our sense of the divine and how we find meaning in the world. Religion, on the other hand, is a set of formalized ideas to define an understanding of the divine. I believe, too, that a person can be spiritual without being religious. One of the best distinctions I've ever heard was a quote by George Bernard Shaw: "There is only one religion, though there are a hundred versions of it."

So wedded is healing to spiritual life that the first professional health-care advisors were doctor-priests in ancient cultures. And healing has been with us throughout religious history. The Bible is filled with stories of miraculous cures, for example. During the Middle Ages, monks in Europe founded many of the first hospitals, and women mystics used medicinal herbs and foods in their ministries to heal people. Many religious groups carry on an active healing tradition today, through the laying on of hands, anointing the sick, and praying for health.

Some in the scientific and medical communities have publicly stated for years that neither religion nor spirituality matters much, yet when I actually looked at the available empirical research on the relationship between spirituality and health, the findings were overwhelmingly positive, and I'll share much of this with you here.

Religions, faith, and spirituality have such vital roles to play in health, prevention, coping with illness, and quality of care. They're part of treating the whole person—body, mind, and, yes, even spirit.

The Science Behind Spiritual Healing

A mound of studies spanning a few decades reveals that if you have some sort of spiritual discipline in your life, from attending church services to prayer to meditation, you are generally healthier. Here are a few examples from the scientific literature:

People who regularly attend church have a 25 percent reduction in mortality—that is, they live longer—than people who are not churchgoers. And people who pray tend to get sick less often.

The health benefits of a regular spiritual practice are so profound that scientists have studied the health differences between believers and nonbelievers. Brain scans reveal that meditation and prayer can change brain activity and improve immune response; other studies have shown that they can lower heart rate and blood pressure, both of which reduce the body's stress response.

People in the hospital who never attended church have longer hospital stays (up to three times longer) on average than those who attend church regularly. And heart patients who undergo surgery are less likely to suffer complications if they are involved in a regular religious practice.

What is the common thread here? Some form of spiritual practice leads to a healthier lifestyle and a healthier life. And it's not just a specific spiritual practice or process, but a spiritual focus in general. Findings like these convince me that there is healing power in spirituality.

Spirituality and Mental Health

Spirituality improves our mental health, and there is a staggering amount of proof. For one thing, there are fewer suicides among religious people, according to data. One study discovered that non-churchgoers were four times more likely to kill themselves than were frequent attendees.

Why would this be? For one thing, several researchers emphasize that the religious people feel that suicide is wrong, because they believe in a moral accountability to God and by killing themselves, they might be eternally condemned.

Religion also plays a role in decreasing other self-destructive behavior such as drug abuse. People of faith tend to drink less alcohol, smoke less, and not abuse drugs. Interestingly, a national survey of 14,000 adolescents found that conservative, churchgoing teens were less likely to use alcohol and drugs. I'd say that for teens living in a society with a high rate of drug abuse, religion may not be so bad after all!

There's more: Not only does religion prevent self-destructive behavior, it also promotes positive life experiences such as good marriages, bonded family relationships, and personal well-being. So if you're spiritually connected and fulfilled, you'll be happy in almost every area of your life—marriage, family, career, and more. There is so much power in faith and spirituality—power that is self-healing.

The Power of Prayer

At age 63, James started having mild chest pain. He hoped that if he just ignored it, the "inconvenient nuisance" would just go away.

After about six months of denial, and with his wife's encouragement, James had an exam.

The medical doctors told James he had some sort of "coronary insufficiency," but they weren't sure of exactly what it was. More testing revealed that his cholesterol, blood pressure, and weight were fine. A CT scan of his chest revealed nothing conclusive. But the pain persisted.

Then, a coronary specialist suggested a series of diagnostics, including a thallium stress test. James was injected intravenously with a mildly radioactive thallium solution and then got on the treadmill. It took ten minutes at full speed before his heart rate got up to the required level—he was in great shape. Then James lay down on his back while a special camera photographed his heart to determine how the various chambers filled up.

The test revealed that his coronary insufficiency was in the left ventricle—particularly the left anterior descending artery emerging from the left ventricle. This "LAD"—also known as the "widow maker" since its complete blockage will, without exception, result in a fatal heart attack—had a 90-degree kink in it. Apparently, he had had this problem since birth. The doctors told him that, had he not been in such good health, he probably would have died in his 50s.

The next step was the installation of a stent to eliminate potential blockage of the LAD. Stents prop arteries open so that blood can flow. In James's case, however, it was discovered during the procedure that the angle in his LAD was so extreme that expansion of the stent could rupture the artery. The procedure was aborted. But the potential widow maker was still lurking.

Next was bypass surgery. Under general anesthesia, with heart-lung machine support, James's ribs were opened up, using a "chest spreader" to provide access to his LAD. Then the surgeons harvested his mammary artery and used it to bypass the LAD.

Following surgery, James continued his regular regimen of daily exercise, whole-food supplements, and weekly adjustments. All was well until six months later, when, during a round of golf, James got really tired and weak.

He went to the emergency room and discovered he was suffering from pneumonia. The doctor ordered a CT scan and discovered an accumulation of blood seepage on the inside of his chest—in the "pleura," or sac the lungs fit into—due to a complication resulting from the surgery. The doctor explained that while the seepage was tiny, "Sooner or later, a dripping faucet can fill a bathtub."

James spent the next five months trying to recover with natural methods. Then he got pneumonia a second time. He couldn't walk more than 50 steps and lost his ability to breathe. He went to the Cleveland Clinic for help.

Doctors diagnosed the problem as "loculated pleural effusion"— a fibrotic mass. The mass occupied 35 percent of his left lung.

Doctors at both the Cleveland Clinic and Brigham and Women's Hospital in Boston recommended that the mass be removed, even though there was no guarantee that the procedure would resolve his breathing problems.

Throughout his medical ordeal, James and Donna, his wife of 44 years, called upon friends and family all over the country to pray for him.

Meanwhile James had agreed to have the mass-removal surgery performed by a surgeon at the Brigham and Women's Hospital. While awaiting surgery, James spent his Christmas holidays in the loving arms of his wife and four adult children and their spouses. They prayed together as a family, and continued to seek out prayer support from their friends across the country.

By the time the New Year rolled around, James had enjoyed a few months of rest, mild exercise, daily whole-food supplements, and weekly chiropractic adjustments. James was feeling very good. His cardiologist suggested that he get another CT scan before scheduling surgery, so he did.

The results of the scan revealed that the mass had resolved itself: down to less than 10 percent, whereas the previous scan had registered 35 percent. The surgeon took one look at the scan and announced that there was no reason to operate! Somehow or other, James's body had reabsorbed most of that mass—a rare phenomenon according to the surgeon, since that particular kind of mass is a fibrous material.

James and Donna burst into tears of relief. "The miracle of it is that I had so many people praying for me. I also believe in natural methods," he said. "If you give the body enough time to heal, it sometimes can heal the most difficult maladies. I know that the body has within it the ability to heal itself. And since God created the human body, I give God the credit for its beautiful design. By His grace, I'm still here."

Healing White Light

Robin was taken to the hospital by ambulance around 9 one evening. A CAT scan of her brain was e-mailed to a neurosurgeon. He took one look at it and rushed to the hospital.

"I'm not sure what we can do," the neurosurgeon told Robin's family. "I will do the surgery anyway, because that is what we do. But you must understand there is little hope Robin will survive the procedure." He commenced the surgery at 10:30 P.M.

Robin's family and friends gathered to hear the sobering reality that this beloved, devoted wife, mother, and office manager of a chiropractic clinic was holding on to life by a thread.

Though shell-shocked, her friends and family got on the floor and held hands. They focused on bathing the neurosurgeon and Robin in white light, and they prayed.

The neurosurgeon walked in, sat down, and took off his surgical cap. Everyone gathered around him, scared and trembling at what he might tell them.

"I can't explain how she lived through the surgery. There were massive amounts of blood on the brain, which is not good. Blood is supposed to flow through the brain, not be on the brain, because this is very damaging to the chemistry balance. We got as much blood out as possible. If she makes it through the next 24 hours, it will be a miracle."

He went on, saying, "I believe she has an AVM, ateriovenous malformation, and she was born with it. It's like a ticking time bomb. You would have never known it was there. It wouldn't be on CT scans or MRIs. Had she ever had a dye study, it might have killed her because of dye going through that section of the brain. Her speech centers and entire right side will be affected, and that's provided she even lives. I have done all we can possibly do. The rest is up to Robin. They're bringing her up in a few minutes so you can see her, but please no stimulation."

The neurosurgeon was adamant that no one touch her or talk to her. This could send neurological stimulation through her brain, and she was not stable enough because of the extent of the brain bleed.

Robin's head was wrapped in white bandages, mummy-style. Attached to her were a breathing tube, drains, and massive amounts of machinery. All anyone could do was continue to bathe her in the white light of prayer.

And each day, Robin continued to live.

Her name was added to hundreds of prayer chains spanning the globe and covering all faiths. On day 24, the night before Mother's Day, Robin opened her eyes for the first time. Her children knew she was in there. They knew it, saw it, and felt it.

The prayers continued.

And as I write this, Robin is still alive, making little pieces of progress every day. She has even spoken her very first words. This story is just another proof to me that prayer heals.

When friends describe to me the benefits of prayer, they say it brings them a sense of well-being, and they've had wonderful healing breakthroughs as a result. Of course, none of this means that spiritual practices are a substitute for traditional medicine, or that prayer will guarantee great health. But what's telling about these stories is that they reveal just how critical of a component prayer can be in our lives.

Prayer and Self-Healing

Prayer comes in many forms. Generally, it can be intercessory or contemplative (reflective). The latter is a personal, one-on-one connection, or communication, with the divine. Intercessory prayer (often called distance healing) is a request to God or a spiritual being, made on the behalf of someone who is sick to bring about a desired end (that is, to heal this person, make him or her well again, help this person recover, and so forth).

Most scientific studies have focused on intercessory prayer, because it is somewhat easier to measure. This type of research has shown that prayer can accelerate and improve the healing process. Probably the best-known prayer study was one conducted at San Francisco General Hospital in 1988. Three hundred and ninety-three heart patients were involved. Half the patients were prayed for by a Christian group, yet were unaware of the prayers on their behalf. The other half (the control group) were not prayed for.

What followed was quite remarkable. The first group, which received prayer, healed much better and required fewer medical interventions than the control group. By contrast, the control group needed more assistance from ventilators, more antibiotics, and more diuretics than the other group. The researchers who conducted this study felt that prayer was therapeutic to heart patients. In short, prayer seemed to be so powerful that it can even help people who are unaware they are being prayed for.

Another study, conducted by Duke University Medical Center, found that people who prayed weekly were 40 percent less likely to have high blood pressure than those who did not have an active prayer life. And a study by Italian researchers found that praying the rosary—the repetition of the Hail Mary prayer—or even reciting a yoga mantra enhanced heart health.

Prayer helped nursing-home residents who suffered from dementia and agitation, according to one study. Under the guidance of a researcher, residents prayed for five minutes on five out of seven days for four consecutive weeks; there was also a control group that did not pray. For the prayer exercise, residents picked a prayer or the researcher provided one of two nondenominational prayers. Those in the prayer group became more verbal, lively, and familiar with their surroundings and the people in it. Prayer definitely had an effect.

In yet another study, Christian, Jewish, Buddhist, American Indian, and other spiritual healers prayed, one hour daily, for 40 AIDS patients. After six months, the patients who had been prayed for had significantly better medical outcomes than a control group, which had not received prayer. Those medical outcomes included fewer new AIDS-associated illnesses, fewer doctor visits, and improved mood.

There is certainly overwhelming proof that prayer helps, and I've only scratched the surface here. Further, I believe this evidence strongly suggests that the divine, to whom prayer is directed, is fact and not fiction. I think most of us know this, but many of us turn to that divine only in a pinch.

My advice is to pray, especially if you think prayer will help you or someone you care about. I've always been taught to pray and trust that everything will work out in the end.

How to Pray

"Daddy," one of my sons said one day after school, "I figured out how to pray. I put my head down, my hands like this, I close my eyes, and I talk to God. At the end I say, 'Amen.'"

That was the best description of how to pray I had ever heard.

I had always been under the impression that prayer was reserved for certain times and under certain circumstances, such as an hour at night before you go to bed or in church. It hadn't occurred to me that prayer could be like a conversation, started spontaneously and for as long or short a time as you want—just as my son taught me.

And so, I pray regularly, and whenever I feel like it. I'm not only comforted by prayer, but I'm also empowered by it. I do know that prayer has a therapeutic effect on me. I feel that I'm actively doing something directly related to my own life, and there's a certain comfort in that.

I pray with my friends who are sick, asking for healing and a strong recovery. I believe in prayer. I believe in divine healing power. I pray to reach outside myself, to position and understand myself against any struggle I might be facing. And I pray to express gratitude for the countless blessings in my life.

To pray, close your eyes so you're not distracted. Forget your personal beliefs or doubts about prayer or whether there is a God. And just start talking, like when you call up a friend on the phone. Ask for what you want, or express gratitude for what you have.

Based on the evidence in favor of prayer and spirituality, I believe that it is vital to maintain a regular spiritual practice, whether it is formal or informal, religious or nonreligious. There are ways to start taking such a journey, no matter what your beliefs. For example:

Reconnect with Something Higher

Reconnect with your faith if you have lapsed: return to the religion of your youth or find another that interests you. If right now spirituality for you is a religion, then try exploring that religion a little more deeply to better understand the lessons within it. If you don't want to become active in a religion or spiritual community, find some disciplined practices to follow "religiously." These might be doing yoga or tai chi, practicing meditation, or even volunteering for a cause you believe in.

One of the most effective things that I have found is to really exercise what I call "quiet time." Even if it's just ten minutes in the morning as soon as you wake up, it is your time to just be still and not talk or allow everyday distractions to seep into your thoughts. Listen to the amazing communication that is happening within yourself. Remember, anything that feeds your spirit will strengthen your body!

Promote Spiritual Harmony

Spirituality is more than praying and worshipping God or a higher power. It can encompass disciplines such as yoga, tai chi, breathing exercises, visualization, or positive thinking—anything that promotes harmony among the body, mind, and spirit. My friend, Monica Wofford, author of the book *Contagious Leadership*, shared with me once that her father was diagnosed with the threat of borderline diabetes—but miraculously, he healed himself. When I asked how he managed to get through his crisis, Monica began to describe her father's own brand of spirituality: a combination of tai chi, a healthy diet, adequate sleep, meditation, and the adoption of an Eastern philosophy and lifestyle. Her father now has no symptoms or threat of diabetes. Monica says he is 64 but looks like he's 45. He created his own spiritual way of being in the world, and it transformed his health. You can do the same.

Explore Nature

I believe one of the easiest ways to connect with your spirituality is to spend more time in nature. A hike up a mountain, a soothing swim in the ocean or a lake, the enjoyment of having pets, a glorious sunset, a butterfly landing on your leg—these are gifts that nurture the soul, a type of divine energy, so to speak.

Nature is the one thing that surrounds us and connects us with the moment. If you're taking a walk in a park, for instance, take the time to observe the beautiful flowers. Look at their texture, their rich colors, and the design that makes it a flower. Or perhaps you see a large tree. It's very old, and you start wondering how long it has been around, how much it has witnessed. Or maybe you see a beautiful sunset or sunrise, and say, "How can this be possible? What intelligence is driving all this to make it so consistent, so beautiful, so powerful?" If you're like me, you'll find yourself awestruck by nature's pattern of promise, change, and life.

When I immerse myself in nature, it never fails to bring me new inspiration. I see my own problems as challenges, not burdens. I see myself as a part of this orderly universe, and I come into closer relationship with the divine and with every living thing. When I am in nature, I am reminded that I am not alone in the world. Dr. Wayne Dyer, one of my mentors and friends, taught me that: "We are not human beings having a spiritual experience, we are spiritual beings having a human experience."

Tap into Your Intuition

Your intuition is spiritual wisdom you carry within. It might manifest as an "Aha!" moment, a gut feeling, a funny feeling, or a hunch—and it is very powerful, if only you'd listen to it more often.

By following your intuition, you can make decisions that are right for you, and learn to express your truest self.

Intuition becomes supremely important when it comes to your personal health. Sometimes you just "know" that something isn't right, because you're listening to the doctor within. If you're not already doing this, try a few of these techniques:

— *Meditate.* Try to get perfectly still, relieving yourself of all anxiety and indecision and clearing your thoughts of all feelings of uncertainty. Pay attention to any messages of pain, soreness, fatigue, or anxiety. Imagine inhaling healing energy, and exhaling these conditions out of your body. Continue meditating in this manner for at least ten minutes. If a sitting meditation doesn't appeal to you, go for a walk in nature. Walking can serve as a "moving meditation" and is very effective.

— *Make intuitive decisions.* Listen to those gut feelings and hunches more often, beyond any facts. Is your gut telling you to go to the doctor, break off a relationship, switch jobs, or cancel an appointment? Trust what you're hearing from within, without barreling through daily decisions. Sometimes it can be difficult to trust your intuition, because it might mean moving out of your comfort zone, but making a change doesn't have to happen abruptly. If you get the feeling that it's time to change jobs, for example, take things one step at a time: update your résumé, interview recruiters, and research the job market before you up and quit.

— *Sleep on it.* This is my favorite way to tap into intuition. Before I go to bed at night, I ask myself a simple yes-or-no question about what path to take, what decision to make, or how to handle a challenge. During sleep my subconscious mind goes to work on the answer. And after I wake up, without fail, I'll have a clear answer. This nighttime ritual is not the same as worrying or ruminating about a challenge or problem—quite the contrary. I simply ask for an answer and turn it over to my subconscious, or to God, to answer it for me.

It's been said that the only time we bother to look up is when we're beaten down. This is because there's nothing at the bottom. *But there is something up there, and within us.* It is the innate intelligence that created our bodies and the innate intelligence that has the power to heal our bodies. Whatever spiritual path we select, a change occurs in us when we trust in it, turn to it, and believe in it. Wonderful things happen to our health. Our immune systems get a boost, our brains release chemicals that serve as natural medicines, our blood pressure decreases, and stress and anxiety are reduced. We sleep better and we feel better. We are, most certainly, healed.

Now I want to offer you the guidance and tools to transform everything I've covered so far into sustainable lifestyle changes, and a renewed sense of health and well-being. In the final part of this book, I'll give you a 21-day program to empower you to take the steps necessary to activate self-healing in your own life.

Part IV

21 DAYS TO
SELF-HEALING

Start today to move from sickness to healing. Begin to raise your expectations and discover what your health potential is. This is something you can begin to accomplish in just 21 days—the period of time known to psychologically form new habits. When you commit yourself to a healing lifestyle, every action generates hope. The final three chapters will help you establish a self-healing plan for your life that includes everything discussed in this book.

CHAPTER TWELVE

WEEK 1: UNLOCK YOUR HEALING POTENTIAL

Before you even start this 21-day program, I want you to get a journal to help you keep track of your progress. Your journaling will not only keep you honest, but it will also be your benchmark to how well you're doing in all areas. You can look back and see where you have strengths and weaknesses, then adjust to improve them. It's a powerful, essential tool on your journey toward self-healing.

Begin by setting some positive goals for yourself. This is an important starting point if you want to live a self-healing life to the fullest. After all, how can you change, get out of a rut, or achieve what you want if you don't have a clear idea of what you're aiming for?

Think about what you specifically want for yourself and write it down in your journal, whether it's to lose weight, stop feeling tired all the time, eat more healthily, or heal a condition that's been bothering you. Include everything from easily attainable goals—taking up yoga, for instance—to things that, at the moment, seem like far-off dreams. Some may be things you haven't dared voice until now, such as: "I want to leave my job and go overseas to do charity work."

Be positive when you describe your goals on paper. For example, instead of writing something negative such as, "I'll never eat cheesecake again," write "I'm going to snack on fruit instead of chocolate."

Next, to make your goals easier to reach, pick one of the smaller ones and put together a detailed plan of action—the more specific, the better. Even small goals are made up of lots of little ones, so concentrate on how you can achieve the achievable—and do so in a sensible time frame. Small successes make you feel like you can achieve larger ones.

If one of your goals is to get more physically fit, for example, you might write: "Tomorrow I will call all the gyms in my area and find out how much the membership costs," or "I will go shopping for a new pair of athletic shoes on Saturday," or "I will walk on Mondays and Wednesdays." Reaching even a small goal is the biggest incentive for working toward the next, bigger one—and that is the best reinforcement for self-esteem and progress.

Now with your goals firmly in mind, let's begin!

The 21-Day Program

My 21-day program provides the framework for creating profound self-healing. Each day, I give you:

- A suggested menu for what to eat

- Advice on supplements to take initially, and ones to add in as needed

- An exercise plan

- A self-healing thought; this is a mantra or affirmation to set your thoughts and emotions in the right spiritual direction

Then as we progress through the program from week to week, I'll show you how to add in various elements of emotional and spiritual healing that will work for you. It's really a simple process. If you follow it, it will work for you, as it has already worked for so many, including myself.

Day 1 begins now!

Day 1

Eat to Heal

Something amazing happens when you begin to eat healing foods and give your body a break from junk foods, bad fats, refined flour, and sugar. Your body may shed up to ten pounds of excess water weight, and your energy soars. You get your digestion working properly again, stop feeling so bloated and congested, and maximize your self-healing potential.

This is the first day of my 21-Day Self-Healing Diet. It incorporates the nutritional principles discussed in Chapter 3. As you start this plan, make sure you are eating the best foods to heal your body, including my top-25 self-healing foods, lots of fresh fruits and veggies, lean proteins, and healthy fats. And drink at least eight glasses of water a day to keep your hardworking body hydrated and energized. If you don't like some of the foods that I recommend, don't force yourself to eat them. Instead, substitute them with other healthy foods you enjoy. Feel free to adapt it to your own preferences. This plan is only a guideline.

Day	Breakfast	Lunch	Snack	Dinner
1	½ cup of whole-grain cereal with 8 oz. almond milk and a cup of berries	A bowl of lentil soup served with 2 cups of steamed veggies	Hummus with sliced cucumbers; 1 piece of fresh fruit	1 cup of gluten-free pasta topped with diced and sautéed zucchini, onions, bell pepper, and portobello mushrooms; and topped with sugar-free marinara sauce and low-fat shredded cheese; salad with 1 Tbsp. vinaigrette dressing

Supplement with Core-Level Healers

I believe that a multivitamin/mineral supplement is the foundation of a supplement program. Multivitamins fill in nutritional gaps—even if your diet is fairly healthy already. Look for a product that has all the essential vitamins and minerals, as well as antioxidant nutrients to preserve well-being and ward off the health-sapping free radicals. Take your multivitamin with meals. The body absorbs the nutrients more effectively that way.

Dosage: While it may be convenient, the best formulation is not the one-a-day variety, contrary to what most people believe. Look for a multivitamin in which you take tablets throughout the day with your meals.

Vitamin D: Another important core-level healer is vitamin D. Check with your physician on correct dosage for you. Usually, people should take enough to total 800 IU of vitamin D per day.

Plant-Based Extract

A plant-based extract is a formulation of concentrated vegetables and fruits made into a powder, and thus full of antioxidants and phytochemicals. This extract can simply be added to water, smoothies, or shakes to provide a quick dose of "liquid nutrition." (For a refresher on all the benefits of this supplement, see Chapter 5.)

Dosage: Follow label directions.

Move to Mend

Today, do some strength training, as it's critically important to include weight training in a self-healing fitness program. First, muscular health provides total-body immunity for reasons scientists are just beginning to understand. Second, you lose muscle as you get older, so you have to work harder to build more. Also, building muscle speeds up your body's metabolism, which means you burn more calories. Another benefit to building strength is increased body definition.

Strength training tones your body and makes you look better in your clothes.

If you've never lifted weights before, begin your program with a personal trainer to make sure that your body posture and positioning are correct. In addition, a qualified trainer will help you get better results and avoid injury. If you're not comfortable with lifting weights or the added expense of consulting a personal trainer, try joining a body-sculpting class. These typically use rubber tubing and body resistance to build muscle.

Do 1 or 2 sets of 8 moves that target your entire body. Aim for 8 to 12 reps. Use a weight that's hard to lift by the last rep.

Do 30 minutes of strength-training work today.

Self-Healing Thought for the Day

Nourishing your body is so simple, so easy. All you need to do is give it the proper food, water, and supplements. Nourish your body daily with these things—and stay aware of how this nourishment gives back to you in all that you need to live fully.

Day 2

Eat to Heal

Keep removing high-calorie, sugar-laden, fatty foods from your diet. Replace them with fresh vegetables and fruit, and high-fiber foods. You'll reduce your disease risk and feel more energetic.

Day	Breakfast	Lunch	Snack	Dinner
2	6 oz. Greek yogurt and a piece of fresh fruit; 1 slice whole-grain or sprouted-grain toast	4 oz. hot or cold salmon served over 2–3 cups mixed greens with 1–2 Tbsp. vinaigrette	Hard-boiled egg sprinkled with sea salt; a handful of almonds	Bowl of vegetarian chili; 1 piece of fresh fruit for dessert

Supplement

Continue taking your core-level healing supplements: multivitamin, plant-based extract, and vitamin D.

Move to Mend

Work on flexibility today. This is the ability to move your limbs through a broad range of motion without feeling too stiff. Flexibility is important because it reduces the risk of strains on your back, legs, and arms. No one wants to pull a hamstring while walking, and gaining flexibility is the way to avoid it.

Also, any kind of twisty, stretchy movement—yoga, basic stretching, Pilates, tai chi—is good for healing because it pushes lymphatic fluid—which drains waste from your cells—through your system in ways that other activities can't. Good lymph flow means you'll have more energy and stronger immunity. Whether or not you like the idea of flexibility exercise, there's no denying that it makes you feel healthier, super-relaxed, and revitalized—especially after a stressful day. One of the best ways to achieve flexibility (and stress reduction) is to participate in a yoga class that teaches these disciplines. (To prevent injury, I urge you to attend flexibility classes taught by a pro.)

Do 30 minutes of flexibility work today.

Self-Healing Thought for the Day

You are vital and alive! With self-healing exercise, you help yourself stay healthy and even improve your health. With activities that increase your heart rate, make you more agile, and invigorate your immune system, you awaken your mind and body.

Day 3

Eat to Heal

Continue your self-healing diet. Remember that you can follow it exactly, improvise, or use any of the breakfast, lunch, dinner, or snack suggestions from other menu days.

Day	Breakfast	Lunch	Snack	Dinner
3	Smoothie: 8 oz. of almond milk, fresh or frozen peaches, ¼ cup of oatmeal, and a handful of spinach	Veggie burger on a whole-grain bun; side salad with 1 Tbsp. vinaigrette dressing	6 oz. Greek yogurt and 1 cup fresh berries	Stir-fried vegetables with 4-oz. chicken breast; ½ cup brown rice

Supplement

Take your supplements: multivitamin, plant-based extract, and vitamin D.

Move to Mend

Work on your cardiovascular system today. Get your heart rate up and blood flowing by doing aerobic activities such as walking, running, biking, swimming, and jumping. The faster you perform the activity, or the longer you perform it, the more calories you burn. A misconception of cardio workouts is that you have to work at a certain pace to reap the calorie-burning benefits. This is not true. If you move at a moderate pace, you will burn calories and help your heart. Over-exertion only leads to injury and burnout. To know if you're pushing yourself too hard, take the "talk test." Try to talk while working out; if you can't, it's time to slow down. Doing cardio activity at high intensity for too long can tear your muscles down and actually make you more flabby.

In order to avoid burnout, progress gradually but steadily in your aerobic workout. You should, however, do as much as you can and increase your time and activity intensity every day. The great thing about cardio workouts is that there is something for everybody. If you like the outdoors, you can walk, run, or ride a bike. If you prefer the comfort of home, get on the treadmill while watching TV or pop in an aerobics video. If you like the gym, there are all sorts of cardio classes: step aerobics, cardio kickboxing, and low-impact aerobics. And if those aren't your thing, then try a class that is as far from traditional as you can get like Zumba.

Do at least 30 minutes of cardio work today. Over time, increase speed, intensity (level of effort), and time as your cardiovascular system improves.

Self-Healing Thought for the Day

Your daily routine is up to you. Maybe it varies. One day you may choose to take a brisk walk, and on another day you may work out in an aerobics class. On a still, crisp day, you may decide to work in your garden. With regular exercise, you are refreshed! Your exercise plan works hand in hand with your desire to self-heal.

Day 4

Eat to Heal

Day	Breakfast	Lunch	Snack	Dinner
4	Veggie scramble: 2 egg whites, diced onion, mushrooms, tomato, and green pepper; 1 slice whole-grain or sprouted-grain toast; 1 orange	Bowl of vegetable soup; side salad with watercress, and 1 Tbsp. vinaigrette dressing	2 oz. reduced-fat cheddar cheese; 1 pear	4 oz. steamed shrimp; 1 baked potato topped with 3 Tbsp. salsa and 1 Tbsp. fat-free sour cream; 3 cups kale, steamed

Supplement

Continue taking your core-level healers.

Move to Mend

Today, do 30 minutes of flexibility work.

Self-Healing Thought for the Day

To say "I am sick" attaches the condition to you. The more often the words are repeated, the more fixed the condition becomes. So wipe out such thoughts. Healing depends a great deal upon your willingness to release from your consciousness the belief in disease. Have faith that you can heal and regenerate. See that nothing but self-healing can be true for you.

Day 5

Eat to Heal

Day	Breakfast	Lunch	Snack	Dinner
5	½ cup fat-free cottage cheese and 4 pineapple rings	Tuna (3 oz. water-packed tuna) in a whole-wheat pita pocket; 1 Tbsp. light mayo; 1 Tbsp. each chopped celery and onion; side salad with 1 Tbsp. vinaigrette dressing	4 dried figs; 8 oz. almond or rice milk	4 oz. roasted pork tenderloin; 1 cup baked acorn squash, mashed with a pinch of cinnamon; 2 to 3 cups salad greens with 2 Tbsp. fat-free dressing

Supplement

Continue taking your core-level healers.

Move to Mend

Today, do strength training: 1 or 2 sets of 8 moves that target your entire body. Aim for 8 to 12 reps. Use a weight that's hard to lift by the last rep.

Do 30 minutes of strength training work today.

Self-Healing Thought for the Day

There may come a time when you get discouraged, question your dedication, or wonder how you'll ever find the time to follow your program. These are understandable thoughts, but all are entirely manageable. You'll have up days and down days. Don't worry. What is important in life is that you stay the course—only then will you gain the rewards of a self-healed life.

Day 6

Eat to Heal

Day	Breakfast	Lunch	Snack	Dinner
6	1 serving high-fiber bran cereal with 8 oz. almond milk or skim milk; 1 sliced banana	1 bowl black-bean soup served with 2 cups of steamed veggies	Celery sticks with 1 Tbsp. almond butter	2 slices vegetable pizza made on gluten-free pizza crust; side salad with 1 Tbsp. vinaigrette dressing

Supplement

Continue taking your core-level healers.

Move to Mend

Today, do 30 minutes of cardio work. Try something new and different.

Self-Healing Thought for the Day

The choices you make today displace illness with health. They bring all cells to healthy activity, strengthening and calming your nerves. They make your whole body powerful and strong.

Day 7

Eat to Heal

Congratulations! You've just about completed one full week of the 21-day plan. I hope you're feeling better as a result of eating more nutritious foods.

Day	Breakfast	Lunch	Snack	Dinner
7	8 oz. cup skim milk/organic soy milk; ½ cup whole-grain cereals like organic oats, and add about 2 Tbsp. chopped walnuts or flaxseed to your cereal; 1 orange or half grapefruit	Turkey sandwich: 3 oz. turkey breast, tomato, and lettuce; 1 Tbsp. Dijon mustard; 2 slices whole-grain or sprouted-wheat bread; 1 banana	Apple with a tsp. of peanut butter	4 oz. baked chicken breast; 1 cup steamed vegetables such as broccoli or Brussels sprouts; 1 medium baked sweet potato

Supplement

Continue taking your core-level healers.

Move to Mend

Today, do 30 minutes of cardio work. Try something new and different.

Self-Healing Thought for the Day

Lift your spirits with activity. If you're feeling low, depressed, or sad, you can do something about it. You can take a walk, clean out a closet, work on a hobby, dig in your garden, or meditate. Activity—mental, physical, and spiritual—will lift your spirits. The specific activity is not important, but getting started is. Once you've made a start, note how energy replaces sadness, and the feeling of achievement replaces the letdown. You are again the cheerful, joyous, enthusiastic person you were meant to be.

In the next chapter, I'll cover what to do from days 8 to 14, and show you how to add in a program of emotional self-healing.

CHAPTER THIRTEEN

WEEK 2: LISTEN TO YOUR BODY

Congratulations—you've entered Week 2! How are you feeling? Energetic? More optimistic? In a better mood? Jot down your responses in your journal. Last week, you were introduced to some basic tools to live a more naturally healthy life. This week is more of the same. Don't worry if you don't do everything perfectly. Listen to your body and your intuition. Both will guide you.

Day 8

Eat to Heal

It's your second week. Continue making improved food choices.

Day	Breakfast	Lunch	Snack	Dinner
8	½ cup oats cooked with 8 oz. fat-free milk; top with 2 tsp. raisins and a sprinkle of cinnamon; ¼ cantaloupe	Spinach salad: toss baby-spinach leaves with 1 hard-boiled egg, sliced; 2 strips turkey bacon; chopped raw mushrooms; 2 Tbsp. light salad dressing (20 to 30 calories per Tbsp.)	1 medium pear or 1 large apple; 8 oz. almond or rice milk or 6 oz. light yogurt	4 oz. grilled salmon; 1 cup steamed cauliflower or broccoli with 2 tsp. Parmesan cheese

Supplement

Depending on your sex, age, activity level, and present health, your supplement needs differ. Today, you might want to consider individualizing your supplement program. If you're a woman, for example, talk to your doctor about taking supplemental calcium to prevent osteoporosis. The usual recommendation is 1,200 milligrams daily. If you're a man, you want to make sure you're taking a men's formula of some kind. This helps ensure you don't get what you don't need. For example, men don't need supplemental iron, as too much can cause heart problems.

As we get older, our nutrient requirements change. People older than 60, for example, have trouble absorbing enough folic acid (a B vitamin), vitamin B12, and calcium. Talk to your health-care practitioner about whether you need more of these nutrients that are typically found in multiples.

You might not realize this, but exercise can increase your need for certain nutrients, such as antioxidants. Regular exercisers require slightly more vitamin C and vitamin E, for example. Both nutrients help muscles regenerate more effectively in the aftermath of a workout. Sports supplements, including sports drinks or protein powders, can be beneficial and may contain added nutrients that support a physically active lifestyle.

Move to Mend

Do strength training today. Increase your level of effort. Do 2 or 3 sets of 8 to 12 reps, working your entire body.

Do 30 minutes of strength training work today.

Decide which healing arts might benefit you. The healing arts I discussed in this book are enjoying growing acceptance by the medical profession. They improve your quality of life, and in many cases, the quantity of your life. They teach you how to decrease stress and cope with unavoidable stresses of daily living. And they give people a sense of control that disease takes away. Each healing art has something to offer, depending on your requirements. Here are some guidelines to help you decide.

When to consider chiropractic care:

Ankle injuries	Chronic ear	Lumbar disc	Scar tissue
Arthritis	infections	herniation	formation
Asthma	Colic	Muscle pulls or	Sciatica
Athletic injury	Foot pain/injury	strains	Sexual dysfunction
prevention	Frozen shoulder	Muscle weakness	Shoulder pain
Back pain/injuries	Headaches	Neck pain	Stomach problems
—and pediatric	High blood	Nerve entrapment	Sports Injuries
lower-back pain	pressure	syndromes	TMJ Syndrome
Bursitis	Hip pain	Painful menses	Vertigo
Carpal tunnel	Ilio tibial band	Repetitive strain	Walking and mo-
syndrome	syndrome	injuries	bility problems
Cerebrovascular	Joint dysfunction	Rib pain	Wellness and
accidents	Knee injuries and	Rotator cuff	prevention
	pain	syndrome	Whiplash injuries

When to consider cold laser therapy:

Arthritis
Back pain
Carpal tunnel syndrome
Foot pain
Hamstring injuries
Neck pain

Neuropathy
Post-surgical healing
Sciatica
Sinus pain
Sprains and strains

Tendon pain, including
   tendinitis and muscle
   injuries
TMJ Syndrome
Wound healing

When to consider energy medicine:

ADD-ADHD
Addictions
Allergies
Eating disorders
Emotional issues

Headaches
Hypertension
Neuropathy
Pain
Panic/anxiety

Phobias and fears
Stress
Vision issues
Weight loss

When to consider massage:

Arthritis
Chronically stiff neck
Depression
Fibromyalgia (stiff, inflamed muscles)

Headache
Low-back pain
Recovery from hospitalization
Stress

Getting the Best Care from the Healing Arts

No matter which healing art you're considering, make sure you:

- *Get a diagnosis.* Any healing art should not be used to just treat symptoms without having a clear idea of the cause behind them. Proper diagnosis is still the most critical component in planning your health care.

- *Know your practitioner.* Ask about certifications, licenses, training, and experience in treating others with your condition. Steer clear of any healer who wants you to stop standard medical care or won't communicate with your other doctors.

- *Find out how many treatments you'll need.* A qualified practitioner will be able to estimate how many sessions it will take for you to feel better.

- *Understand your individuality in self-healing.* Not everyone benefits from the same techniques or protocols. One thing doesn't work for everybody.

- *Change your lifestyle to enhance the healing art.* Most healing-arts practitioners won't just work on you in their office; they'll advise you to make changes in your exercise and diet habits at home and find ways to reduce your stress. Follow their advice.

Self-Healing Thought for the Day

Realize that it is natural to be healthy. Think in terms of health. Words have power, so speak positive words of health and healing to yourself.

Day 9

Eat to Heal

Here is your menu for today. Feel free to improvise!

Day	Breakfast	Lunch	Snack	Dinner
9	Smoothie: Blend together 1 cup berries (any type), 6 oz. light yogurt, and ½ cup fat-free milk; 1 slice light whole-wheat bread spread with 2 tsp. peanut butter	Avocado chicken salad: Toss salad greens (include chicory and watercress) with 3 oz. skinless chicken or turkey breast, cut into strips; 1 orange, peeled and sectioned; ¼ ripe avocado, cut into chunks; 1 Tbsp. toasted almonds, chopped; 2 slices red onion. Sprinkle with flavored vinegar.	Apple or pear; 6 oz. Greek yogurt	4 oz. grilled salmon, 8 steamed asparagus spears, 1 small baked sweet potato, 1 tsp. grated cheese

Supplement

Continue to take your core-level healers, along with any extra supplements you need.

Move to Mend

Work on flexibility today. Increase your time to 45 minutes of exercise.

Recognize Anti-Healing Thought Patterns

Negative thoughts can obstruct healing. An important way to prevent that is to make a list of your typical negative messages that play in your head; next to those, jot down the opposite positive message. Practice repeating those in your mind. Here are some examples:

- I can't get well. / I am a self-healing creation. I am healing.

- I can't change. / I can change. My choices for change are under my control.

- I'm a couch potato. / I used to be inactive, but now I'm exercising.

- I've tried, and I always fail. / I don't always fail. Every healthy choice I make is a major success.

- I'm too fat. / Every moment I exercise and eat right, my body is healing and becoming better at burning fat for fuel.

— *Reframe negatives into positives.* Some examples: You're unemployed? No, you're just between jobs. You're broke? No, you're just well on your way to making a big financial comeback. Be a problem solver. Instead of asking yourself, *Why isn't my life going the way that I want it to?* ask, *How can I make it better? How can I get a better job? How can I get in shape?*

— *Practice optimism.* Someone once asked me, "Fab, how come we're supposed to be so optimistic, when we're all going to die?" Well, the answer has to do with the quality of our lives. Whether we live 40 years, 70 years, or 100 years, we still seek to live life optimally. And the quality of our life is directly related to our state of mind, particularly if it's one of hope and optimism.

— *See yourself in a good light.* List your strengths and skills. Refer to this list every day for the next week.

—*Take the words "health problem" out of your vocabulary.* Replace them with *health challenge*. Along those same lines, try not to see yourself as a victim or sufferer of an ailment, or to become a professional patient. Use language to help your positive healing energy flow. For example, do not tell yourself: *I'm asthmatic*, or *diabetic*, or *epileptic*. You are a person who has this illness. You are not your illness.

What I strongly urge you to do is this: Before you go to sleep at night, think about all the positive changes you're making in your life and how they're vitalizing your health. Try meditating on any mantra that has strengthened you thus far. When you do this, your healing potential will strengthen, day by day.

Self-Healing Thought for the Day

Are you an optimist? Do you live each day cheerfully, positively, and rationally, anticipating only good? Let nothing destroy the confidence you have in your ability to self-heal, unless you let it. Build your capacity to find good in every situation.

Day 10

Eat to Heal

Enjoy the following self-healing menu today.

Day	Breakfast	Lunch	Snack	Dinner
10	¾ cup low-fat calcium-fortified cottage cheese; 1 slice light whole-wheat bread, toasted, with 1 tsp. fruit jam; ½ cantaloupe	Mediterranean salad: Toss together 15 grape tomatoes, halved; eight ¾" chunks of part-skim mozzarella cheese; and 3 fresh basil leaves, chopped. Sprinkle with flavored vinegar; 1 medium pear	1 red pepper, sliced, with 3 Tbsp. hummus	Sprinkle fajita seasoning mix on top of a 6-oz. boneless pork-loin chop or a 6-oz. piece of flank steak. Grill or broil: ½ cup Mexican-style canned corn, drained, seasoned with ½ tsp. ground cumin; 1 zucchini, cut into wedges, lengthwise; or 8 asparagus spears. Spray with cooking spray, then grill or roast.

Supplement

Taking core-level healers and nutrients for your special needs is a great way to protect your health. But going above and beyond these supplements may be in order. Let's start that process today.

Depending on your physical health, you may want to look into "disease-specific" supplements—those that have been shown in scientific research to prevent, treat, and even reverse, certain diseases. Here's a review of health issues that might be improved by taking certain supplements:

Boost Immunity

- *Omega-3 fatty acids:* 2–3 grams daily. Note: If you eat a diet rich in wild fish (four or more times a week), you'll need a smaller dosage.
- *GLA:* 500 milligrams daily.
- *Curcumin:* 750 mg capsules; take two to three times daily.
- *Reishi mushroom extract:* During cold and flu season; follow label directions.
- *Whey protein:* Use in smoothies daily, or several times a week; follow label directions.
- *Licorice (Glycyrrhiza glabra):* 1–10 milligrams of glycyrrhizin or 1–5 grams of licorice is estimated to be a safe dose for most healthy adults.

Also, consider these immune-boosting vitamins and minerals in additional amounts:

- *Selenium:* 200 mcg daily. This mineral appears to be effective against viruses; it keeps them from replicating.
- *Vitamin C:* Up to 1,000 mg daily during flu season or to prevent a cold during cold season.

- *Zinc:* 50 mg daily to boost immunity; zinc lozenges appear to help shorten the duration of colds.

Blood-Sugar Support

Increasingly, supplements are being used, along with diet, to help control blood sugar. There are two supplements in particular that help:

- *Alpha lipoic acid:* 600–800 milligrams daily. Supplementation may alter dosage requirements for insulin and oral diabetes medications, so check with your doctor.
- *L-glutamine:* 500 milligrams daily.

Anti-Stress

- *L theanine:* 200–500 milligrams when under stress.
- *B-complex:* Daily. Each pill should supply 100 micrograms of vitamin B12 and biotin, 400 micrograms of folic acid, and 100 milligrams of all the other B vitamins. Take it along with food to enhance absorption.
- *Magnesium:* 300–600 milligrams of magnesium daily to counter the effects of stress.

Digestive Repair

- *Probiotic supplements:* Follow label directions. One serving should be at least 1 billion CFU (Colony Forming Units).
- *Digestive enzymes:* Follow label directions.

Joint Support

- *Hyaluronic acid (HA):* 40–80 milligrams daily for joint problems.
- *Glucosamine/chondroitin:* 1,500 milligrams daily for joint problems.
- *MSM:* 1,000–3,000 milligrams daily, with meals, for osteoarthritis.

Prevent Heart Disease

- *CoQ10:* 50 to 200 milligrams daily.
- *Red yeast rice extract:* 1,200 milligrams daily taken with food.

Brain Support

- *Choline:* 425 milligrams per day for women and 550 milligrams per day for men.
- *GPC:* 1,200 milligrams daily.
- *Vinpocetine:* Up to 10 milligrams a day in two doses paired with food.
- *ALC:* 500–1,500 milligrams two or three times a day, preferably on an empty stomach.
- *Ginkgo biloba:* 120–240 milligrams daily.

Move to Mend

Today, perform your favorite cardio exercise. Shoot for 45–60 minutes at a moderate pace.

Self-Healing Thought for the Day

Perseverance—seeing a task through to its completion—is a valuable trait. Often we feel we do not have the time to accomplish the things we should like to do. But once we set our sights on something important, and learn to persevere, we go forward to meet it with success.

Day 11

Eat to Heal

Day	Breakfast	Lunch	Snack	Dinner
11	6 oz. Greek yogurt topped with 1 cup berries and 2 Tbsp. chopped almonds or walnuts	Sandwich: 2 slices light whole-wheat bread; ¼ avocado, mashed; 1-oz. slice Swiss or Jarlsberg cheese; 2 strips turkey bacon; tomato slices; 1 cup berries or 1 peach	1 apple with 1 Tbsp. peanut butter	Baked fish: Sprinkle top of 6-oz. white-flesh fish (such as flounder, sole, or snapper) with 1 Tbsp. Parmesan cheese and 2 tsp. dried bread crumbs. Sprinkle with paprika, salt, and pepper, then spray with cooking spray. Bake in preheated 500-degree F oven until fish is opaque throughout; 5-oz. sweet potato, baked; 1–2 cups steamed cabbage.

Supplement

Take all the supplements in your program that you and your health-care practitioner feel are necessary for your individual situation.

Move to Mend

Today, it's time again for flexibility exercises, and it's also another good time to meditate. Consider yoga or tai chi. Do it for 45 to 60 minutes.

Get Stress Under Control

Every day the world bombards us with stress. Today, I just want you to think of the areas in which stress may be intruding in your health and well-being. Some things to consider:

— *Get your finances under control.* Develop a plan to curb spending and overspending, and reduce debt. Seek help from a financial advisor if you can't do this on your own.

— *Take control of your time.* Make daily to-do lists. On each, rank them in order of importance. Do them in that order but don't stress out if you don't finish everything.

— *Walk away from stress.* A massage or a hot bath is a great way to relieve stress. But don't overlook the benefits of a brisk walk or some other type of physical activity that you enjoy. Exercise, nature's tranquilizer, burns off excess adrenaline, a stress hormone that is a by-product of your body's response to stress.

— *Love your enemies.* Often our biggest stresses in life come from people who frustrate us. Learn to love those people. If you allow someone's behavior to anger you, then you give your power away to that person. You allow him or her to make your heart beat faster and raise your blood pressure. Why should you let anyone do that to you? So now if somebody cuts you off in traffic, if your boss makes you mad, or if a friend hurts your feelings, throw him or her a kiss.

— *Stop doing everything yourself.* Start delegating tasks at work and at home.

— *Prioritize and focus.* Decide what is truly important to you. Take time occasionally to make clear choices about what you want from life. Take an active role in deciding how you'll spend your time; don't just let things happen.

— *Say no sometimes.* When something is asked of you, take time to consider the request instead of agreeing immediately. Can you handle it with relative ease? What must you put aside in order to do it? What is it going to cost in terms of time?

— *Create a routine.* Make sure you schedule time daily to relax, take care of yourself, and spend time with those you love. Recreation and fun are as important as hard work, responsibility, and success. Get the balance right and give yourself permission to do so.

Unloading stress is an incredibly healing process. Once you do so, along with everything else, your body will continue to heal.

Learn to Meditate

Meditation can help you find inner peace. The best way to begin is to sit on a soft spot such as a pillow or mat in a quiet place. Close your eyes. Take a deep inhalation, then exhale. Continue this pattern of breathing for a few minutes. Really focus on your breathing. If there are distractions around you—like noise or thoughts—accept them and gently allow your attention to come to your breathing. Those thoughts are simply in the background. This technique helps you learn that basically you can allow your thoughts to roam without being hijacked by them.

Next, imagine waves of comfort and peace moving through your body. Let the muscles in your face soften, your shoulders relax. Turn your attention inward to "watch" those waves flowing throughout your body with each exhalation and inhalation.

Visualize peaceful scenes: a full moon against a starry night, a breeze floating through a meadow . . . ocean waves lapping on the seashore. Or journey in your mind to some pleasant place that you hold dear. Hold these images in your mind as you meditate. Do this each day for about 20 minutes.

If formal meditation isn't your thing, try looking for meditative moments in everyday activities. For example, some people find housework or yard work a calming practice. Or if you take the train or bus to work, use that time for reflection. Or meditate while doing exercise. Whatever calms you down, do it each day.

Self-Healing Thought for the Day

Tension in your mind and body comes through thinking thoughts that cause mental and physical anguish. Negativity causes nerves to get taut and the muscles to contract. Relief comes from getting rid of such thoughts and relaxing by thinking more productively. Go within, breathe deeply, and turn away from the thought that makes you tense.

Day 12

Eat to Heal

You are halfway through the program. I hope you're feeling healthier, more energetic, and more at peace. Here is your menu for today.

Day	Breakfast	Lunch	Snack	Dinner
12	2 eggs, cooked in nonstick skillet; 2 strips turkey bacon;1 slice light whole-wheat bread, toasted; ½ grapefruit	Chef's salad: Top salad greens with 2 ounces extra-lean ham, turkey breast, or chicken breast, cut into strips; 1-oz. slice of Swiss or Jarlsberg cheese, cut into strips; tomato wedges; cucumber and onion slices; and 2 Tbsp. light salad dressing	6 oz. Greek yogurt; 1 medium banana, or 1 large apple	Chicken and couscous: Arrange 4 oz. skinless rotisserie chicken breast over ½ cup cooked couscous. Top with 3 Tbsp. salsa. Avocado salad: On lettuce leaves, arrange 1 small orange, peeled and sectioned; ¼ ripe avocado, thinly sliced; and 1 slice red onion. Drizzle with a mixture of 2 Tbsp. balsamic vinegar, 1 Tbsp. orange juice, and 1 tsp. olive oil.

Supplement

Continue to take your full complement of supplements.

Move to Mend

Today, do your strength-training routine. Do 2 or 3 sets of 8 to 12 reps, working your entire body. Do it for 45 to 60 minutes.

Build Your Trust Factor

Today, analyze your relationships with your health-care practitioners. Become an active participant in your care mentally, physically, and emotionally. Work with your regular physician, but also choose the best that both traditional and alternative medicines have to offer. Believe that there are healing powers within you that can be tapped. Meditate on this.

Self-Healing Thought for the Day

Trust your healer, trust your treatment, and trust in your capacity to self-heal. Trust brings about health and healing.

Day 13

Eat to Heal

Day	Breakfast	Lunch	Snack	Dinner
13	Breakfast ham and cheese sandwich: top 2 slices of light whole-wheat bread with ¼ cup of grated Swiss or Jarlsberg cheese, and broil until cheese melts. Layer 1 oz. extra-lean deli-sliced ham between the bread; 1 orange	Black-bean salad: toss ½ cup canned black beans, ½ cup mandarin orange sections, and chopped red bell peppers, red onion, and scallions with 1 tsp. vinegar. Serve over salad greens. 1 pear	1 slice whole-wheat bread with 2 tsp. almond butter; 1 apple	4 oz. grilled beef tenderloin; 6 steamed asparagus spears, tossed with 1 tsp. olive oil; 1 cup mixed salad greens; 2 Tbsp. low-cal dressing

Supplement

Don't forget to take all your supplements today.

Move to Mend

Do 45 to 60 minutes of cardio at a moderate pace. Choose a different activity than you've done before.

Make Peace with the Doctor Within

By now you understand that you are a self-healing creature. Yet many of us are at odds with "the doctor within," and we spoil our healing potential with damaging habits. This week, I want you to make peace with the doctor within—and begin to think about changing detrimental lifestyle habits that are interfering with your self-healing potential.

Bad habits cause emotional and physical discomfort and can diminish your self-esteem, health, productivity, work, family, and other relationships. To overcome a bad habit, you've got to put into place more effective ways of coping, and build healthy habits instead.

I want you to really analyze why you're mired in certain bad habits. This is your first step toward change, and I believe you're emotionally strong enough to do this now. With your negative behavior or bad habit in mind, write your answers to the following questions in your journal. Your answers will be very revealing to you.

- *What is it I like about my habit?*
- *What good does it do for me?*
- *What am I afraid my life would be like if I did not engage in this behavior?*
- *What bad feelings (anger, frustration, stress, depression) does my habit help me deal with?*
- *How painful would it be to stop engaging in this behavior?*
- *How much does this behavior help me in my relationships with others?*
- *How much do I need this habit in order to feel good?*

A Break-That-Habit Action Plan

Step 1. Look over your answers to the previous questions. Identify what triggers your habit. List these triggers in your journal.

Step 2. With those triggers in mind, plan ahead. Devise some productive and positive ways that you can respond when those vulnerable moments occur. Consider things like talking to a supportive friend, going for walk, spending a few moments in meditation, or anything that redirects you away from your bad habit.

Step 3. Consider actions that can help you strengthen your self-healing power, develop an optimistic outlook, and create a more positive view of yourself. These changes can range from very simple things like getting up earlier each morning and reflecting on your day, to keeping a gratitude log in your journal, to more complex ones like seeking out resources required to achieving a long-held personal goal.

Self-Healing Thought for the Day

Every day, you make decisions that define your life. You may feel stuck in a job, an addiction, a bad relationship, or just a rut in life. If you know you are stuck, then you are stuck. If you believe you can get out, you can. You have the power to free yourself.

Day 14

Eat to Heal

Here's another delicious menu that will do wonders for your health.

Day	Breakfast	Lunch	Snack	Dinner
14	Express breakfast sandwich: cook 1 egg and 1 slice turkey bacon in a nonstick skillet. Place egg, bacon, and 1 slice fat-free cheese between two halves of a light multigrain English muffin. Heat sandwich in a toaster oven until cheese melts, about 1 minute; 1 orange	Greek salad with grilled chicken: grill and dice a 3 oz. chicken breast; toss together with 2 oz. reduced-fat feta cheese, 2 cups romaine lettuce, and ½ cup each tomato, cucumber, and roasted red peppers. Top with 2 Tbsp. light vinaigrette; 2 whole-wheat crackers	6 oz. Greek yogurt; 1 cup fresh berries	4–5 oz. grilled salmon topped with 2 Tbsp. teriyaki sauce; 1 cup zucchini sautéed in 1 Tbsp. olive oil; ½ cup steamed brown rice

Supplement

Take all supplements again today: core-level healers and personalized supplements.

Move to Mend

You have choices today: do 30 to 60 minutes of cardio, rest, or do something fun and active (hike, golf, play tennis, walk on the beach, bike around town, or whatever you can think of).

Ignite Your Creative Spark

Creativity is healing. Think about what you can do to be more creative—then do it! Some ideas:

- Sign up for a painting or pottery class.
- Take up a new hobby or craft.
- Try photography.
- Redecorate a room in your house.
- Plant some colorful flowers.

Self-Healing Thought for the Day

Creativity springs from doing something we love and giving it our best. Creativity is something we do every day, whether we realize it or not. Did you choose the clothes you have on today? That took creativity! Did you solve a problem at work? That took creativity! So today and every day, tap into your creativity. It brings joy, happiness, and healing to life.

Up next is the final part of the self-healing paradigm: how to nourish your spirit.

CHAPTER FOURTEEN

WEEK 3: NOURISH YOUR SPIRIT

I hope that these tools and strategies are becoming a part of your lifestyle now. This week, I'll introduce you to some other ways to slow down and discover what's really important to you. Keep in mind, too, the goals you set for yourself at the beginning of this program. At the end of this week, review them and see which ones were met.

Day 15

Eat to Heal

Enjoy your next self-healing menu. Meditate on all the wonderful things healthy food is doing for your body.

Day	Breakfast	Lunch	Snack	Dinner
15	6 oz. Greek yogurt mixed with ¾ cup Kashi Go Lean Crunch Cereal; 1 cup blueberries	Turkey burger: On the stovetop, cook a 4 oz. lean turkey burger. Add 1 slice fat-free cheese and heat until cheese melts. Serve burger on a toasted whole-wheat roll with lettuce, tomato, and mustard or ketchup; 1 cup fruit salad	2 whole-wheat crackers with 2 wedges Laughing Cow Light cheese; 1 cup grapes	1 cup whole-wheat pasta with ½ cup pasta sauce and 3 turkey meatballs; tricolor salad (top 1 cup mixed greens with 3 canned artichoke hearts, 2 Tbsp. grated Parmesan, 2 Tbsp. balsamic vinegar, and 1 tsp. olive oil); fresh strawberries with 1 Tbsp. fat-free whipped topping

Supplement

Take your supplements, and as you did with food, meditate on how these supplements are enhancing your health.

Move to Mend

Do your strength-training routine today. Do 2 or 3 sets of 8 to 12 reps, working your entire body. Marvel at how much stronger you feel. Do it for 45 to 60 minutes.

Develop a Forgiving Spirit

Let go of a grudge. Write on a piece of paper about an incident that hurt your feelings. Then wad up the paper and throw it away.

Recall a time in your life when you hurt someone and later asked for forgiveness. How did it feel to be forgiven?

Think of someone, past or present, you need to forgive. Then write out at least three reasons why you might want to forgive this person. Then forgive.

Self-Healing Thought for the Day

Forgiveness is letting go, tossing aside personal pride, and giving up unpleasant memories. The process is purely a personal and mental one. Until you release something from your mind, it will always have power over you. Yet when you forgive, you gain more benefits and blessings yourself than will the one whom you forgave.

Day 16

Eat to Heal

Here is your self-healing menu for today. By now, this way of healing should feel like second-nature!

Day	Breakfast	Lunch	Snack	Dinner
16	"Light" scrambled eggs (in a small bowl, whisk together 1 whole egg and 2 egg whites. Add ¼ cup each sliced mushrooms, spinach, and onions. Cook in a pan over medium heat until eggs are fluffy); 1 cup cubed cantaloupe	Ham and cheese sandwich (layer 3 oz. deli-sliced ham, 2 fat-free cheese singles, 1 Tbsp. mustard, 2 lettuce leaves, and 2 slices tomato between 2 slices reduced-calorie whole-wheat bread); 1 cup light minestrone soup; 1 apple	6 oz. Greek yogurt with 1 cup fresh berries	Chicken Parmesan (Top a 4 oz. cooked chicken breast with ½ cup marinara sauce and 3 Tbsp. shredded low-fat mozzarella. Bake at 400°F until cheese melts, about 4 minutes); small whole-wheat roll; 1 cup steamed broccoli

Supplement

Be sure to include all your supplements today.

Move to Mend

Today, do 60 minutes of flexibility work. Incorporate meditation into your moves.

Look for the Blessings

Finding meaning in my own tragedies has helped release me from the pain and bitterness. I no longer look at tragedies in my life as negatives, even though they were painful. Going through what I did with my father has made me stronger and more compassionate. I can now connect with others better. Had I not lost my father, how could I ever relate when somebody said to me, "I just lost my brother/my sister/my loved one"? The tragedy changed my perspective on my life for the better.

To find the blessings in a tough situation, ask yourself a few questions, such as: What did you learn from your experience? How did it affect you? Are you a more resilient, more compassionate, or more courageous person as a result? Write the answers down in your journal.

At the end of each day, take a few minutes to journal at least three things in your life for which you are grateful or thankful. Continue this exercise nightly. In a week or so, you may notice that you have a very different outlook toward life; you'll feel more positive and hopeful—attitudes that contribute to self-healing.

Self-Healing Thought for the Day

When you are grateful for your blessings, your gratitude attracts extra good to you. Gratitude is a powerful magnet that draws friends, love, peace, and health into your life.

Day 17

Eat to Heal

Day	Breakfast	Lunch	Snack	Dinner
17	1 cup oatmeal with 8 oz. almond or skim milk; 2 Tbsp. sliced almonds; a pinch of cinnamon; ½ grapefruit	3 oz. tuna served over mixed greens with 2 Tbsp. low-cal dressing; 1 pear	2 cups low-fat popcorn sprinkled with 2 Tbsp. Parmesan	Turkey taco (in a medium sauce pan, brown 4 oz. turkey meat. Add 1 Tbsp. taco seasoning and 4 oz. canned, diced tomatoes. Cook over high heat until liquid is absorbed. Serve in a whole-wheat soft flour tortilla with ½ cup fat-free cheese shreds, 2 Tbsp. salsa, and 1 Tbsp. fat-free sour cream.)

Supplement

Take all your regular supplements today. Note how much better you feel because you're giving your body what it needs, and supplements are a big part of that.

Move to Mend

Get your heart pumping and your blood flowing with 45 to 60 minutes of your favorite cardio activity. Make it a moving meditation.

Tune In to Supportive, Loving Relationships

We need relationships to enrich our lives, as long as they are *healthy* relationships. A healthy relationship, whether family, friendship, or romance, is one that helps you become the best version of yourself. This is reciprocal, too. You're helping someone else become the best version of him- or herself. And by "best version," I mean that you help each other feel secure, comfortable, valued, respected, and protected in the relationship.

Today, I'd like you to take a look at key relationships in your life and try to answer the following questions in your journal: Who are the most important people in your life? What do these people mean to you, and why?

In an average week, how much time do you actually spend with these people? Is that enough time or not? Either way, figure out, and write down, new ways to spend more time with them.

Make it a point to get in touch each day with someone special in your life—with a phone call, a text, an e-mail, or other communication. Schedule a time to get together. Don't let obligations force you to cancel. You need loving, supportive relationships in your life; they're a part of a self-healing lifestyle.

Self-Healing Thought for the Day

Relationships are an undeniable part of life. Be open to the good that others are willing to share with you. Return that good in kind. Cherished relationships can be a priceless investment in your health and happiness.

Day 18

Eat to Heal

Don't worry about doing everything perfectly. Just follow your plan as closely as you can, and congratulate yourself for your effort.

Day	Breakfast	Lunch	Snack	Dinner
18	1 slice toasted raisin bread with 1 Tbsp. reduced-sugar jam; 6 oz. Greek yogurt; 1 medium peach or 1 kiwifruit or 1 cup strawberries; For more calories: Add an extra slice of toast with 1 Tbsp. reduced-sugar jam.	Bean-and-beet salad: Toss 2 cups bagged salad greens with 12 canned beet slices, drained, and 1 cup canned three-bean salad with its liquid (no more than 70 calories per ½ cup); 2 sesame breadsticks; 1 cup fresh strawberries	Baked apple: Peel ½ way down; core; place 1 tsp. raisins and 2 tsp. brown sugar in center of apple, sprinkle with cinnamon. Cook in microwave oven in small bowl, covered, 2–3 minutes on high.	4–5 oz. cooked turkey breast; 1 medium sweet potato, baked; 1 cup green beans, steamed; 1 small whole-grain roll

Supplement

Supplements are a simple way to make big improvements in your health. Be thankful that you've chosen to make supplements a part of your self-healing plan, and remember to take your usual regimen.

Move to Mend

Do 60 minutes of flexibility work today. It offers a great opportunity to meditate, so try to incorporate it into your workout. It helps lower stress and strengthens your immune system.

Nurture Your Spirit

Whether you are religious or not, nourish your spirit. Find something that gives you inner peace. Maybe it is meditation or prayer, reading spiritual books, practicing yoga, bicycling, hiking a mountain, sitting quietly by a river, or getting involved in an organized religion or house of worship. Remember, people who are affiliated with a religious or spiritual group are usually tapped into the healing triad: forgiveness, gratitude, and love. Follow your personal definition of spirituality and practice it.

Self-Healing Thought for the Day

Pray and anticipate good. When you ask for something good to come into your life, make yourself open and receptive to it. The best way to do this is to drop some undesirable thing from your life and make room for something good. Look for the good, and know that it will manifest. Then give your thanks for what you have received.

Day 19

Eat to Heal

Keep in mind any goals you've set for healthy eating. Let today bring you one step closer to those goals.

Day	Breakfast	Lunch	Snack	Dinner
19	1 toasted multigrain English muffin with 1 Tbsp. reduced-sugar jam; ½ cup 1 percent fat cottage cheese; 1 cup melon balls (fresh or frozen, thawed)	Stuffed potato: 1 medium (5½ oz.) baked potato topped with 1/3 cup canned kidney beans, chopped and cooked broccoli, diced raw tomato, 2 tbsp. salsa; 1 cup fresh or ½ cup juice-packed pineapple chunks	Fruit smoothie: Mix in blender 4 oz. low-fat milk; ¼ cup strawberries, sliced; ½ very ripe medium banana; 1 tsp. sugar or honey; 3 ice cubes	4–5 oz. broiled flank steak; 1 cup steamed green beans or 1 cup steamed asparagus; 2 steamed ears of corn (each 3½ inches)

Supplement

Supplementation helps transform your nutritional habits. This in turn helps you feel better, mentally and emotionally.

Move to Mend

Today, do 2 or 3 sets of 8 to 12 reps for strength training, working your entire body. Strength training offers another wonderful opportunity for meditation. As you do each exercise, focus on the body part you're working. Visualize how the move is making your body healthier and more fit. Do it for 45 to 60 minutes.

Focus on Your Purpose

Spiritual people want to make the world a better place, not only through prayer, meditation, and other activities, but also through their actions. They have a sense of purpose that may be felt as a "call" or "mission" to fulfill. I urge you to ask yourself such questions as: *What is my purpose for being here? What is my journey all about? Am I here to take what I can from society, or am I here to contribute?* Answer these questions in your journal.

Self-Healing Thought for the Day

You need a sense of purpose! If there is something you long to do, go within and pray. Act upon what you want to do. Know in your heart that something better is on its way to you. Prepare yourself and get ready to fulfill your purpose. Eventually, your life will be so full that you'll wonder how anyone could feel that life has no meaning.

Day 20

Eat to Heal

I'm sure by now you've transitioned from eating an unhealthy diet to a healthy, naturally delicious one. Your improved food choices and more-active lifestyle is setting an example for others.

Day	Breakfast	Lunch	Snack	Dinner
20	Banana Shake (whirl together in blender): ¾ cup skim or 1 percent milk, ½ medium banana, ½ tsp. vanilla extract, 3 or 4 ice cubes	On 2 slices light whole-grain bread, spread 2 Tbsp. hummus and top with 2 oz. sliced turkey breast and tomato slices; 1 cup grapes	6 oz. Greek yogurt, flavored with herbs and seasonings; lots of fresh, cut-up veggies for dipping	4–5 oz. chicken breast baked with 1 tsp. olive oil; ½ cup cooked rice; 1 cup steamed broccoli with lemon juice; 1 cup melon balls (fresh or frozen)

Supplement

Take your usual complement today. Some people believe supplements are too expensive. In the long run, they're less expensive than the money you'll spend to treat a chronic disease with drugs and other treatments. Look at supplements as a value-added necessity to your life. If there's an extra expense, just know you're worth it!

Move to Mend

Do 45 to 60 minutes of a fun cardio activity. If the opportunity presents itself, try something different. Or look into some fun technology to chart your progress, like a heart-rate monitor or a pedometer to count your steps.

Live Your Spirituality

One way to live your spirituality is to help others. A truly spiritual person thrives on turning thoughtful words and feelings into action. Reciting Bible passages is one thing, but helping others achieve true spirituality is quite another. It's the familiar adage: "Actions speak louder than words."

When I was a freshman in high school, I was asked to volunteer with the Special Olympics. I was so afraid to do it; I didn't think I was adequate. But with the encouragement of the other volunteers, I signed up. I was paired with a child. I supported that child, and we went to every event together. The smile on that child's face will be a memory I will always cherish. It was a very bonding experience, and it touched my life immeasurably.

Once you get involved in something like Special Olympics, you get caught up in it. That experience changed me so much that I asked to be the leader in recruiting other students to join us the next year. All I did was go from classroom to classroom and share my own experience. I was honest about my own inhibitions—my own fears, worries, and anxieties. I said that since I was able to surpass them, my fellow classmates could, too. We recruited 250 volunteers; the following year, 400; and the next year, 1,000. Several years later, I coordinated the Special Olympics back in Miami, Florida. Volunteering reminded me that as long as I have something to give, I have something to be thankful for.

Self-Healing Thought for the Day

Share your gifts with others—your family, friends, and associates. Your whole life will be enriched through the gifts you give. As you give from love, these gifts will return to you a thousandfold.

Day 21

Eat to Heal

This is the last day of the plan. But it's not the end. It's the beginning of a new healing lifestyle for you that will inspire you to keep going!

Day	Breakfast	Lunch	Snack	Dinner
21	Smoothie: In blender, combine 1 cup fat-free milk, ½ cup bran flakes cereal, 1 banana, 8 strawberries, a dash of vanilla extract, and 4 ice cubes	Tortilla melt: (heat in microwave) 1 small corn tortilla topped with ½ cup canned kidney beans, diced tomato and green pepper, 1 Tbsp. shredded cheddar cheese	6 oz. Greek yogurt; 1 cup fresh strawberries	4–5 oz. broiled flounder or sole (thin fillet about 5 inches long), cooked with 1 tsp. olive oil; 1 cup steamed spinach with lemon; 3 small potatoes (each 1¼" diameter) boiled, steamed, or roasted; 1 cup of cherries or grapes

Supplement

Continue taking your supplements daily. I hope you can see and feel how supplementation has improved your life. Meditate on this and feel grateful that you've started this positive new habit.

Move to Mend

Have some fun today. Do some fun cardio, or something active (hike, golf, play tennis, walk on the beach, bike around town, and so on). Or just rest!

Reach Out

Starting now, and each day going forward, give someone a hug. The need to be touched is essential to your health and well-being.

Laugh with someone. When you do that, you create a bond. Laughter and humor give you a better perspective on situations and make them more tolerable. What makes you laugh? Today write in your journal about a subject that makes you laugh.

How well do you know your neighbors? If you don't know them too well, it's time to make the effort. Today think of how you'd like to spend time with your neighbors. Invite someone over for coffee . . . start a walking group or organize a book club . . . set up a play date if you have kids . . . organize a block party . . . connect with those on your street.

Self-Healing Thought for the Day

Think of each new day as a clean, unwritten page. It doesn't have to be scratched up by yesterday's mistakes. Write on this page only the thoughts and the actions that will bring your self-healing potential to its highest and best level.

AFTERWORD

When I turned 15 years old, my parents gave my brother and me two tickets for Christmas to go back to Colombia for New Year's. We were so excited; we would get to see our friends and relatives. We stayed with my aunt, uncle, and my cousins.

One particular evening, my uncle had to travel for business, leaving my aunt, two cousins, my brother, and me home alone. My brother and I slept in different guest rooms. At around 1 A.M., I was awakened by a gun hitting my head, repeatedly. The room was dark, but I could see the shadowy figures of three men in the room. The guy hitting my head kept saying, "Where's the safe? Where's the safe?"

"I don't know where the safe is. I don't even live here. This is my uncle's house," I pleaded.

"Where's the safe? I know you know where the safe is." Then they tied my hands, they tied my legs, and they tied both of them together.

"If you don't tell us, we're going to kill your brother."

I cried, "I don't know where the safe is!"

What we were subjected to must be everyone's nightmare: to be woken up by intruders, assaulted with a gun, have your life threatened, and be told that someone you love would be killed. It was truly horrific.

All of a sudden I heard a noise from my brother's room. The men came into my room with blood all over their hands.

"We just killed your brother!" they shouted.

This ripped me apart; it was an absolute nightmare. To my mind those men had no heart. They had no conscience.

Then the intruders started yelling to each other. In the confusion, I heard the scarcely believable message: "It's the police." The men scattered and escaped.

A security guard next door had seen a car he didn't recognize in the front of the house and called the police. The police untied me, and all I could think about was that my brother was dead.

But he wasn't, thank God. He had been hit severely in the head and later required over 20 stitches. It was a miracle that we survived the terrifying assault. My relief was immense. But I want you to know what that lesson taught me—to be grateful for everything, for life, and to never take anything for granted. And I have lived that way ever since.

I don't look at the tragedies in my life as "negatives," even though they were painful. I've always come out a better person because I've grown. These are opportunities to learn about myself and others; opportunities to experience the level of pain that so many have experienced so I can connect with others better. If I hadn't been close to dying in that robbery in Colombia, how could I ever understand when somebody says, "I was robbed today; I was violated. I was . . ." So those experiences have allowed me to understand and relate to others more.

What keeps me so inspired is that every day of my life is about serving others. If I'm not serving, then I couldn't be as excited and motivated, because that's my destiny in life. I believe that everyone's destiny is to utilize whatever gifts they were given, whatever experiences, whatever riches . . . so that they can share what they've learned. That's my life. I wake up thinking, *How can I do that?* every single day.

As a parting thought, I would encourage you to take the time to evaluate your life. For example:

- What are you doing for your physical health?
- How are you changing your thoughts and expressing your emotions?
- How do you calm your mind and find peace?

- Do you have faith in your own power to self-heal?

- Who have you forgiven?

- What are you thankful for?

- What is your spiritual practice?

- How will you enrich your life?

Maybe you need to give up bad influences. By "bad influences," I'm talking about the people and behaviors that subtract from living a self-healing lifestyle. Are there people in your life who diminish you instead of encouraging, supporting, and nurturing you? If so, you must let them go.

Do you have negative habits, such as an addiction to tobacco, alcohol, or drugs, that have taken root in your life? Don't allow this to continue; you are worth more than this. Be aware of bad influences in your life; they are destructive forces that are anachronistic to who you are and what you're trying to achieve.

Keep your goals at the forefront. It's easy to lose sight of your goals, and they become obscured. Ask yourself, *What is it I want to achieve? How willing am I to keep striving, no matter how much I am met with disappointment? What are my biggest dreams? What am I willing to do to make them come true?* Think through your answers, and write them down in your journal.

Let go of old attitudes. A lot of us carry old, largely unconscious attitudes with us about health, healing, and, really, life in general. These attitudes vividly color your ability to stay well and set limits on your self-healing potential. For example, if placing your fate fully in the hands of a healer was a part of your mind-set, you might find it hard to make empowering health decisions. Take a look at your old notions and see how they might be affecting your health and well-being. Recognize that some may not be serving you well today.

Release hidden resentments. Holding grudges always constricts self-healing. A good rule of thumb is to forgive yourself and others. Hurts of the past and present are usually not important enough to stay angry about, so let them go. Forgiving is not a coward's way out; it is the way of courage. In any relationship, there are countless conflicts and hurts that we simply must forgive, for there is really nothing we can do about them. To hold resentment is destructive and negates self-healing. It only results in our feeling less alive and less loving toward others.

Reach for your highest potential. The world is full of people who just get by, never distinguishing themselves and always letting obstacles stay in their path. If you feel inhibited or self-conscious, it might be because you don't feel you're enough—not attractive enough, not smart enough, not healthy enough, or not lovable enough. Don't let negative self-doubts become facts. Not allowing yourself to be dominated by self-doubt will help you feel more empowered and alive. If you act on your desire to be attractive, smart, healthy, and lovable, you will come to feel—and be—that way. Do what it takes, and you'll attract the best results.

Today is a very special time in your life. Most of your options are all open. There are many things in life that can be started new today, including a dynamic new health regime; a rewarding love life; more positive, stimulating thoughts; or all of the above. Right now, the present, is the one time in your life when you truly have control. You can do something about your health and your life right now—change their direction, supercharge them, and reform them. This is not a time to take for granted. It is a time to act!

I leave you with a final thought: *If self-healing is to be, it's up to me.* Recognize that right now, regardless of the issues that you're facing, you're not alone. All of us, in some way or another, are going through similar circumstances and experiences. Please seek out the loved ones around you for guidance. Don't feel that you're out there by yourself. You're not. The people who care for you want to support you. But ultimately understand that you are the one who will decide whether there is change or no change, whether your life becomes exactly what you dream of, or whether it stays the same, whether you decide to do different things so you can have different results.

Once you make these changes, you'll find that they are a part of your everyday life, and it will seem only natural to continue. You have been given your body as a gift; a body with powers to self-heal. Take care of it, and it will take care of you.

❖　❖　❖

SELF-HEALING
REFERENCES

Body Heal Thyself

Gold, M. 2006. Commercial health insurance: smart or simply lucky? *Health Affairs* 25: 61490–61493.

Healing Versus Curing

Arnaert, A., et al. 2005. Stroke patients in the acute care phase: role of hope in self-healing. *Holistic Nursing Practice* 20:137–146.

Chapter 1: Self-Healing Foods

Edwards, R.L., et al 2007. Quercetin reduces blood pressure in hypertensive subjects. *The Journal of Nutrition* 137:2405–2411.

Gerhauser, C. 2008. Cancer chemopreventive potential of apples, apple juice, and apple components. *Planta Medica* 74:1608–1624.

Kanner, J., et al. 2001. Betalains--a new class of dietary cationized antioxidants. *Journal of Agricultural Food Chemistry* 49:5178–5185.

Adams, L.S., et al. 2010. Blueberry phytochemicals inhibit growth and metastatic potential of MDA-MB-231 breast cancer cells through modulation of the phosphatidylinositol 3-kinase pathway. *Cancer Research* 70:3594–3605.

Kahkonen, M.P., et al. 2001. Berry phenolics and their antioxidant activity. *Journal of Agriculture and Food Chemistry* 49:4076–4082.

Howell, A.B., et al. 2002. Cranberry juice and adhesion of antibiotic-resistant uro-pathogens. *Journal of the American Medical Association* 287:3082–3083.

Jenkins, D. J., et al. 2002. Dose response of almonds on coronary heart disease risk factors: blood lipids, oxidized low-density lipoproteins, lipoprotein(a), homocysteine, and pulmonary nitric oxide: a randomized, controlled, crossover trial. *Circulation* 106:1327–1332.

Wiberg, B., et al. 2006. Metabolic risk factors for stroke and transient ischemic attacks in middle-aged men: a community-based study with long-term follow-up. *Stroke* 37:2898–2903.

Dojousse, L., et al. 2001. Relation between dietary linolenic acid and coronary artery disease in the National Heart, Lung, and Blood Institute Family Heart Study. *American Journal of Clinical Nutrition* 74:612–619.

Torabian, S., et al. 2010. Long-term walnut supplementation without dietary advice induces favorable serum lipid changes in free-living individuals. *European Journal of Clinical Nutrition* 64:274–279.

Bosetti, C., et al. 2002. Olive oil, seed oils and other added fats in relation to ovarian cancer (Italy). *Cancer Causes and Control* 13(5):465–470.

Knekt, P., et al. 2002. Flavonoid intake and risk of chronic diseases. *American Journal of Clinical Nutrition* 76:560–568.

Voutilainen, S., et al. 2006. Carotenoids and cardiovascular health. *American Journal of Clinical Nutrition* 83:1265–1271.

Chu, Y.F., et al. 2002. Antioxidant and antiproliferative activities of common vegetables. *Journal of Agriculture and Food Chemistry* 50:6910–6916.

Geleijnse, J.M., et al. 2002. Inverse association of tea and flavonoid intakes with incident myocardial infarction: the Rotterdam Study. *American Journal of Clinical Nutrition* 75:880–886.

Wu, C.H., et al. 2002. Epidemiological evidence of increased bone mineral density in habitual tea drinkers. *Archives of Internal Medicine* 162:1001–1006.

Kucuk, O. 2002. Chemoprevention of prostate cancer. *Cancer Metastasis Review* 21(2):111–24.

Riccioni, G., et al. 2008. Protective effect of lycopene in cardiovascular disease. *European Review for Medical and Pharmacological Sciences* 12:183–190.

Hecht, S.S., et al. 1999. Effects of watercress consumption on urinary metabolites of nicotine in smokers. *Cancer Epidemiology, Biomarkers & Prevention* 8:907–913.

Worthington, V. 2001. Nutritional quality of organic versus conventional fruits, vegetables, and grains. *The Journal of Alternative and Complementary Medicine* 7:161–173.

Chapter 3: Self-Healing Supplements

Holmquist, C. 2003. Multivitamin supplements are inversely associated with risk of myocardial infarction in men and women - Stockholm Heart Epidemiology Program (SHEEP). *Journal of Nutrition* 133:2650–2654.

Mohr, S.B., et al. 2008. Relationship between low ultraviolet B irradiance and higher breast cancer risk in 107 countries. *Breast Journal* 14:255–260.

Roll, S., et al. 2011. Reduction of common cold symptoms by encapsulated juice powder concentrate of fruits and vegetables: a randomised, double-blind, placebo-controlled trial. *British Journal of Nutrition* 105:118–122.

Zhang J., and Oxino, G. The effect of fruit and vegetable powder mix on blood pressure and heart rate variability. Poster and abstract presentation. Association of Chiropractic Colleges Convention, March 2007, St. Louis, Mo.

Jiang J., et al. 2004. Ganoderma lucidum inhibits proliferation and induces apoptosis in human prostate cancer cells PC-3. *International Journal of Oncology* 24:1093–1099.

Cao, Q.Z., and Lin, Z.B. 2004. Antitumor and anti-angiogenic activity of Ganoderma lucidum polysaccharides peptide. *Acta Pharmacologica Sinica* 25:833–838.

Wachtel-Galor, S., et al. 2004. Ganoderma lucidum ("Lingzhi"); acute and short-term biomarker response to supplementation. *International Journal of Food Sciences and Nutrition* 55:75–83.

Kim, L.S., et al. 2006. Efficacy of methylsulfonylmethane (MSM) in osteoarthritis pain of the knee: a pilot clinical trial. *Osteoarthritis and Cartilage* 14:286–294.

Heber, D., et al. 1999. Cholesterol-lowering effects of a proprietary Chinese red-yeast-rice dietary supplement. *American Journal of Clinical Nutrition* 69:231–236.

Barbagallo Sangiorgi G., et al. 1994. alpha-Glycerophosphocholine in the mental recovery of cerebral ischemic attacks. An Italian multicenter clinical trial. *Annals of the New York Academy of Sciences* 717:253–69.

Le Bars, P.L., et al. 1997. A placebo-controlled, double-blind, randomized trial of an extract of Ginkgo biloba for dementia. North American EGb Study Group. *Journal of the American Medical Association* 278:1327–1332.

Chapter 4: Active Healing

Lees, B.J., and Booth, L.W. 2004. Sedentary death syndrome. *Canadian Journal of Applied Physiology* 29:447–460.

Li, J.X., et al. 2001. Tai chi: physiological characteristics and beneficial effects on health. *British Journal of Sports Medicine* 35:148–56.

Neiman, D.C., et al. 1993. Physical activity and immune function in elderly women. *Medicine and Science in Sports and Exercise* 25:823–831.

Irwin, M.L., et al. 2008. Influence of pre- and postdiagnosis physical activity on mortality in breast cancer survivors: the health, eating, activity, and lifestyle study. *Journal of Clinical Oncology* 26:3958–3964.

Chen, K., and Yeung, R. 2002. Exploratory studies of Qigong therapy for cancer in China. *Integrative Cancer Therapies* 1:345–370.

Lee, M.S., et al. 2007. Tai chi for cardiovascular disease and its risk factors: a systematic review. *Journal of Hypertension* 25:1974–5.

Chapter 5: The New Healing Arts

Shekelle PG, Adams AH, et al. The appropriateness of spinal manipulation for lowback pain: project overview and literature review. R-4025/1-CCR/FCER. Santa Monica: RAND; 1991.

Fanuele JC, Birkmeyer NJ, Abdu WA, Tosteson TD, Weinstein JN. The impact of spinal problems on the health status of patients: have we underestimated the effect? *Spine.* Jun 15 2000;25(12):1509–1514.

Bigos S, Bowyer O, Braen G. Acute Lower Back Pain in Adults. Clinical Practice Guideline, Quick Reference Guide Number 14. AHCPR Pub. No, 95–0643. Rockville: U.S.

Department of Health and Human Services, Public Health Service, Agency for Healthcare Policy and Research; 1994.

Manga P. Enhanced chiropractic coverage under OHIP as a means of reducing healthcare costs, attaining better health outcomes and achieving equitable access to health services. Report to the Ontario Ministry of Health. Ottawa: Ministry of Health, Government of Ontario; 1998.

Choudhry N, Milstein A. Do Chiropractic Physician Services for Treatment of Low-Back and Neck Pain Improve the Value of Health Benefit Plans? An Evidence-Based Assessment of Incremental Impact on Population Health and Total Healthcare Spending. San Francisco: Mercer Health and Benefits; 2009

Bakris G, Dickholtz M, Sr., Meyer PM, et al. Atlas vertebra realignment and achievement of arterial pressure goal in hypertensive patients: a pilot study. *J Hum Hypertension.* May 2007;21(5):347–352.

Hawk C, Khorsan R, Lisi AJ, Ferrance RJ, Evans MW. Chiropractic care for nonmusculoskeletal conditions: a systematic review with implications for whole systems research. *Journal of Alternative and Complementary Medicine.* Jun 2007;13(5):491–512

Hernandez-Reif, M., et al. 2001. Lower back pain is reduced and range of motion increased after massage therapy. *The International Journal of Neuroscience* 106:131–145.

Bauer, B.A., et al. 2010. Effect of massage therapy on pain, anxiety, and tension after cardiac surgery: a randomized study. *Complementary Therapies in Clinical Practice* 16:70–75.

Field, T., et al. 2009. Pregnancy massage reduces prematurity, low birthweight and postpartum depression. *Infant Behavior & Development* 32:454–460.

Chapter 6: You Think, Therefore, You Heal (or Not)

Helgeson, V.S., et al. 1999. Applicability of cognitive adaptation theory to predicting adjustment to heart disease after coronary angioplasty. Health Psychology 18:561–569.

Riley, K.P., et al. 2005. Early life linguistic ability, late life cognitive function, and neuropathology: findings from the Nun Study. *Neurobiology of Aging* 26:341–347.

Giltay, E.J., 2004. Dispositional optimism and all-cause and cardiovascular mortality in a prospective cohort of elderly Dutch men and women. *Archives of General Psychiatry* 61:1126–1135.

Maruta, T., et al. 2000. Optimists vs pessimists: survival rate among medical patients over a 30-year period. *Mayo Clinic Proceedings* 75:140–143.

Brummett, B.H., et al. 2006. Prediction of all-cause mortality by the Minnesota Multiphasic Personality Inventory Optimism-Pessimism Scale scores: study of a college sample during a 40-year follow-up period. *Mayo Clinic Proceedings* 81:1541–1544.

Chapter 7: Emotions That Heal, Emotions That Harm

McClelland, A.B., et al. 2009. Psychological and cumulative cardiovascular effects of repeated angry rumination and visuospatial suppression. *International Journal of Psychophysiology* 74:166–173.

Kiecolt-Glaser, J.K., et al. 2005. Hostile marital interactions, proinflammatory cytokine production, and wound healing. *Archives of General Psychiatry* 62:1377–1384.

Harburg, E., et al. 2003. Expressive/suppressive anger-coping responses, gender, and types of mortality: a 17–year follow-up (Tecumseh, Michigan, 1971–1988). *Psychosomatic Medicine* 65:588–597.

Matthews, K.A., et al. 1998. Are hostility and anxiety associated with carotid atherosclerosis in healthy postmenopausal women? *Psychosomatic Medicine* 60:633–638.

Katon, W.J., et al. 2005. The association of comorbid depression with mortality in patients with type 2 diabetes. *Diabetes Care* 28:2668–2672.

Cohen, S., et al. 1998. Types of stressors that increase susceptibility to the common cold in healthy adults. *Health Psychology* 17:214–223.

Tan, M.A., et al. 2007. Humor, as an adjunct therapy in cardiac rehabilitation, attenuates catecholamines and myocardial infarction recurrence. *Advances in Mind-Body Medicine* 22:8–12.

Miller, M., and Fry, W.F. 2009. The effect of mirthful laughter on the human cardiovascular system. *Medical Hypotheses* 73:636–9.

Frey, W., et al. 1981. Effect of stimulus on the chemical composition of human tears. *American Journal of Ophthalmology* 92:559–567.

Kabat-Zinn, J., et al. 1998. Influence of a mindfulness meditation-based stress reduction intervention on rates of skin clearing in patients with moderate to severe psoriasis undergoing phototherapy (UVB) and photochemotherapy (PUVA). *Psychosomatic Medicine* 60:625–632.

Chapter 9: Creative Forces

Cohen, G., et al. 2006. The impact of professionally conducted cultural programs on the physical health, mental health, and social functioning of older adults. *The Gerontologist* 46:726–34.

Keith, D.R., et al. 2009. The effects of music listening on inconsolable crying in premature infants. *Journal of Music Therapy* 46:191–203.

Janata, P., et al. 2002. The cortical topography of tonal structures underlying Western music. *Science* 298:2167–2170.

McGuire, K.M., et al. 2005. Autonomic effects of expressive writing in individuals with elevated blood pressure. *Journal of Health Psychology* 10:197–209.

Chapter 10: The Healing Triad

Waltman, M.A., et al. 2009. The effects of a forgiveness intervention on patients with coronary artery disease. *Psychology & Health* 24:11–27.

Van Oyen Witvliet, C., et al. 2001. Granting forgiveness or harboring grudges: implications for emotion, physiology, and health. *Psychological Science* 12:117–123.

Rein, G., et al. 1995. The physiological and psychological effects of compassion and anger. *Journal of Advancement in Medicine* 8: 87–105.

Emmons, R.A., and McCullough, M.E. 2003 Counting blessings versus burdens: an experimental investigation of gratitude and subjective well-being in daily life. *Journal of Personality and Social Psychology* 84:377–389.

Kashdan, T.B., et al. 2006. Gratitude and hedonic and eudaimonic well-being in Vietnam war veterans. *Behaviour Research and Therapy* 44(2):177–199.

Chapter 11: The Healing Spirit

Byrd, R.C. 1988. Positive therapeutic effects of intercessory prayer in a coronary care unit population. *Southern Medical Journal* 81:826–829.

Koenig, H.G., et al. 1998. The relationship between religious activities and blood pressure in older adults. *International Journal of Psychiatry in Medicine* 28:189–213.

Bernardi, L., et al. 2005. Cardiorespiratory interactions to external stimuli. *Archives Italienne de Biologie* 143:215–221.

Koenig, H.G., et al. 1997. Religious coping in the nursing home: a biopsychosocial model. *International Journal of Psychiatry in Medicine* 27:365–376.

Kudel I,, et al. 2011. Spirituality and religiosity in patients with HIV: a test and expansion of a model. *Annals of Behavioral Medicine* 41:92–103.

ACKNOWLEDGMENTS

Writing this book was possible due to the love, patience, and support of my wife, Alicia, and my sons, Gianni and Luciano.

I would also like to thank the following people:

My editor, Maggie Greenwood-Robinson, for your passion, insight, and guidance. You are the best in the industry.

The fabulous team at Hay House: Reid Tracy, Louise Hay, Jill Kramer, Lisa Mitchell, Patrick Gabrysiak, Gail Gonzales, and Christy Salinas. You are gifted and brilliant.

The greatest literary team in the world: Jan Miller, Shannon Marven, Nena Madonia, Ivonne Ortega, Nicki Miser, and Lacy Lynch.

My attorney, Eric Rayman from Miller Korzenik Sommers. You are very talented.

The board, faculty, students, staff, and alumni of Parker University. You inspire me every day.

My mentor and friend, the late Dr. James W. Parker, for introducing me to chiropractic and the natural healing concepts that opened a new world for me.

My brothers and sisters-in-law, Pier, Robin, Aldo, Erin, and Paolo Mancini.

My loving mother, Gladys Mancini, for your advice and love.

All my friends and transformational leaders for always encouraging me to contribute at a higher level.

All of the contributors of the inspiring stories in this book. Thank you for sharing your healing experiences.

And, you, the reader, for embracing the paradigm of self-healing.

❖ ❖ ❖

ABOUT THE AUTHOR

Dr. Fabrizio Mancini is an internationally acclaimed bilingual speaker, author, educator, philanthropist, and the president of Parker University in Dallas, Texas.

His childhood dreams of serving humanity were ignited in Texas, where he pursued pre-medicine studies at the University of Dallas in preparation to become a doctor. He later enrolled as a student at Parker College of Chiropractic as his passion for life was redefined to empower individuals to take responsibility for their own health and well-being; and in 1999, Dr. Mancini became one of the youngest presidents of a college or university when he was chosen to lead the institution.

Since that time, and while leading Parker University through historic educational and professional achievements, Dr. Mancini has developed his life's passion through a variety of arenas. His enthusiasm for life is contagious and has earned him numerous recognitions that include Heroes for Humanity, Humanitarian of the Year, CEO of the Year, and many others.

As a highly sought-after guest of radio and television programs, he inspires thousands of individuals each year with his innovative messages of success, service, health, and wellness. He is the co-author of *Chicken Soup for the Chiropractic Soul* and *The Well-Adjusted Soul* and the author of *Feeling Fab: Four Steps to Living a Fabulous Life.*

Dr. Mancini has also given testimony to the White House Commission for Complementary and Alternative Medicine and had the honor to serve on the Texas Governor's Advisory Council on Physical Fitness.

His satisfies his commitment to keeping the Hispanic community informed on the benefits of healthy habits by serving as a frequent guest of CNN Español and Univision; and he recently received the honor of having Mexico's new leading university, UNEVE, name their library after him.

In addition, because of his contributions to the field of chiropractic and for his dedication to spreading a proactive message regarding health and wellness, Dr. Mancini has been inducted into the Wellness Revolutionaries Hall of Fame and is a noted active member of the National Speaker's Association.

Website: **www.drfab.net**

HAY HOUSE TITLES OF RELATED INTEREST

YOU CAN HEAL YOUR LIFE, the movie, starring Louise L. Hay & Friends
(available as a 1-DVD program and an expanded 2-DVD set)
Watch the trailer at: **www.LouiseHayMovie.com**

THE SHIFT, the movie,
starring Dr. Wayne W. Dyer
(available as a 1-DVD program and an expanded 2-DVD set)
Watch the trailer at: **www.DyerMovie.com**

*THE ART OF RAW LIVING FOOD: Heal Yourself and the Planet
with Eco-delicious Cuisine,* by Doreen Virtue and Jenny Ross

FRIED: Why You Burn Out and How to Revive, by Joan Borysenko, Ph.D.

INSIDE-OUT HEALING: Transforming Your Life Through the Power of Presence,
by Richard Moss

RESONANCE: Nine Practices for Harmonious Health and Vitality,
by Joyce Whiteley Hawkes, Ph.D.

SEEDS OF FREEDOM: Cultivating a Life That Matters,
by Heather Marie Wilson

*UNLOCK THE SECRET MESSAGES OF YOUR BODY! A 28-Day Jump-Start
Program for Radiant Health and Glorious Vitality,* by Denise Linn

YOU CAN CREATE AN EXCEPTIONAL LIFE,
by Louise Hay and Cheryl Richardson

All of the above are available at your local bookstore,
or may be ordered by visiting:

Hay House USA: **www.hayhouse.com**®
Hay House Australia: **www.hayhouse.com.au**
Hay House UK: **www.hayhouse.co.uk**
Hay House South Africa: **www.hayhouse.co.za**
Hay House India: **www.hayhouse.co.in**

We hope you enjoyed this Hay House book. If you'd like
to receive our online catalog featuring additional information
on Hay House books and products, or if you'd like to find
out more about the Hay Foundation, please contact:

Hay House, Inc., P.O. Box 5100, Carlsbad, CA 92018-5100
(760) 431-7695 or (800) 654-5126
(760) 431-6948 (fax) or (800) 650-5115 (fax)
www.hayhouse.com® • **www.hayfoundation.org**

Published and distributed in Australia by: Hay House Australia Pty. Ltd.,
18/36 Ralph St., Alexandria NSW 2015 • *Phone:* 612-9669-4299
Fax: 612-9669-4144 • www.hayhouse.com.au

Published and distributed in the United Kingdom by: Hay House UK, Ltd.,
292B Kensal Rd., London W10 5BE • *Phone:* 44-20-8962-1230
Fax: 44-20-8962-1239 • www.hayhouse.co.uk

Published and distributed in the Republic of South Africa by: Hay House SA (Pty),
Ltd., P.O. Box 990, Witkoppen 2068 • *Phone/Fax:* 27-11-467-8904
www.hayhouse.co.za

Published in India by: Hay House Publishers India, Muskaan Complex,
Plot No. 3, B-2, Vasant Kunj, New Delhi 110 070 • *Phone:* 91-11-4176-1620
Fax: 91-11-4176-1630 • www.hayhouse.co.in

Distributed in Canada by: Raincoast, 9050 Shaughnessy St.,
Vancouver, B.C. V6P 6E5 • *Phone:* (604) 323-7100
Fax: (604) 323-2600 • www.raincoast.com

Take Your Soul on a Vacation

Visit **www.HealYourLife.com®** to regroup, recharge, and
reconnect with your own magnificence. Featuring blogs, mind-body-spirit
news, and life-changing wisdom from Louise Hay and friends.

Visit **www.HealYourLife.com** today!

Free e-newsletters
from Hay House, the Ultimate
Resource for Inspiration

Be the first to know about Hay House's dollar deals, free downloads, special offers, affirmation cards, giveaways, contests, and more!

 Get exclusive excerpts from our latest releases and videos from *Hay House Present Moments*.

 Enjoy uplifting personal stories, how-to articles, and healing advice, along with videos and empowering quotes, within *Heal Your Life*.

 Have an inspirational story to tell and a passion for writing? Sharpen your writing skills with insider tips from *Your Writing Life*.

Sign Up Now!

Get inspired, educate yourself, get a complimentary gift, and share the wisdom!

http://www.hayhouse.com/newsletters.php

Visit www.hayhouse.com to sign up today!

HAY
HOUSE

HAYHOUSE
RADIO))
radio for your soul®

HealYourLife.com